Paradox

Central Problems of Philosophy
Series Editor: John Shand

This series of books presents concise, clear, and rigorous analyses of the core problems that preoccupy philosophers across all approaches to the discipline. Each book encapsulates the essential arguments and debates, providing an authoritative guide to the subject while also introducing original perspectives. This series of books by an international team of authors aims to cover those fundamental topics that, taken together, constitute the full breadth of philosophy.

Published titles

Causation and Explanation
Stathis Psillos

Free Will
Graham McFee

Knowledge
Michael Welbourne

Meaning
David E. Cooper

Mind and Body
Robert Kirk

Ontology
Dale Jacquette

Paradox
Doris Olin

Perception
Barry Maund

Relativism
Paul O'Grady

Scepticism
Neil Gascoigne

Truth
Pascal Engel

Universals
J. P. Moreland

Forthcoming titles

Action
Rowland Stout

God
Jay Wood

Modality
Joseph Melia

Philosophy and Science
James Logue

Realism and Anti-Realism
Stuart Brock & Edwin Mares

Rights
Duncan Ivison

Self
Stephen Burwood

Value
Chris Cherry

Paradox

Doris Olin

McGill-Queen's University Press
Montreal & Kingston • Ithaca

© Doris Olin 2003

ISBN 0-7735-2677-3 (bound)
ISBN 0-7735-2678-1 (paper)

Published simultaneously outside North America
by Acumen Publishing Limited

McGill-Queen's University Press acknowledges the financial support of
the Government of Canada through the Book Publishing Development
Program (BPIDP) for its activities.

National Library of Canada Cataloguing in Publication Data

Olin, Doris, 1943-
   Paradox / Doris Olin.

(Central problems of philosophy)
Includes bibliographical references and index.
ISBN 0-7735-2677-3 (bound).—ISBN 0-7735-2678-1 (pbk.)

   1. Paradox. 2. Logic. I. Title. II. Series.

BC199.P2O45 2003   165   C2003-902775-9

Designed and typeset by Kate Williams, Abergavenny.
Printed and bound by Biddles Ltd., Guildford and King's Lynn.

In memory of my parents,
Joseph and Gertrude Finkel

Contents

Preface

How quaint the ways of Paradox!
At common sense she gaily mocks!
                              W. S. Gilbert, *The Pirates of Penzance*

Paradoxes are fascinating: they baffle and haunt. They are among the most gripping of philosophical problems, for as we struggle through the maze of argument and counter-argument, there is the sense that the solution, the crucial insight, lies just beyond the next turn of the path. Still, most of the paradoxes of interest to philosophers are not mere intellectual puzzles. They raise substantive philosophical issues, and their resolution offers the prospect of increased philosophical knowledge.

This book begins by considering what a paradox is, and what the possible avenues are for resolution of a paradox. Chapter 2 examines a challenge to the analysis based on the view that contradictions can be true, and that the conclusion of a paradox may thus be both true and false. In subsequent chapters, the focus is on a detailed study of paradoxes that are particularly riveting and seductive (or, at least, strike me as so), and that appear to have considerable philosophical depth. The paradoxes studied are also linked by the theme of rationality: they raise difficult issues about the rationality of belief, the rationality of action and the coherence of our language.

The permission granted by editors and publishers to reprint material previously published is acknowledged at the beginning of the relevant chapters, and is much appreciated. A special note of thanks is due Bernard Katz for his invariably sound advice and philosophical insight; I have benefited greatly from both. I also want to thank Steven Gerrard of Acumen Publishing for his understanding and patience. To the family and dear friends who have provided unstinting support, encouragement, and dinners out, I am more grateful than I can say.

This book is not finished. I make this admission not for the sake of creating a new paradox of the preface, but to acknowledge that each time I review the manuscript, there are further considerations and responses I feel inclined to add. Practical considerations, however, dictate that it is time to stop.

1 The nature of paradox

Paradoxes can be fun. They can also be instructive, for the unravelling of a paradox may lead to increased philosophical knowledge and understanding. The paradoxes studied in this work offer promise of both these features. But paradoxes may be also disturbing; their study may reveal inadequacies, confusion or incoherence in some of our most deeply entrenched principles and beliefs. The reader is forewarned: some of the material that follows may prove unsettling.

It seems wise to begin at the beginning, with the questions "What is a paradox?" and "How does one resolve a paradox?" But first we need some examples of paradoxes at our disposal.

The Monty Hall paradox

You are invited to be a contestant on a fabulous game show. The host of the show, Monty Hall, explains how the game works. After some initial banter and scintillating chat, you will be presented with three doors, *A*, *B* and *C*. Behind one of the doors will be the car of your dreams – a Porsche, a Jaguar, whatever you wish. Behind each of the other two doors is a worthless goat. Which door conceals the car is decided randomly. You will first be asked to pick a door; then Monty, who knows what is behind each door, will pick, from one of the other two doors, a door that has a goat behind it, open that door, and show you the goat.

At that point, you will be offered a second option. You may stay with your original choice, and keep whatever is behind that door. Or, you may switch to another door, and keep whatever lies behind it.

Naturally, you are delighted to accept the invitation. With a week to go before the show, you feel there is nothing to deliberate about other than what you will wear. It seems clear that it is all a matter of luck. The first choice is entirely arbitrary. It is equally likely that the car is behind any one of the three doors; the probability that the car is behind any given door is 1/3. Similarly, the second choice is a matter of whim; there is no reason to prefer either switching to another door or staying with your original choice. Suppose, for example, you first pick door A, and Monty then shows you the goat behind door C. That means the car is either behind door A or behind door B. But it is equally likely that it is behind either door; there is no reason to prefer one to the other. So the probability that the car is behind either door is now 1/2, and there is nothing to gain either by switching or by not switching.

It's all a matter of common sense, you tell yourself. How could being shown that one of the doors I did not choose has a goat behind it give me any reason to prefer one of the two remaining doors?

The night before your television appearance, a mathematician friend appears at your door, seemingly agitated. "Do whatever you want on the first choice", he says. "But on the second choice, you *must* switch! It's just become clear to me", he continues. "Look at it this way. Suppose you pick door A on the first round, and that Monty then shows you that door C has a goat behind it. Monty had to choose between doors B and C, and he wanted to pick a door that concealed a goat. He might have been in a position where he could pick either door (both were 'goat doors'); or he might have *had* to pick door C. Initially, the probability that the car was behind either door B or door C was 2/3. So the probability that his choice was *forced* was 2/3. But his choice was forced only if the car is behind door B. So if you switch to door B, your chance of winning is 2/3. You can't do better than that!"

Panicked, you start to protest, but he interrupts. "Let me put it another way. Suppose you get to play the game many times and you are going to pick a strategy. If you consistently pick a door (say door A) and stay with it, you will win 1/3 of the time (the 'car door' is determined randomly). But 2/3 of the time the car will be behind either door *B* or door *C*, in which case Monty will, in effect, show you which of the two it is not behind. So you will win 2/3 of the time if you follow the strategy of switching – twice as often as if your strategy were not switching."

What should you do?

Other paradoxes

The barber paradox

Imagine a charming village, as yet untouched by the tourist trade, in which there is only one barber. He is extremely busy, for he cuts the hair of all and only those villagers who do not cut their own hair. But who, we may wonder, cuts the barber's hair? Suppose he cuts his own hair. If he does, then, since he is a villager, he does not cut his own hair. Suppose, alternatively, that he does not cut his own hair. If he does not, then, since he is a villager, it follows that he does cut his own hair. So the barber in this village cuts his own hair if and only if he does not cut his own hair.

The Achilles and the tortoise paradox

The tortoise and Achilles are to have a race. Of course, the tortoise is much slower than Achilles; Achilles, at his best, can run ten times faster than the tortoise. To make the contest interesting, the tortoise is given a head start of 10 metres; the racetrack is 100 metres. Can Achilles overtake the tortoise? Consider. By the time Achilles reaches the tortoise's starting point (point 1, which is 10 metres ahead of Achilles' starting-point), the tortoise will have travelled another metre to reach point 2 (since Achilles runs ten times as fast as the tortoise). But once Achilles has reached point 2, the tortoise will have travelled another tenth of a metre to reach point 3. By the time Achilles has reached point 3, the tortoise will still be one hundredth of a metre further ahead at point 4. And so on. It seems that whenever Achilles has caught up to where the tortoise *was*, the tortoise is still some tiny distance ahead. Thus, Achilles cannot pass the tortoise and cannot win the race.

The ship of Theseus paradox

Theseus, an experienced sailor well aware of the hazards of the sea, has a ship that he decides needs complete renovation. The ship – call it "*T*" – consists of 1,000 old planks. When the renovation begins, Theseus' ship is placed in dock *A*. The crew is ordered to work as follows. In the first hour of renovation, they are to remove one plank from *T*, replace it with a new one, and carry the old plank to dock *B*. In the second hour of renovation, they are to remove an adjoining plank, replace it with a new one, and carry the old plank to dock *B*, where it is appropriately fastened to the plank that has been removed in the previous hour. They are to remove a third plank in the third hour. And so on. After 1,000 hours, a ship has been assembled in dock *A*, call it "*X*", that consists of 1,000 new planks; there is also a ship in dock *B* – call it "*Y*" – that consists of the 1,000 old planks removed from Theseus' ship and then reassembled in exactly the same way they had been arranged prior to the renovation. Which ship is Theseus' ship? Which ship is *T*?

If you methodically took apart the ship, and then reassembled it exactly as it was, surely you would say that it was the same ship.[1] But that is exactly what has happened here. *T* was first taken apart, then reassembled and is now in dock *B*. So *Y* is *T*. Note that *Y* is made out of exactly the same materials, arranged in exactly the same fashion, as *T* was when Theseus brought it into port.

On the other hand, if you remove one plank from a ship and replace it with a new one, you still have the same ship. Such a slight change cannot affect the identity of the object. So after one hour, the ship in dock *A* is still *T*. But again, removing one plank from a ship and replacing it does not affect the identity of the ship. Thus, after two hours the ship in dock *A* is *T*. And so on. Finally, after 1,000 hours, the ship in dock *A* is *T*. Thus, *X* must be *T*.

The taxi-cab paradox

In the town of Greenville there are exactly 100 taxis, of which 85 are green and 15 are blue. A prominent citizen witnesses a hit-and-run accident that involves a taxi, and testifies that the taxi was blue. The witness is subjected to tests that determine that, in similar circumstances, he is 80 per cent reliable in his colour reports. Is it likely that the taxi in the accident was blue?

First, it seems clear that we are entitled to accept what the witness says as highly likely. He has proved 80 per cent reliable in similar circumstances, and there is no reason to think there is any relevant difference in this situation. Surely what he says can be considered highly probable, and should be regarded as such in a court of law.

On second thought, if we take the long view, it seems unlikely that the witness was correct in his colour identification. To see this, consider 100 randomly selected taxi accidents in Greenville. About 85 of these accidents will involve a green taxi and about 15 will involve a blue taxi. If the witness were to report on the 85 green taxi accidents, he would report correctly in about 80 per cent of the cases and incorrectly in 20 per cent. This means that of the 85 green taxi accidents, he would report about 17 as involving a blue taxi. The 15 blue taxi accidents would presumably also yield 80 per cent correct reports, or 12 reports of blue taxis involved in accidents. Were a witness of 80 per cent reliability to report on 100 randomly selected taxi accidents in Greenville, then, there would be about 29 ($= 17 + 12$) blue taxi reports, only 12 of which would be accurate; that is, only 41 per cent of the blue taxi reports would be correct. So it seems more likely than not that the witness in our original case was mistaken in his report of a blue taxi.

What is a paradox?

In order to appreciate why these scenarios seem baffling, confusing and yet absorbing, it is necessary to have a better understanding of the sort of problem they pose. Using these few paradoxes as background, let us consider the question: what is a paradox?

One striking feature of these problems is that they present a conflict of reasons. There is, in each, an apparently impeccable use of reason to show that a certain statement is true; and yet reason also seems to tell us that the very same statement is utterly absurd. Apparently letter-perfect operations of reason lead to a statement that reason is apparently compelled to reject.

Let us unpack what this means. It should first be noted that each paradox presented above contains an argument; this feature is central to the philosophical notion of paradox. The popular use of the term "paradox", by contrast, is undoubtedly broader. A recent newspaper report, for instance, says that the rosier health picture for those with HIV-AIDS has "sparked a paradoxical response, a disturbing trend to unprotected sex among young gay men".[2] Here "paradoxical" seems to have the force of "irrational" or "unfitting". Statements that seem absurd at first sight, but on closer examination are seen to be true, are also referred to as "paradoxical" in popular usage. In Gilbert and Sullivan's *The Pirates of Penzance*, for instance, the following is taken to be paradoxical: Frederic is 21 years old, but has had only five birthdays. (The clue is that Frederic was born in a leap year on February 29.)

But we are pursuing the philosophical notion of paradox. We might say with Quine that "a paradox is just any conclusion that at first seems absurd, but that has an argument to sustain it".[3] This seems to be essentially in line with the traditional definitions in the literature. It should be made explicit, however, that the argument in question must seem strong or compelling; arguments that are clearly fallacious do not yield paradox. Revising Quine's definition, we can say: a paradox is an argument that appears flawless, but whose conclusion nevertheless appears to be false.

But what is meant by speaking of an argument as flawless? Evaluating an argument normally requires assessing two components: the premises, and the reasoning from the premises. For an argument to be without fault, the premises must be true and the reasoning correct. So we have:

> A paradox is an argument in which there appears to be correct reasoning from true premises to a false conclusion.

This is to be understood as saying that the appearance of each of three elements is required: correct reasoning, true premises and a false conclusion.

Is this an adequate account of the notion of paradox? It is easy enough to see how this traditional definition fits the example of Achilles and the tortoise. There we have what seems to be a meticulous argument leading to the obviously false conclusion that Achilles can never pass the tortoise. However, some of the other paradoxes considered above do not fit quite so neatly into this mould. In the ship of Theseus paradox, for instance, there are seemingly compelling arguments for two different conclusions.

And while neither conclusion may appear clearly false, the two conclusions (X is T, Y is T) certainly appear to be inconsistent. The Monty Hall paradox and the taxi-cab paradox also seem to share this feature: two apparently faultless arguments lead to two apparently inconsistent conclusions.

This points to the need to distinguish two types of paradox. A type I paradox, such as Achilles and the tortoise, has one argument and one conclusion; a type II paradox, such as the ship of Theseus, involves two arguments and two conclusions. The definition just given may do for type I paradoxes, but type II paradoxes require a more complex account as follows:

> A type II paradox occurs when there is one argument in which there appears to be correct reasoning leading from true premises to a conclusion A, and another argument in which there appears to be correct reasoning leading from true premises to a conclusion B, and A and B appear to be inconsistent.

Since it would be tedious to express every point made in the following discussion as it applies both to type I and to type II paradoxes, I shall sometimes illustrate just with one type, and allow the reader to work out the corresponding point for the other type.

The discussion began by noting that a paradox presents us with a conflict of reasons; the successive accounts of "paradox" just offered are to be understood as attempts to unpack or spell out just what is meant by this initial characterization. It remains to be considered whether *any* conflict of reasons constitutes a paradox. Is it always the case, for instance, that when there are two apparently strong arguments leading to apparently inconsistent conclusions, there is an intellectual problem to be solved, or a conflict about what to believe?

Consider the following two arguments:

99% of Texans are rich.	99% of philosophers are poor.
Jones is a Texan.	Jones is a philosopher.
∴ Jones is rich.	∴ Jones is poor.[4]

Suppose that the premises of the two arguments appear to be true. Certainly, the conclusions are inconsistent. So each of the two arguments appears to be an instance of good inductive reasoning, and (let us assume) to have true premises, but the conclusions are clearly incompatible.

Nonetheless, it is it is quite clear that this sort of conflict of reasons does not constitute a paradox.[5] Situations of this sort, situations in which there is strong evidence for two competing claims, are commonly encountered. But there is nothing mysterious or baffling here, nothing to puzzle or confound. The example trades on a well-known feature of inductive arguments: they are defeasible. That is, certain premises may *in themselves* provide strong inductive support for a conclusion, and yet further evidence may "defeat" the argument; even if the premises are justifiably believed to be true, they may not, *given further information*, warrant belief that the conclusion is true. So in the Texan/philosopher case, there is no difficulty in granting that, given only this evidence, we are not entitled to regard either conclusion as true. The evidence provided by one set of premises defeats the evidence provided by the other. The rational course is clear: suspend belief in each conclusion. There is no sense here, as there is in a paradox, that we are *compelled* to accept the conclusion of each argument, despite recognition of the inconsistency. Thus there is nothing troubling or problematic about this sort of conflict of reasons; there is no intellectual problem to be solved.

Note that the same sort of difficulty may arise with regard to the account of a type I paradox. Consider an argument of the form:

99% of *A*s are *B*.
x is an *A*.
∴ *x* is a *B*.

Suppose that the premises seem to be true, and yet you apparently can see that *x* is not a *B*. Again, there is a conflict of reasons. In such a case, it may be that the perceptual evidence takes priority; or, in some extreme cases, it may be that the inductive evidence is taken to be stronger. Or, finally, it may be that the two sorts of evidence are considered roughly equal in strength, in which case you must suspend belief concerning whether or not *x* is a *B*. But in none of these cases is there anything paradoxical.

The account of the notion of paradox thus requires further refinement. Happily, there is a simple revision that suffices to handle cases of this sort. Up to now, it has been implicitly allowed that the argument(s) in a paradox might be either inductive or deductive. But what seems essential now is that the paradox-generating argument appears to be deductively correct, that is, that the premises appear to logically imply the conclusion. So we have:

> A type I paradox is an argument in which there appears to be valid reasoning from true premises to a false conclusion.

The same sort of qualification is to be understood in the account of a type II paradox. Valid arguments, it should be noted, do not share with inductive arguments the feature of defeasibility. Given premises we are entitled to accept as true, valid reasoning will yield a conclusion we are entitled to accept as true, *no matter what further information we have*. Clearly, if there is an apparently valid argument from apparently true premises to an apparently false conclusion, then we do indeed have an affront to reason; we are entitled to feel baffled and confounded. In a paradox, what appears to be cannot possibly be.

One matter remains. What may seem puzzling, in this series of definitions, is a presupposition that is made here, and in the philosophical literature generally, that the premises of a paradox-generating argument can be, or appear to be, true. The paradoxes presented thus far all involve a description of *a situation that does not exist*; they all involve a story that is not factual. How then can statements about these situations be, strictly speaking, true? In the taxi-cab paradox, for example, a premise of the second argument is: in 100 randomly selected accidents in Greenville involving one taxi, about 85 will involve a green taxi and about 15 will involve a blue taxi. But how can we regard this premise as true when, as far as we know, Greenville does not exist?

Most paradoxes start with a story (although not all do, as we shall see later). This suggests that the notion of truth we use in evaluating the premises of a paradoxical argument, in such cases, is not the everyday, straightforward sense, but is more analogous to fictional truth. As in the taxi-cab paradox, we can discuss what is true in Tolstoy's *Anna Karenina* even though we are clear that the events and situations described never occurred. Moreover, when we speak of the character of Vronsky, our comments can be understood as

prefaced by "In the novel *Anna Karenina* ...".[6] Similarly, our statements about Greenville, it could be argued, are to be taken as prefaced by "In the taxi-cab paradox ...". Of course, there are
significant disanalogies between fictional truth and truth in a paradox; nonetheless, the comparison is suggestive.

"Narrative-paradox" is the term I shall use for those paradoxes
based on descriptions of nonexistent situations, or stories. To say
that a statement is true in a narrative-paradox is to say that it is true
in the story or narrative N that is the basis of the paradox. But how
is this to be understood? We need an account of "true in N" that is
appropriate for the context of paradoxes.

To begin with the obvious, truth in the story of the taxi-cab paradox is clearly a function of the description of the story that gives
rise to the paradox. Let D be the conjunction of statements that
describe the narrative N. Then we might suggest:

(I)   A statement S is true in N just in case S is logically implied by D.

Put differently, this says that any possible world in which D is true
is a world in which S is true.

It might be objected, however, that this first analysis is too
restrictive. The condition that S be implied by D is sufficient for truth
in N, it might be argued, but it is not also necessary. Recall that in the
taxi-cab paradox, we want to say that it is true that in 100 randomly
selected accidents involving one taxi, about 85 will involve a green
taxi and about 15 will involve a blue taxi. But this is not implied just
by the data concerning the colour of taxis in Greenville. At the least,
we also need a statement that is a matter of common knowledge: the
colour of a car is irrelevant to how accident-prone it is.

There are two possible responses here. The first is to grant the
force of the objection, and attempt to revise the account so as to get
around the difficulty. For instance, it might be proposed that:

(II) A statement S is true in N just in case S is logically implied by D,
      or by the conjunction of D and C, where C is a contingent true
      statement.

("True" used without a qualifier here means "true *simpliciter*").
The chief drawback of this proposal is that it is hard to see

exactly what restrictions should be placed on C. Clearly, C must at least be consistent with D. But more than this seems to be required. Otherwise, we will have to say that in the taxi-cab paradox, it is true that, for instance, Glendon College has a bilingual curriculum. This surely does not conform exactly to our intuitions concerning truth in a narrative-paradox.[7] A still further qualification might be suggested in response, to the effect that C be an item of common knowledge. But this is not a very precise notion, and, in any case, the analysis still appears too weak. The statement "George Bush is president of the United States" seems to qualify as common knowledge yet, again, is not true in the paradox.

The alternative, which I favour, is to maintain that the objection to the first proposal does not go through. To do so, we must insist that the statement "The colour of a car is irrelevant to how accident-prone it is" is properly part of the description of the situation envisaged in the taxi-cab paradox, although it is not normally made explicit. It is by no means surprising that this should be so, for it is often no trivial matter to say exactly how the story should be specified, to see precisely what is necessary for the argument.[8] Part of the work demanded by a paradox is to determine how the description must be filled out, sharpened or refined, and this may emerge gradually as the result of ongoing analysis. So there is nothing implausible in the suggestion that a statement not normally made explicit is nonetheless intended as part of the story.

Thus far, the truth of a statement S in N is straightforwardly a function of D. However, one further consideration remains. Paradoxical arguments sometimes appeal to abstract general principles. In evaluating the argument for switching in the Monty Hall paradox, for instance, we grant that if there are two possible outcomes of your doing either A or B, O is the preferred outcome, and B is more likely to yield O than A is, then it is rational to do B rather than A. If this principle is a necessary truth (true in all possible worlds), then it need not be added explicitly to the premises of the argument. If the argument is valid with it, then it is also valid without it. But such principles are often included in the paradoxical argument, and this may make it easier to assess the validity of the argument. So we may say:

(III) A statement S is true in N just in case S is logically implied by D, or by the conjunction of D and $T_1, ..., T_n$, where each T_i is a necessary truth.

Assuming that such general principles, if true, are necessarily true, (III) seems the most promising account thus far.[9]

Let us recast the definition of "paradox" in light of the above. We now have a distinction between "true" ("true *simpliciter*") and "N-true". Thus we may say:

> A type I paradox is an argument in which either (i) the premises appear to be true, the conclusion false and the argument valid or (ii) the premises appear to be N-true, the conclusion N-false and the argument valid.

Finally, a word on terminology. When we say that a particular statement is true in a narrative N, we are not using the ordinary, everyday notion of truth. Still, there seems to be no danger of confusion if we use the word "true" with no further qualification in discussing paradoxes based on stories. In contexts where it seems wise to remind the reader that we are using a special sense of "true", the term "N-true" will be used. For paradoxes that do not begin with a story, of course, we need only the ordinary sense of "true". The reader should easily adapt to supplying the appropriate sense of "true" in a given context.

Types of paradox

We have already seen that paradoxes may be classified as type I or type II. Before going on to consider how a paradox may be resolved, further distinctions will be helpful. First, the notion of a veridical paradox:[10]

> A type I paradox is veridical just in case its conclusion is true (N-true in the case of a narrative-paradox, true *simpliciter* otherwise).

> A type II paradox is veridical just in case the conclusions of the two arguments are both true.

Of course, the truth of the conclusion(s) does not provide a logical guarantee that the reasoning is impeccable, nor that the premises are true (although one might search in vain for a veridical paradox in which there is a flaw in either). Still, what is deceptive in a veridical paradox, at the very least, is the appearance of falsity in the conclusion (or the appearance that at least one of the conclusions is false).

The notion of a falsidical paradox is understood analogously. A type I paradox is falsidical provided that its conclusion is false; a type II paradox is falsidical if at least one of its conclusions is false. So in a falsidical paradox, the fault lies in the paradox-generating argument (or in at least one of the arguments), either in the premises, or in the reasoning.

Of the paradoxes we have to draw on, only the barber paradox can be considered to be veridical, for it is generally conceded that there is no flaw in the paradoxical argument, either in the premises or in the reasoning. But the conclusion of the barber paradox is:

> The barber cuts his own hair if and only if he does not cut his own hair.

How can we say that this conclusion is true, as required by the definition of "veridical"? After all, any statement of the form "P if and only if $\sim P$" is necessarily false.

Here it is essential to remember that in classifying the barber paradox as veridical, we are committed only to saying that the conclusion of the paradoxical argument is N-true, true in the barber story. This is guaranteed if the conclusion is implied by the statements in the description of the paradox. But it is now generally recognized that the story that gives rise to the paradox (there is a village in which there is a barber who cuts the hair of all and only those villagers who do not cut their own hair) is incoherent, that it is impossible for there to be such a village. Hence, there is no problem in granting that the description implies an impossible conclusion, and thus no problem in granting that the conclusion is N-true. A necessarily false premise may imply a necessarily false conclusion.

The same sort of thing may occur in a type II veridical narrative-paradox. Given that the paradox is veridical, the conclusions of both arguments will be N-true. One might naturally assume, in such a case, that the conclusions must be consistent. But if the description of the paradox is itself necessarily false, then the conclusions may both be implied by the description, and yet be inconsistent.

A clear example of a type I falsidical paradox is provided by the Achilles and the tortoise paradox. Of the type II paradoxes already introduced, all seem to be falsidical: the two conclusions, in each case, are unquestionably inconsistent and yet the descriptions seem logically coherent.

The final distinction to be drawn here is between controversial and uncontroversial paradoxes:

> A type I paradox is uncontroversial if either there is general agreement that its conclusion is true or general agreement that its conclusion is false.

Note that to say that a paradox is uncontroversial does not mean that there is *no* controversy surrounding it. There may be broad agreement that the conclusion of an argument is false, even though there is no consensus concerning the diagnosis of the flaw in the argument. Both the barber and Achilles and the tortoise provide examples of uncontroversial paradoxes. The corresponding definition for type II paradoxes is:

> A type II paradox is uncontroversial if either there is general agreement that both conclusions are true or there is general agreement that a particular conclusion is false.

Looking at the type II paradoxes, the Monty Hall paradox can fairly be regarded as uncontroversial, since it is generally recognized that it is rational to switch one's choice of door. But the taxi-cab and the ship of Theseus are both controversial.

To sum up, the distinctions drawn is this section can be illustrated as follows:

Barber	type I, veridical, uncontroversial
Achilles and the tortoise	type I, falsidical, uncontroversial
Monty Hall	type II, falsidical, uncontroversial
Ship of Theseus	type II, falsidical, controversial
Taxi-cab	type II, falsidical, controversial

How to resolve a paradox

At this point, we have an account of what constitutes a paradox, and an understanding of the different types of paradox. What remains to be dealt with is the question of how to respond to a paradox, how to provide a resolution.

Paradoxes present us with apparently impeccable operations of reason that nonetheless lead to apparent absurdity. They are upsetting because, while the illusion persists, we have a challenge to the supposed veracity and reliability of reason. If this is where logic can lead, then why would we recommend logic or respect its dictates? The threat to reason can be overcome only by puncturing the illusion created by the paradox.

To resolve a paradox it is necessary to show that the paradoxical argument does not in fact present us with an impeccable use of reason leading to a patent absurdity. There are thus two principal options in providing a resolution for a type I paradox: (i) we may dispel the illusion that the argument is air-tight by isolating and diagnosing a flaw or fallacy in the argument; or (ii) we may *explain away* the appearance of falsity in the conclusion. This is accomplished by explaining why the conclusion appears to be false even though it is in fact true. In pursuing alternative (i), attempting to find a flaw in the argument, there are two further options: (a) show that at least one of the premises is not true; or (b) show that the argument is invalid.

Briefly, the options for resolving a type II paradox are as follows. One sort of resolution will consist in finding a flaw in one of the two paradox-generating arguments, either in the premises or in the reasoning. Alternatively, we may explain why it *appears* that the conclusions cannot both be true even though, in fact, both are.

Later chapters will study instances of the different types of resolutions in detail. For now, let us look at some of the paradoxes already introduced in order to illustrate these distinctions. Of necessity, the discussion will be limited to the uncontroversial paradoxes.

The barber paradox has been cited as an instance of a veridical paradox. This despite that the fact that its conclusion, that the barber cuts his own hair if and only if he does not, is a contradiction. To make sense of this, it is essential to keep in mind, as was pointed out earlier, that it is strictly N-truth and N-falsity that are relevant to the assessment of the argument of a paradox based on a story. The real issue is whether the conclusion is N-true, that is, whether the description of the village implies the premises of the argument, which, in turn, imply the conclusion. It may at first seem that this could not be, since the description of the village seems perfectly consistent, and a consistent set of statements does not imply a contradiction. But it is not difficult to convince oneself that the description is, in fact, contradictory. After all, it refers to, among others, the barber himself, and says of him that he cuts his own hair if and only if he does not. So there is no problem in granting that the conclusion of the paradoxical argument is N-true, that it is implied by the description of the village. It appears to be N-false only because it is contradictory and the description of the village appears, at first, perfectly consistent. Thus, we can explain the *appearance* of falsity while granting that the conclusion is true.

This treatment of the barber paradox exemplifies one basic approach to veridical paradox resolution: showing that the description of the paradox is inconsistent. If it is, then there need be no surprise or shock at what the description implies, since anything follows from an inconsistency.

The Monty Hall paradox provides an example of an uncontroversial falsidical paradox, for it is generally agreed that the correct strategy is to switch your choice of door after Monty shows you a goat door. This means that there must be a flaw in the argument that there is no good reason to switch – in the "no switching argument". But what, precisely, is wrong with it? Suppose you pick door A, and then Monty shows you that door C has a goat behind it. A key premise in the no switching argument is that after door C is revealed as a goat door, it is *as likely* that the car is behind door A as it is that it is behind door B; the two possibilities are equally likely. To find a fallacy in the no switching argument and thereby resolve the paradox, it is this premise, I believe, that must be successfully rebutted.

Consider. If Monty's intent had been simply to open one of the three doors at random, and this intent had resulted in his opening door C, and revealing a goat behind it, then it would be equally likely that the car was behind door A and that it was behind door B. But Monty's choice was in fact restricted to door B or door C, and his intent was to choose a goat door. So you know something about door *B* that you do not know about door *A*; there is an asymmetry in your knowledge of the two doors. In a choice between door *B* and another door, where the intent was to choose a goat door, door *B* was not chosen. How is this knowledge relevant to the assignment of probabilities? Well, there was a 2/3 chance that Monty's choice was forced – that only one of the two doors was a goat door. Since you knew that Monty's intent was to open a goat door, and that he could do this, *his opening door C and revealing it to be a goat door does not change this probability*. But if Monty's choice was forced, then the car is behind door *B*. Thus, there is a likelihood of 2/3 that the car is behind door *B*; and, accordingly, there is only a 1/3 likelihood that it is behind door *A*.

If this analysis is correct, then we have dissolved the paradox, dispelled the illusion, by showing that one of the premises in one of the paradox-generating arguments is false. Of course, the reasoning is subtle; the flaw in the no switching argument is not easy to discern. Indeed, some mathematicians and probability theorists have been initially taken in by the no switching argument, although none has persisted in defending it.

Further illustrations of the resolution of a paradox must await the more detailed treatment of individual paradoxes. But, at this point, some words of caution are in order. First, to be satisfactory, the resolution of a paradox should be robust: it should stand up to strengthened versions of the paradox. For instance, the paradox-generating argument may initially be presented with an extremely strong premise, a premise that makes a very broad, sweeping claim. If so, it may take no great acumen to point out counter-examples to the premise. However, before declaring the paradox vanquished, we need to be sure that it cannot simply be reinstated when a suitably weakened version of the critical assumption is provided. To be robust, the attack on a paradoxical argument should be focused on the strongest, most impregnable version of the argument available.

A related point concerns different versions of the same paradox. The Achilles and the tortoise paradox, for example, seems to be essentially the same as the racetrack paradox (see the Appendix). If so, then any solution to the one should also be applicable, with the appropriate changes, to the other. An attempted resolution of a paradox that cannot be applied successfully to *every* version of the paradox must be off the mark in that it focuses on some inessential feature of the paradox. This is not to say that it is always evident whether one paradox is a variant of another. In fact, the criteria for two arguments being versions of the same paradox are far from obvious. One can even imagine cases in which the fact that a solution applies to one argument, but not to the other, would be cited as reason for denying that these are just two versions of the same paradox. Nonetheless, as we shall also see, there are many cases in which it is entirely clear that different scenarios are all versions of the same paradox, and thus require a unified solution.

What does *not* count as a resolution of a paradox? The negative may be almost as significant as the positive here. One very common and natural response to a stated paradox is *to present another argument*. More specifically, the response is an attempt to present an even more compelling or persuasive argument for (or against) the conclusion (one of the conclusions) involved in the original paradox. Consider the Monty Hall paradox, for example. Suppose a mathematician friend, having announced that she has a solution to the paradox, proceeds to give a very clear, very explicit, and very powerful argument for the conclusion that one ought to switch doors. Whatever the merits of her argument and the worth of her contribution, they do not constitute a *solution* to the paradox, for the argument in favour of not switching is left untouched. So there is still an apparent conflict of reasons: two ostensibly strong arguments for inconsistent conclusions. Consequently, there is still a sense of confusion, of being befuddled, which can be cleared up only by an analysis of an error or flaw in one of the arguments. A paradox is not unravelled by attempting, however successfully, to prove that one "side" in the conflict is correct. Later chapters will provide examples of philosophers responding to the challenge of a paradox in this way.

The ideal, in treating a paradox, is to puncture the illusion of letter-perfect reasoning leading to clear absurdity. But short of achieving this ideal, there are still worthwhile contributions one can make. The mathematician's argument alluded to in the previous paragraph may convince us that the rational response in the Monty Hall scenario is indeed to switch, when previously we had been uncertain. While such an argument does not suffice to dissolve the paradox, it may convert a previously controversial paradox to the status of uncontroversial. Assuming the argument to be correct, this constitutes an advance in the understanding of the problem, and progress in the search for a solution. If it is known that the correct strategy is to switch doors in the Monty Hall game, then the focus must be squarely on the no switching argument, and the attempt to locate a flaw in it. The range of possible solutions has been narrowed.

One other way to move a controversial type I paradox into the uncontroversial category is worth mentioning here (and will be illustrated in Chapter 4). Suppose we construct an argument that is strongly analogous to the original paradoxical argument, but that leads to a conclusion even more preposterous or bizarre than that of the paradoxical argument; so bizarre, in fact, that it is *completely clear* that the conclusion, and therefore the argument, have to be rejected. Since the new argument is strongly analogous to the original paradoxical argument, it is now apparent that the original argument must also be rejected. Again, the set of possible options for a solution has contracted.

There is, finally, one other way to make progress on a paradox, short of resolving it or narrowing the range of possible solutions: progress can be made by clarifying one of the central arguments. This may be achieved in a variety of ways. Among the more significant are: analysing one of the key concepts; setting out, fully, rigorously and explicitly, the premises necessary for the argument; ensuring that the premises are just as strong as needed, but no stronger, so that the argument is as immune to criticism as possible; and making clear exactly what the inferential steps are that take us from the premises to the conclusion, so that any logical gaps in reasoning will be more apparent.

This section has considered how to resolve a paradox, how not to resolve a paradox and how to make progress on a paradox short of resolution. To conclude, let us consider the question of why we feel a pressing need to untangle a paradox, why we care about paradoxes. One answer has already been suggested. An unresolved paradox is a threat to the trustworthiness of reason. How can reason command our respect if it leads to absurdities? But another motivation stems from the fact that the proper resolution of a paradox may give us greater philosophical knowledge. Faulty assumptions concerning, for instance, justified belief, or rational action, may be uncovered in the unravelling of the paradox.

Of course, some paradoxes, of which the barber is one, have little, or no, philosophical punch. The ship of Theseus, on the other hand, may reveal a good deal about the principles governing our concept of the identity of a physical object. The depth of a paradox is generally considered to be a function of the sort of philosophical impact its resolution will have. At one extreme of the spectrum, a paradox may reveal an incoherence that necessitates a fundamental revision of our conceptual scheme; at the other end of the spectrum there is the barber. Unfortunately, a proper appreciation of the depth of a paradox frequently must await its resolution.

2 | Paradox and contradiction

Dialetheism

Paradoxes are baffling. Faced with an apparently impeccable argument that leads to an apparently outrageous conclusion, we are confused and confounded. On the one hand, the conclusion appears false; on the other hand, it apparently must be true. What appears to be cannot be, we assume. This is the source of our fascination; this is why there is a problem.

Recently, impressive arguments have been advanced that this underlying assumption is mistaken. A statement can be *both true and false*, it is maintained; further, it can be rational to believe that a given statement and its negation are both true. Contradictions (statements of the form "A & $\sim A$") can be true, and can be rationally believed.[1] If this view, known as "dialetheism", prevails, there are clear consequences for the account of paradox. In Chapter 1, three strategies for dealing with a paradox were distinguished: show that the argument is invalid; show that a premise is false; and explain away the appearance of falsity in the conclusion. But if contradictions can be true, and can be rationally believed, then there is another legitimate response to a paradox: accept everything that appears to be the case, that is, grant that the conclusion of the paradoxical argument is both true and false.

This is an apparently fantastic proposal. Until recently, dialetheism would have been dismissed out of hand as a simple conceptual confusion. Largely because of the work of philosopher Graham Priest, however, it has come to be regarded as at least deserving of serious consideration and response.

The aim of this chapter is to give the reader an understanding of the intricacies of the theory as developed by Priest, and an awareness of some of the sophisticated responses Priest has developed to traditional objections. What seem to be some of the outstanding difficulties for dialetheism will also be presented. I do not suggest that any of following is likely to subdue the committed dialetheist; however, the implications and the cost of accepting true contradictions should emerge more clearly in the end.

The radical nature of dialetheism is best appreciated by contrast with the prevailing view. Classical logic, the logic that currently represents the orthodox view, maintains that every statement must be either true or false; truth and falsity are *exhaustive* categories. It also holds that no statement can be both true and false; truth and falsity are *exclusive* categories. To put it a little more graphically, according to classical logic, there are no truth-value gaps (every statement falls into one of the two categories); and there are no truth-value gluts (no statement falls into both categories). The possibilities, for classical logic, may be represented as in Figure 2.1.

But for the logic of dialetheism, "paraconsistent logic" as it is called, an accurate representation is as in Figure 2.2. Area 2 represents statements that are true and not false; area 3 represents statements that are false and not true; and area 4 represents statements that are both true and false. Each of these areas contains statements; only area 1 is empty. There are no statements that lack a truth-value, that are neither true nor false. In short, there are truth-value gluts, but no truth-value gaps.[2]

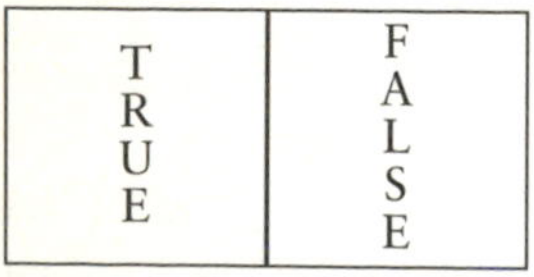

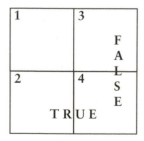

Figure 2.1

Figure 2.2

One first wonders, quite naturally, what might have prompted such a radical view. The principal source of dialetheism, for Priest, is an ancient paradox, the liar paradox. Let "*S*" refer to the sentence:

This sentence is false.

It seems that if *S* is true, then, since *S* asserts its own falsity, *S* is false. On the other hand, if *S* is false, then, since *S* asserts its own falsity, *S* must be true. It follows that *S* is true if and only if it is false. But this implies that *S* is both true and false. It seems that a contradiction can be derived from unquestionably true premises.

The liar paradox has been known for over two thousand years, and has been the subject of intense debate, especially in recent times. In Priest's view, all the solutions to the paradox that have been offered (other than his own) face serious problems: they are often *ad hoc*; they are complex; they seem vulnerable to strengthened versions of the paradox. Since every attempt to avoid the conclusion of the paradoxical argument faces difficulties, we are warranted, according to Priest, in thinking it cannot be avoided. That is, we are warranted in accepting the conclusion: *S* is both true and false. This is the main argument Priest offers for dialetheism.[3]

Dialetheism, we should be clear, does not maintain that all contradictions are true, only that some are. On Priest's version, few contradictions are true. Nor is it claimed that accepting both the conclusion of a paradox-generating argument and its negation is the proper response to *every* paradox. But it is a possible response to a paradox, since it is possible for a statement to be both true and false.

If the possibility of true contradictions is countenanced, then the classical system of logic must be abandoned. But is there an acceptable alternative? The current attitude toward dialetheism, which is more receptive or at least more tolerant, stems largely from the fact that Priest has constructed a system of paraconsistent logic that is remarkably similar to classical logic, and yet is apparently not "infected" with contradictions; that is, not all contradictions are true. An awareness of at least the skeleton of this paraconsistent system is essential to a full appreciation of the strength of dialetheism.

Let us see how the truth-functional connectives may be defined. Paraconsistent logic admits three truth-values:

t: true only (true and not false)
f: false only (false and not true)
b: true and false

How can negation be understood in terms of these three truth-values? The controlling intuition here comes from classical logic, which takes the negation of a statement to be true if and only if the statement is false. In paraconsistent logic, negation behaves as in the classical system provided the statement is true only or false only. But the negation of a statement that is both true and false will itself be both true and false. Thus the truth-table in Figure 2.3 defines negation.

The understanding of conjunction is also built on classical logic, where a conjunction is true if and only if both conjuncts are true, and false just in case at least one conjunct is false. In paraconsistent logic, if neither conjunct is both true and false, the conjunction behaves as in the classical system. The only issue is how to understand a conjunction in which one conjunct has both truth-values. Suppose *A* is true only, and *B* is both true and false. First, *A* and *B* are both true, so the conjunction is true. However, since *B* is also false, one conjunct is false, and the conjunction is therefore false. So the conjunction is both true and false. The defining truth-table is shown in Figure 2.4. Note that whenever one conjunct is false only, the conjunction is false only.

A	*~A*	*A & B*
t	*t*	*t*
t	*b*	*b*
t	*f*	*f*
b	*t*	*b*
b	*b*	*b*
b	*f*	*f*
f	*t*	*f*
f	*b*	*f*
f	*f*	*f*

A	*~A*
t	*f*
b	*b*
f	*t*

Figure 2.3

Figure 2.4

It is now clear how dialetheism will treat disjunctions. As in classical logic, a disjunction is true if and only if at least one disjunct is true, and false if and only if both disjuncts are false. Novelty arises only in the case in which one disjunct has both truth-values. Suppose A is false only, while B is both true and false. Since one disjunct is true, the disjunction is true; but since both disjuncts are also false, the disjunction is also false. Similarly, the truth-table for the conditional will deviate from the classical truth-table only when one component has both truth-values. In paraconsistent logic, as in the classical system, a conditional is false if its antecedent is true and consequent false, and true otherwise. But if the antecedent is both true and false, and the consequent false only, then the conditional will be both true and false.

This is sufficient to enable us to understand how the dialetheist can construe the statement connectives in terms of the three truth-values. The understanding of validity is also based on the classical system. An argument is considered truth-functionally valid if and only if it is truth preserving, that is, for any assignment of truth-values to the simple statements in which the premises are all true, the conclusion is also true. But the traditional definition has startling implications here: a valid argument, in paraconsistent logic, may have true premises and a false conclusion. What is impossible is a valid argument with true premises and a *false only* conclusion. Finally, a tautology is understood as a statement that is true under any assignment of truth-values to its simple statements. It is a remarkable fact that the tautologies of classical logic are all tautologies in Priest's system of paraconsistent logic as well. Clearly, the close fit between the classical and the paraconsistent systems that Priest has achieved is impressive, and is responsible, in large measure, for the new respectability of dialetheism.

Does Priest's paraconsistent logic constitute a fundamental conceptual revision to which we must simply adapt? Is there merit in the comparison of this new logic to the Copernican hypothesis that the earth revolves around the sun? Despite its technical success, there are still major hurdles facing dialetheism. Let us survey some of them.

An apparently knockdown objection to any theory that countenances true contradictions claims that a contradiction implies any statement whatsoever. The derivation is as follows:

(1) $A \,\&\, \sim\!A$
(2) A from (1)
(3) $A \lor B$ from (2)
(4) $\sim\!A$ from (1)
(5) B from (3) and (4)

This seems to show that any statement follows from a contradiction, since the second disjunct in (3) can be any statement you like. Thus, if even one contradiction is true and can be rationally believed, then every statement is true and can be rationally believed.

Not even the dialetheist can tolerate rational belief in everything; nor is he compelled to. The derivation offered above is certainly valid in classical logic. But in paraconsistent logic, the inference from (3) and (4) to (5) is not licensed; that is, the rule known as "disjunctive syllogism" is invalid. To see this, consider a situation in which both A and $\sim\!A$ are true, while B is false only. The *possibility* of this truth assignment is sufficient to establish the invalidity of disjunctive syllogism in Priest's system, for on this assignment, the premises of the inference are true and the conclusion false. The possibility that A is both true and false, while B is false only, also provides a direct proof that not every statement follows from a contradiction in paraconsistent logic. Hence, this traditional objection to true contradictions has no weight in Priest's system.

Are there more damaging objections to dialetheism? Three potentially troublesome areas for the dialetheist will be examined: (i) the notions of accepting and rejecting a statement; (ii) classically valid rules of inference that are invalid in dialetheic logic; and (iii) the requirement that a meaningful statement must rule out some possibility.

Accepting and rejecting a statement

Priest distinguishes three cognitive attitudes that you may have to a statement: you may accept A, reject A, or be agnostic about A (neither accept nor reject A). This tripartite distinction is, of course, familiar. Most of us accept the claim that the earth revolves around the sun, reject the view that all heavenly bodies revolve around the earth and are agnostic on the issue of whether there is life on other planets.

To accept a statement is to believe it. But what is it to reject a statement? The classical view is that to reject A is to disbelieve A, and to disbelieve A is to believe $\sim A$. Priest, however, cannot subscribe to this identification. According to him, contradictions can be true and can be believed. Thus we can believe A and also believe $\sim A$. So if dialetheism adopted the classical view, it would be possible both to accept and reject a statement. But Priest insists that acceptance and rejection are exclusive, that one cannot both accept and reject A. His reason for maintaining this exclusivity is that there are dispositions to certain behaviour patterns associated with accepting and rejecting a statement, and these dispositions, he claims, cannot be manifested simultaneously.

Priest's positive thesis concerning rejection is as follows. To reject A is not just to fail to believe it, nor to believe $\sim A$, but to *refuse* to accept A.[4] No gloss is given of "refuse to accept A", but it is clear that the phrase is intended to convey something more than just not accepting A. One possible reading is that to refuse to accept A is to first consider A seriously, take it as a "live option", and then decline to accept it. This, however, is hardly a satisfactory interpretation. I may seriously consider whether Bernard loves Sara, and then decline to believe it; but this is quite compatible with my being agnostic on the issue of whether Bernard loves Sara. Certainly, it does not follow from the above that I reject the claim that he loves her. So this is not, for Priest, an acceptable reading of "refuse to accept".

Another possible interpretation of Priest is that to refuse to accept A is to not believe A and to be committed to not believing A; that is, to believe that no further evidence will be forthcoming that will (or should) get you to believe A. The difficulty here again is that I may, in this sense, refuse to accept that there is life on other planets, and yet be agnostic on this issue. For I may be agnostic on this matter while believing that we will never have adequate evidence for or against the existence of extraterrestrial life.

Let us give up the attempt to clarify Priest's account of rejecting a statement in terms of refusing to accept for the moment, and briefly consider other options. An alternative suggestion is that to reject A is to believe $\sim A$ *and* not also believe A. This, one might think, will get around the difficulties of the classical view. But even this somewhat desperate manoeuvre does not succeed as an account of rejection in a dialetheist system. If I now believe ~*A*, and do not believe *A*, this may be because I am agnostic on the issue of *A*'s truth, because I regard *A*'s truth as an open issue. But if this is so, we surely cannot say that I reject *A*.

The most promising proposal may be that to reject *A* is to believe that *A* is untrue, that is, to believe that *A* is *false only*. A difficulty with this proposal will emerge in the final section of this chapter. For now, it suffices to say that one outstanding issue for dialetheism is whether the theory can make sense of what it is to reject a statement.[5]

Invalid rules of inference

A second predicament for dialetheism concerns rules of inference. In Priest's paraconsistent logic, several classically valid argument forms are no longer valid, that is, no longer truth-preserving. Some of the more important examples include:

$A \lor B$	$A \supset B$	$A \supset B$	$A \supset (B \;\&\; \sim B)$
$\sim A$	A	$\sim B$	$\therefore \sim A$
$\therefore B$	$\therefore B$	$\therefore \sim A$	

The first three argument forms are, respectively, disjunctive syllogism, *modus ponens* and *modus tollens*. The last is a plausible representation of *reductio ad absurdum*. We have already noted that disjunctive syllogism cannot be considered valid in dialetheic logical theory. If *A* is both true and false, while *B* is false only, both the premises will be true, but the conclusion will not be true, and the form is thus invalid. The same truth assignment will show *modus ponens* invalid. The last two argument forms can be seen to be invalid by considering the case in which *A* is true only, while *B* is both true and false. That these basic argument forms cannot be counted valid seems to be a mark against paraconsistent logic, and a serious obstacle for dialetheism. The cost of accepting true contradictions appears to be escalating.[6]

But the dialetheist is not easily subdued, and not without response. Note that these classically valid argument forms fail to be truth-preserving *only* when the truth-values involved are not classical (true only or false only). Argument forms that are truth-preserving only under such conditions are referred to by Priest as "quasi-valid".[7] One might expect the dialetheist simply to dig in his heels at this point, and insist that quasi-valid rules of inference are not to be used, that they are invalid and reasoning in accord with them is not rational. This, however, is a sacrifice Priest is not prepared to make; for renouncing *modus ponens*, disjunctive syllogism and other quasi-valid rules would, he contends, have a paralysing effect on both everyday and mathematical reasoning. Instead, Priest aims to provide a *pragmatic justification* of these rules, to show that it is normally acceptable (rational) to reason in accordance with them, despite their invalidity.

What sort of pragmatic justification can be offered for disjunctive syllogism? This rule of inference fails to preserve truth only when some statement in the argument is both true and false. However, according to Priest, statements that are both true and false ("paradoxical statements", he calls them) are rare; the probability of any given contradiction being true is, *ceteris paribus,* very low (although it is not 0, as classical probability calculus has it). This statistical infrequency provides the basis for the rationale of disjunctive syllogism, which runs as follows. Since true contradictions are rare, we are entitled to presuppose there are no paradoxical statements in an argument as long as there is no positive case for thinking there are. Consequently, it is reasonable to employ an argument of the form disjunctive syllogism provided there is no positive reason for thinking that some statement in the argument is paradoxical.

The same sort of considerations justify the use of other quasi-valid rules. With regard to *reductio ad absurdum*, note that the low statistical frequency of true contradictions grounds the claim that inconsistency in one's beliefs is, prima facie, a rational transgression. If certain views imply a contradiction, then there is probably error in those views. So a *reductio* does not provide definitive grounds for regarding one's hypothesis as mistaken, but it does give reasonable assurance that it is not true. The benefits of classical logic seem to have been recaptured.

The claim that paradoxical statements are statistically rare is pivotal to the pragmatic justification of quasi-valid rules of inference, and merits closer scrutiny. Priest's case for dialetheism is based primarily on his analysis of the sort of sentences that give rise to the liar paradox; but he contends that there are true contradictions in the empirical world as well as in the realm of logic. As I walk out of a room, there is an instant when "I am symmetrically poised, one foot in and one foot out, my center of gravity lying on the vertical plane containing the center of gravity of the door".[8] Am I in the room or not? According to Priest, the only possible answer is that I am both in the room and not in the room. Again, when I write, there is a time at which my pen is in contact with the paper, and a time when it is not. At the instant when it leaves the paper, it is, according to Priest, both on and off the paper. Finally, note that these examples are not limited to cases of physical change. Suppose you have been puzzling over a problem for days. Suddenly the answer occurs to you. At the instant the solution strikes you, Priest says, you both know and do not know the solution.

These examples all have to do with the instant of change. But it seems that similar examples could be produced in vast numbers. Assuming the correctness of Priest's analysis, then, one wonders if true contradictions are so exceedingly rare.

Leaving aside these qualms, there remain deeper perplexities concerning the issue of warrant. How can the claim that true contradictions are statistically rare be justified? Grant that Priest's philosophical work acknowledges relatively few true contradictions. Still, this shows, at best, that he has thus far *discovered* only a small number of true contradictions. To some dialetheists, it may seem just obvious that true contradictions are rare. After all, sense perception never reveals to us cases of true contradictions; we never see that a person is both tall and not tall. But consider Priest's example in which Socrates is said to be both sitting and not sitting at the moment he rises. Here, he says, the contradiction is revealed to us only by a priori analysis, not by observation.[9] And presumably he would say the same of the person halfway in and halfway out of the room. The point is that even in the empirical realm, there are true contradictions that elude observation.

In a recent paper, however, Priest maintains that if α is an observable state of affairs, then it is possible *to perceive that α & $\sim\alpha$ does not obtain*.[10] If this is so, it should be immensely helpful in establishing that true contradictions are rare, since Priest can then argue that, on the basis of perception, we know that great stretches of the observable world contain no true contradictions. Priest begins with the assertion that the contents of your visual sense experience can be contradictory; that is, it can visually appear to you that a contradiction is true. This he takes to be established by appeal to an Escher-like drawing, and to two other visual illusions: one in which, as he understands it, something appears to be both at rest and in motion, and one in which something appears (although extremely briefly) to be both red and green. Priest then argues that if an object, say a cup, appears to me to be at rest, I can *see that* it is not also in motion, for I know what it looks like for a thing to be both at rest and in motion, and that is not how it now looks.

One critical difficulty with this line of thought lies in the claim that we know, in general, how things would appear if a contradiction were true. For Priest has given, at best, three cases in which the contents of our visual experience are contradictory. Even granting what he has to say about these examples, they have no bearing on other perceptual properties. That is, there is still no reason to think that it is possible, or that we know what it would be like, for a thing to appear both round and square, tall and not tall, shiny and dull. So there is a problem in extrapolating to other perceptual properties, in generalizing. Further, Priest seems to assume that there is only one way a thing can appear to be both, say, at rest and in motion: the way his example illustrates. The fact that things do not look *that way* is the reason I can supposedly see that the cup is not both at rest and in motion. But perhaps there is another way, one that I do not know, that things might look if this particular contradiction were true. Clearly, the argument does not establish that for any observable α, α & $\sim\alpha$ can be perceived not to obtain.

Priest also has an entirely different route to establishing the low frequency of true contradictions, one that is more direct, and that is based on the normal success of quasi-valid reasoning. His argument runs as follows. We use arguments such as disjunctive syllogism all the time, and they have rarely led us astray; that is, they have rarely led from true premises to a conclusion that is not true. Disjunctive syllogism is the form: $A \lor B$, $\sim A$, $\therefore B$. An argument of this form will lead from true premises to a conclusion that is not true only when A and $\sim A$ are both true, and B is not true, that is, only when a contradiction is true. Thus, Priest concludes, the normal success of disjunctive syllogism is best explained by the infrequency of true contradictions.[11,12]

This line of reasoning, however, is also less than decisive; for there is a very simple alternative explanation for the apparent success of disjunctive syllogism. Note that the argument form *never* (as opposed to rarely) appears to lead us astray. A possible explanation for this is that whenever we seem to have an instance of disjunctive syllogism leading to a conclusion that is not true, *we infer* that one of the premises must also be not true. That is, we reason according to classical logic in which disjunctive syllogism is valid, and this of course affects our evaluation of the truth-value of the premises and conclusion. Thus, the lack of *apparent* counter-examples to disjunctive syllogism can be adequately explained by our adherence to classical logic. Priest has somehow to eliminate this alternative explanation.

Priest's pragmatic justification of quasi-valid reasoning requires an adequate defence of the infrequency of true contradictions, which has yet to be supplied. Reflection on his attempted justification, however, points the way to deeper problems with the epistemology of dialetheism. Surely it will be possible to establish the low frequency of true contradictions only if it is possible to justify a claim, concerning *at least one particular statement*, that it is not both true and false. But there are epistemic difficulties at this very basic level. Paradoxical statements do not wear their truth-value on their sleeve, and neither do non-paradoxical ones.

It is a standard assumption in epistemology that there is a general conceptual connection linking evidence and justification, a connection that presupposes nothing about what constitutes good evidence. Good evidence might include, for instance, perception, testimony, considerations of simplicity or the fact that the hypothesis in question provides the best explanation of some accepted fact. Let us see what sorts of principles linking evidence and justification might be appropriate if dialetheism is correct.

Suppose it is claimed that A is true, and not paradoxical – not also false. What sort of evidence is required for this assertion that A is only true to be justified? Clearly, the fact that there is strong evidence for A is not sufficient to justify the statement that A is true and not false, for such evidence shows at best that A is true. Once A's being true is split apart from A's not being false, evidence for one is not automatically evidence for the other.

One might therefore suggest the following principle:

(O)   If there is strong evidence for A and no (or weak) evidence for $\sim A$, then we are warranted in believing that A is only true (true and not false).

Of course, it would be circular to attempt to justify (O) on the basis of the infrequency of true contradictions. To establish the generalization, we noted earlier, it is first necessary to be able to decide a particular case. For the same reason, a more limited version of (O), which restricts A to certain subject areas, cannot be justified on the basis of where true contradictions are likely (unlikely) to occur.

The fact is that, in the context of dialetheism, (O) is highly suspect as an epistemic principle, for what (O) seems to presuppose is:

(O_1)   If there is no (or only weak) evidence for $\sim A$, then we are warranted in believing that A is not false.

But why should the absence of evidence for $\sim A$ entitle us to think that A is not false? Why would it not warrant us instead in being agnostic about A's falsity, in being agnostic about $\sim A$? (O_1) is surely wrong; the fact that we have no evidence for something does not entitle us to think that it is not so. The principle seems to license a form of argument from ignorance. But it is entirely unclear how to improve on (O_1).

We have been considering what sort of evidence could justify belief that a statement is true and not false. It is worth noting that difficulties also arise if one asks what sort of evidence justifies belief in a contradiction. The following might be suggested:

(O_2)   If there is strong evidence for A and equally strong evidence for $\sim A$, then we are warranted in believing that A is both true and false.

But why would this equally strong evidence for A and for $\sim A$ not warrant suspension of belief concerning A? Let us be a little clearer. Strong evidence for a statement justifies a belief only if the *total evidence* strongly supports the statement. But if there is equally strong evidence for A and for $\sim A$, then it seems that the total evidence supports neither. And if that is so, then we are warranted in believing neither.

A key issue, then, in attempting to construct an adequate epistemology to mesh with paraconsistent logic is how to specify the sort of evidence that would count as adequate epistemic grounds for asserting that a statement is true only (or true and false). There is a significant lacuna here in the theory of dialetheism; the prospect of filling it seems dim.

A meaningful statement must exclude some possibility

A traditional objection to true contradictions, which can perhaps be traced back to Aristotle's *Metaphysics*, is that if contradictions could be true, nothing would be meaningful. In order for a statement to be meaningful, the argument runs, it must rule out some possibility. A claim that rules out nothing is meaningless. But according to dialetheism, a statement *A* and its negation can both be true. So *A* does not rule out ~*A*, and thus rules out nothing. Since any contradiction can be true, no statement rules out its negation, and thus no statement has meaning.

The requirement that a meaningful statement must rule out something seems intuitively quite plausible. But the notion of one statement ruling out another is surely in need of clarification. One way to understand it is:

> *A* rules out *B* if and only if it is logically impossible for both *A* and *B* to be true.

On this interpretation of "rules out", the dialetheist must grant that, in his system, *A* does not rule out ~*A*, and thus rules out nothing. He is then left with the rest of the argument. Presumably, he will have to try to deny that ruling out something is a necessary condition for meaningfulness.[13]

But there is another possible interpretation of "ruling out":

> *A* rules out *B* if and only if it is logically necessary that if *A* is true, then *B* is false.

On this reading, the dialetheist's problem dissolves. *A* does rule out ~*A*, for if *A* is true, then ~*A* must be false. In classical logic, the two interpretations are equivalent – not so in paraconsistent logic. Each seems a plausible and natural reading, perhaps because they are equivalent in orthodox logic. So the traditional objection is incomplete until a case is made that meaningfulness requires that a statement rule out something in the first sense of "rules out".

Reflection on this argument, however, leads to a full appreciation of the mind-boggling quality of dialetheism. Consider. The classical logician proposes two truth-values that he takes to be exclusive (no statement can have both) and exhaustive (every statement must have one). It is because truth and falsity are exclusive that it can be maintained that A rules out $\sim A$ in the first sense given above. The dialetheist, however, denies they are exclusive, and instead asserts three truth-values: true only (t), false only (f) and both true and false (b). It is natural to assume that he intends these new truth-values to be exclusive. That is, we take it that it is logically impossible for "A is true only" and "A is false only" to both be true; logically impossible for "A is true only" and "A is both true and false" to both be true; and so on. When we read the dialetheist's truth-tables, we assume that if a statement is assigned a particular truth-value, then this is the *only* truth-value it has; there is nothing more to be said.

But these assumptions cannot be (and are not) endorsed by the dialetheist. For while not every contradiction is true, it is *possible* for any contradiction to be true. Hence

A is true only, $\sim$(A is true only)

can both be true. Since "$\sim$(A is true only)" implies "A is false", it also follows that

A is true only, A is false

can both be true.

The dialetheist opens the door to the possibility of true contradictions and, it gradually dawns on us, there is no point at which the door can be closed tight. We began by taking seriously the idea that the truth-values of classical logic are not exclusive: two truth-values were replaced by three. But now we see that the dialetheist's three truth-values also cannot be considered to be exclusive.[14]

What this means is that when I say "A is true only", I leave it an *open possibility that A is false*. But if "A is true only" does not exclude the truth of "*A* is false", then what does it mean? I, for one, cannot fathom what it might mean. To put the point a little differently, I cannot see how to express what I want to express when I say "*A* is true *only*". At this point, the Alice-through-the-looking-glass feeling of dialetheism becomes impossible to repress.

Earlier we argued that it is difficult to see how the claim that *A* is true only can be justified by the dialetheist; now we have doubts as to what it can mean in the context of dialetheism. Perhaps these doubts can be assuaged. But for the moment, at least, it seems entirely unwarranted to add accepting a contradiction as true to the list of possible options for responding to a paradox.

Believing in surprises:
the prediction paradox

I think that this flavour of logic refuted by the world makes the paradox rather fascinating. The logician goes pathetically through the motions that have always worked the spell before, but somehow the monster, Reality, has missed the point and advances still.[1]

The paradox

A teacher announces to her student *S* that she will give him exactly one examination during the next week, and it will be a surprise: *S* will not be able to predict, prior to the day of the examination, on which day it will be held.[2] The student, a star logician, objects that this is impossible. He argues as follows. "If the exam were held on Friday, then on Thursday evening, realizing that no examination had yet been given, I would reasonably expect it on Friday; hence a Friday examination would not be a surprise. But, if the examination were given on Thursday, then on Wednesday evening I would be aware that no examination had yet been given and, recognizing that it cannot be given on Friday, would expect it on Thursday; so a Thursday examination would not be a surprise. Similarly for the remaining days. Consequently, the surprise examination cannot be given – you cannot do what you said you would do."

The teacher, visibly shaken, declines to answer, and cancels the class in order to think. On Tuesday of the next week, she presents the student with an examination whose first question is "Is this test a surprise?" Grudgingly, S recognizes that he must answer in the affirmative.

This is the paradox of the surprise examination: there is an apparently impeccable argument for a conclusion that seems patently false. Clearly the teacher can give a surprise examination on, for instance, Tuesday.

Variations of the paradox abound. One version involves a sadistic judge who sentences a man to be hanged, but adds a twist concerning the date. He is to be hanged, the judge decrees, on one of the three following days at noon, and he will not know beforehand which day it will be. The condemned man reasons as follows. "If I am to be hanged on the third day, then on the evening of the second day, I would expect the hanging on the third day; so the decree cannot be fulfilled on the third day. If the judge has in mind the second day, then on the evening of the first day I would realize the sentence cannot be carried out on the third day, and thus would expect it on the second day. And so on. So the judge's decree cannot be carried out." The prisoner is at peace until the hangman arrives on the morning of the second day.

Another variation has a friendly philosophy student carefully arrange a deck of cards, and then announce that he will turn over the cards one by one, showing you the face, until he arrives at the jack of spades; you will not be able to predict when that card will appear, he says, before actually seeing it. You think to yourself that he cannot leave the jack of spades to the end of the deck, because then its appearance would not be a surprise. Nor can he leave it to the second to last card, since after 50 cards have been turned over, knowing that it cannot be the last card, you would expect it to appear as the second to last card. Before long, you realize that it is possible to continue in this way until all 52 cards have been eliminated.

These are all versions of what has come to be known as "the prediction paradox". One rather delightful feature of the paradox is that it appears to have had its origin in a historical event. Sometime during 1943–44, it was announced on Swedish radio that a civil defence exercise would take place one day of the following week, and that in order to provide a proper test of the civil defence system, no one would be able to predict the day of the test in advance. A Swedish mathematician, Lennart Ekbom, is apparently to be credited with having first detected the paradox lurking behind the announcement.[3]

How does the prediction paradox fit into the classification scheme developed in the first chapter? Clearly, it is a type I paradox. It is also apparent that the paradox is falsidical, since a surprise examination, or a surprise hanging, is surely possible in the circumstances described. Finally, the paradox is uncontroversial: there is virtually complete agreement that the conclusion of the argument is false. So there is a general consensus that to dissolve the paradox, it is necessary somehow to defuse the paradoxical argument, to reveal the fallacy or error. In particular, it is pointless to construct further arguments that the surprise examination is possible; that is something we already know. It is also worth noting that the paradox-generating argument is one we all find seductive; so we are likely to be off the mark if our solution consists in isolating and refuting a premise that is initially implausible or highly controversial.

Before considering possible solutions, it will be helpful to get more clarity on the paradox itself. Note first that the announcing of the surprise examination is crucial to the problem, for it must be plausible to suppose, at certain points in the argument, that the student has good reason to believe that a surprise examination will be given; and the sole reason to suppose this is that the teacher, who is generally reliable, has said so. Epistemic concepts such as "has good reason to believe" and "is entitled to believe" seem central to the paradox. In fact, the relevant issue, in determining whether the exam will be a surprise, is what the student is *justified* or *warranted* in believing. That is, to say that the examination will be a surprise is to say that the student will not be justified in believing, before the day of the examination, that the examination will occur on that day.

It might be suggested, with some plausibility, that the notion of surprise can be unpacked in terms of knowledge: the student will not *know* the day of the examination in advance. An adequate solution to the paradox should, I believe, be applicable to *either* interpretation of the central concept. However, the interpretation in terms of justified belief is the minimal one, given that knowledge implies justified belief. Further, the *reason* the student apparently does not know the day of the examination in advance is that he is not justified, before that day, in believing that it will be on that day. Thus the interpretation in terms of justified belief enables us to focus on the key issue, rather than get tangled up in irrelevant questions concerning the more complex concept of knowledge.

The details of the paradoxical situation must also be sharpened, and made more explicit. The teacher, let us suppose, said to S, "An examination will be held on exactly one of the days Monday to Friday; and if an examination is held on day D, you will not be justified in believing this before that day." Now, if the student's argument is not to be open to trivial objections, at least the following assumptions concerning S's memory, reasoning powers and evidence are needed.

(A_1) The student is an expert logician: if he is justified in believing $P_1, \ldots, P_n$, which jointly imply (or strongly confirm) Q, then he sees that $P_1, \ldots, P_n$ jointly imply (or strongly confirm) Q.

(A_2) On Sunday evening, and throughout the next week, the student remembers what the teacher said, and also remembers that she is generally reliable and trustworthy.

(A_3) On Sunday evening, and on any evening of the week, the student knows what evening it is and, on any evening of the week, he remembers whether an examination has been held on that or any previous day of the week.

(A_4) Throughout the week, the student has no source of evidence relevant to the teacher's announcement other than that given by (A_2) and (A_3).

With this background understood, the steps of the paradox-generating argument can be stated as follows:

(1) If the only examination of the week is held on Friday, then on Thursday evening the student will be justified in believing that an examination will be held on Friday.

(2) If the only examination of the week is held on Thursday, then on Wednesday evening the student will be justified in believing (1), and therefore also justified in believing that the examination will be on Thursday.

And so on. Eventually, we reach the conclusion that the examination cannot be given. Notice that the argument is expressed in the third person, not the first. This helps us to keep in mind that the argument can be worked through by a bystander who happens to hear the announcement addressed to the student, as well as by the student.

At this point, ideas for a solution may be percolating in the reader's mind. Let me anticipate some initially appealing responses.

Response I

It is often maintained that the solution to the paradox lies in recognizing that the student has presented a compelling argument that no surprise exam can be given, and therefore cannot believe the teacher's announcement. So the student has no reason to expect any examination next week, and a surprise examination can therefore be held on any day of the week.

This, however, is hardly a solution. For one thing, as was noted earlier, what is wanted as a solution is not an argument or proof that the surprise examination can be given; that is something we already know. Even more important, this line of thought requires us to "give in" to the paradox-generating argument – to grant that it is a good argument. But no coherent solution can find the fallacy in the student's argument while granting that the argument is sound.[4]

Response II

Another initially appealing response is that the flaw in the argument has something to do with temporal order, and with the fact that the argument moves backwards in time. True enough, the argument must proceed by first eliminating Friday, then moving back to Thursday, and so on. But is there anything illegitimate about this? The intuition that the temporal direction of the argument is critical, that something akin to time travel is going on, might be defended as follows. In the first step of the argument, the student assumes that he already knows, when working through the argument, that no exam has been held on the first four days of the week. But this is something he couldn't know until Thursday night. Hence, he begins with an assumption of knowledge to which he is not entitled.

Here there is simply a misunderstanding of the argument. The argument begins with "If the examination is held on Friday, then on Thursday evening, . . .". The statement that the examination is held on Friday is an assumption only in the sense that it is taken as the antecedent of a conditional that is affirmed. But to affirm "If *P*, then ..." you do not need to know that *P*.

That the paradox does not essentially involve reasoning backwards in time can also be demonstrated by considering a rather ingenious variation.[5] Of five students, Art, Bob, Carl, Don and Eric, one is to be given an examination. The students are lined up in alphabetical order, so that each can see the backs of those before him. The teacher has four silver stars and one gold star which will be placed on the students' backs; the gold star designates the student who will be examined. The teacher tells the students this, and also informs them that the designated student will not be entitled to believe that he is the designated student until after the students break formation.

The students then generate the following argument. If Eric is the designated student, then he will see four silver stars ahead of him and will thus be able to infer that he is the designated student; so he cannot be the designated student. But if Don is the designated student, then since he will see three silver stars ahead of him, and will realize that Eric is not the designated student, he will be entitled to believe that he is the designated student; so he cannot be the designated student. And so on. The students conclude that the specified examination cannot be given. They then break formation, and Carl is surprised to learn that he is the designated student.

This variation suffices to show that *any* analysis that focuses on the temporal factor will not be a comprehensive solution.[6]

Response III

It is tempting to view the paradox as resulting from a misunderstanding of the teacher's announcement that the exam will be a surprise. It has been suggested, for instance, that the surprise component of the teacher's assertion should be understood as implicitly qualified, as claiming that the exam will be a surprise *unless it takes place on the last day.*[7] Construed this way, the announcement certainly does not support the paradoxical argument. For in the very first step of the argument, we can say that if the exam is held on Friday, it will not be a surprise; but this now gives us no reason to rule out Friday as a possible day for the exam. This sort of reinterpretation of the announcement is unsatisfying, however, because although the teacher might have intended the qualified assertion, there seems no reason to suppose she could not have intended the unqualified assertion. And if she is understood as intending the latter, it still seems possible that the exam should be a surprise. So the original paradox remains.

Another reinterpretation has it that the surprise clause of the announcement should be construed as saying that the student will not know the day of the exam *before the week begins*.[8] Again, no paradox will result on this interpretation. But again there seems no reason why the teacher could not intend the stronger claim that the students will not know the day of the examination *at any time before* that day. Nor does understanding the announcement in terms of this stronger claim seem to preclude the possibility of there being a surprise exam.

Since the paradox proves resistant to these attempts at a "quick fix", we turn now to an examination of the more prominent approaches to the paradox found in the philosophical literature. Initially, the paradox may appear to be a mere puzzle, a brainteaser, that can be disposed of in a few pages. But decades of controversy and a voluminous, still growing, literature suggest otherwise. In fact, I shall argue, this is a paradox of some depth, with much to teach us about familiar epistemic principles.

Quine's contribution

An influential early contribution by Quine regards the problem as not particularly taxing; it is remarkable, he says, that the solution to the puzzle is seldom clearly apprehended.[9] The problem occurs, according to Quine, at the very first step of the argument. The student looks ahead to Thursday evening, and discerns just two possibilities: (a) the exam will have already occurred; or (b) the exam will occur on Friday, and the student will be aware of this on Thursday evening (in which case the teacher's announcement will be false). The student rejects (b) on the grounds that it falsifies the announcement, and opts for (a), thus beginning the process of whittling down the possible days till none remain. But, says Quine, the student should have discerned not two possibilities for Thursday evening, but four. Apart from (a) and (b), the student should also consider: (c) the exam will fail to occur on Friday, thereby falsifying the announcement; and (d) the exam will occur on Friday and the student will not know this before Friday. If each of these is recognized as a possibility, then the student will find the path to eliminating Friday blocked.

What Quine seems to mean, in speaking of each of the four situations as a possibility, is that, for all the student knows, any one of them might obtain; that is, he does not know, of any one of them, that it does not obtain. But only two of them, (a) and (d), are compatible with the teacher's announcement. If the student does not know that the other two do not obtain, this must mean that he does not know the truth of the teacher's announcement. So the core of Quine's analysis is that the student does not know the truth of what the teacher has said.

But the teacher is a reliable and trustworthy person, and she is in a position to know the statement she asserts. Why should the student not believe her? Why does he not know the truth of what she says? Quine has nothing to say on this score. True, the announcement is a statement about the future; true also that the only grounds the student has for it is the testimony of the teacher. But surely we (and Quine) do not want to deny all knowledge or warranted belief about the future (do I not know that my desk will be in my office when I arrive in the morning?); and testimony provides the basis for great quantities of what we normally claim to know. We can readily grant that if Quine is right, the paradoxical argument collapses. However, in the absence of any reason to deny the student knowledge that, on the face of it, he would seem to have, Quine does not appear to have laid the paradox to rest.

The logical approach

The single most popular approach to the paradox, over the decades since it first surfaced, has been to construe it in purely logical terms by interpreting the teacher's statement in terms of deducibility. The origin of the paradox, it is then argued, lies in self-reference, and it thus bears some resemblance to the liar paradox.

The core of this approach was first presented in a seminal paper by R. Shaw.[10] Shaw's version of the paradox has it that the students are told, at the end of term, that it is an unbreakable rule of the school that an examination will be given on an unexpected day of the next term. To say that the day of the examination will be a surprise, Shaw insists, is to say that it is *not deducible from the rules of the school* (in conjunction with background information concerning whether or not an examination has yet been given).

How exactly should the rules of the school be stated? Suppose we try:

> Rule 1: An examination will take place on one day of the next term.
>
> Rule 2: The examination will be unexpected, in the sense that it will take place on a day such that on the previous evening it will not be possible for the students to deduce *from Rule 1* that the examination will be on the next day.

Given these two rules, the last day of term is eliminated, since it would violate Rule 2. But any other day will satisfy the rules. An attempt to run the paradoxical argument will succeed only at the first step, if this is how the rules are interpreted. But suppose now that we add a third rule:

> Rule 3: The examination will take place on a day such that on the previous evening it will not be possible for the pupils to deduce *from Rules 1 and 2* that the examination will take place on the next day.

On this understanding of the rules, the last two days of the term can be eliminated by the student's argument. Consider the situation the evening before the second to last day. The examination has to be on one of the next two days, by Rule 1. By Rule 2, it can be deduced that it will not be on the last day. Hence, by Rules 1 and 2, it follows that it will be on the second to last day. But this deduction means that Rule 3 would be violated if the examination were on the second to last day. The last two days, then, are not possible given these three rules; but any other day of the term is possible. In general, it will take $n + 1$ rules of this sort to eliminate the last n days of term.

Provided that the teacher's statement is understood in terms of these rules, and that there are at least as many days in the term as there are rules, the paradoxical argument will be stopped before every day is eliminated. Thus there will be days on which the surprise examination is possible.

The paradox-generating argument, Shaw suggests, is seductive because we interpret the teacher's announcement in terms of Rule 1 and the following:

> Rule 2*: The examination will take place on a day such that on the previous evening the pupils will not be able to deduce from *Rules 1 and 2** that the examination will take place on the next day.

Rule 2* is self-referential (like the sentence of the liar paradox), and clearly does imply a contradiction. If we rely on this interpretation, the paradoxical argument will unquestionably go through; but this should not be troubling, for self-referential sentences are widely regarded as illegitimate or defective. The key to resolving the paradox, according to Shaw, is to recognize that we are interpreting the teacher's statement as the self-referential Rule 2* when we work through the argument; but in judging that the exam is possible, we interpret the teacher as asserting something like Rules 1 and 2.

The difficulty with this general approach, however, is that it does not go to the heart of the paradox. More specifically, the paradox does not arise from construing the announcement as Rules 1 and 2*. Notice that the teacher, as well as the student, can work through the paradoxical argument. But she can do so only if she assumes that the surprise exam has been previously announced to the student. Without this tacit premise, the argument cannot even begin. But from 1 and 2* it can be deduced that the exam cannot be given, without having to make *any other assumptions*. So the teacher's having announced the exam plays a role in the paradox for which this approach has no room. The teacher's announcement is not being interpreted as 1 and 2* in the paradoxical argument.

The (KK) thesis

The argument of the prediction paradox requires, as we have already noted, certain assumptions about the student's cognitive abilities and situation. Call these the factual assumptions. But there are also philosophical assumptions at work in the background that have not yet been brought to light.

One influential approach to the paradox has it that the paradoxical argument makes essential use of the philosophically controversial (KK) thesis, which says:

(KK) If S knows that p, then S knows that S knows that p.

The (KK) thesis apparently licenses unlimited iterations of knowledge. But according to this approach, (KK) is not viable, and the flaw in the argument is thus its reliance on this principle.

To begin, let us try to understand why (KK) seems necessary as an assumption.[11] As noted earlier, the paradox, and the notion of surprise, may be expressed either in terms of knowledge, or in terms of justified belief. Those who focus on (KK) take knowledge to be the central concept of the paradox. But an adequate solution should apply to both the knowledge and the justified belief versions of the paradox. The analogue to (KK), which would presumably be essential for justified belief versions of the paradox, is:

(JJ) If S is justified in believing that p, then S is justified in believing that S is justified in believing that p.

Most of what follows will apply, with appropriate changes, to (JJ). The argument, couched in terms of knowledge, begins with:

(1) If the only examination of the week is held on Friday, then on Thursday evening the student will know that an examination will be held on Friday.

The reasoning underlying this step is that the student knows, after the announcement, that there will be an exam during the week and retains this knowledge throughout the week, and also knows at any point in the week whether an exam has yet been given. At this stage, there is no need for the (KK) thesis. But now consider the next two steps:

(2) If the only examination of the week is held on Thursday, then on Wednesday evening the student will know (1), and thus know that the examination will be held on Thursday.

(3) If the only examination of the week is held on Wednesday, then on Tuesday evening, the student will know (1) and (2), and thus know that the examination will be held on Wednesday.

The pattern is clear. Each step of the argument, after the first, requires that the student have knowledge, at the appropriate times, of the preceding steps.

It is here that (KK) is thought to play a role. Step (1) rests, in part, on:

(a) The student knows on Sunday evening that there will be exactly one examination during the week.
(b) The student retains this knowledge throughout the week.
(c) The student knows, on every evening, what day of the week it is and whether an examination has yet been given.

In order to know (1) on Sunday evening, then, the student must know (a). That is, it must be the case that:

(a*) The student knows on Sunday evening that he knows on Sunday evening that there will be exactly one examination during the week.

To ensure the truth of (a*), it is argued, we must appeal to (KK).[12]

Two philosophers whose diagnosis centres on the role of (KK) are James McLelland and Charles Chihara.[13] They grant that in the intuitive, unformalized version of the paradox, no explicit appeal is made to (KK). Rather, we reason from assumptions concerning what the students know in the situation to a statement P (A Friday exam will not be a surprise). Since the students, we think, can deduce whatever we can, we then attribute to them *knowledge* of P. But this will follow only if they also *know* the premises concerning what they know in the situation. Thus, we are in effect reasoning in accord with (KK).

McLelland and Chihara attempt to refute (KK), and thereby show that the paradoxical argument rests on a false premise. One criticism they advance is that (KK) implies that if we know P, then we can disregard any evidence that would indicate that we do not know P. For if we know that we know that P, then we know that any such evidence is misleading (is evidence for something false), and thus may reasonably be disregarded. But this is rarely true in the ordinary situations in which one claims to know. The (KK) thesis would thus set the standards for knowing very high: it would require something like conclusive evidence.

If successful, however, this sort of reasoning tells not just against (KK). It is essentially the reasoning of Harman's paradox of dogmatism, which makes no reference to (KK).[14] If P is true, then any evidence against P is misleading evidence. If I know that P is true, then I know that any further evidence I may encounter against P is misleading, and I may therefore disregard it. So, once I know that P is true, I am in a position to disregard any future counter-evidence against P.

The fallacy in this sort of reasoning emerges clearly once explicit reference to time is introduced. If I know at time t that P, then I know at t that any evidence against P is misleading. However, if at a later time t_1 I acquire evidence E against P, I may well *not know at* t_1 that E is misleading. For, given my new body of evidence, I may not be justified in believing P at t_1, and thus may not know at t_1 that P. Knowledge and justified belief may shrink, as well as grow, with the acquisition of new evidence.

There are, in any case, several reasons to suppose that refuting (KK) (or (JJ)) will not suffice to resolve the paradox. First, the paradoxical argument does not require (KK) in its full generality; (KK) is a premise far stronger than necessary. In the argument, Friday is first eliminated and then it is assumed that *the student* could also eliminate Friday. This obviously does not follow, given just the factual assumptions specified earlier. There is a gap in reasoning that could be filled by (KK). But much less than this is required.

Consider a three-day version of the paradox. The first step requires no iteration of the student's knowledge (or justified belief). It assumes that the student knows that P (There will be exactly one exam in the three-day period). The second step requires that the student know that he knows that P (one iteration); the third step requires two iterations. All that is necessary, then, is that the student have the kind of epistemic self-awareness that would permit two iterations of his knowledge. And it surely seems *possible* that the student, who is credited with superb memory and logical skills, in general, with all the intellectual assets of an ideal knower, should have this level of epistemic self-knowledge.

In short, to stop the argument in the three-day case, one would have to show that it is *impossible* for the student to have two iterations of knowledge. Merely showing that (KK) is not, in its full generality, true, is inadequate.

The second reason for deeming (KK) irrelevant to the prediction paradox is that there are variations that do not require any iterations of the subject's knowledge (or justified belief). Consider again the designated student variation. The first step of the argument in this variation assumes that Eric knows that exactly one of the five students will be given an exam (*P*). The second step, to eliminate Don, requires that *Don* knows that *Eric* knows that *P*. (KK) has no bearing on this sort of iteration, which involves a change of subject (*D* knows that *E* knows that *P*), or change of cognitive viewpoint.

Clearly, (KK) is not directly relevant to this variation. Still, it has recently been maintained by Timothy Williamson that no sufficiently lengthy iteration of knowledge, including those *that involve a change in cognitive viewpoint*, can be true; and that this impossibility provides the basis of a solution to the prediction paradox.[15] However, although this broader approach is more likely to be relevant to the designated student variation, there is yet another ingenious variation that escapes even Williamson's wider net.

Consider the sacrificial virgin paradox.[16] The inhabitants of a tropical island observe an annual ritual of sacrificing a virgin to the local volcano. A number of virgins are blindfolded and brought before the volcano. They all hold hands in a line and can only communicate the statement: "No one to your right is a sacrificial virgin". This is done by squeezing the hand of the virgin to one's left. The virgins are logically skilled and reliable, and will give the signal if and only if they know the truth of what is communicated. The chief takes the leftmost virgin to the mouth of the volcano and, if the offering is acceptable, sacrifices her and sends the others home. If not, he tries again with the new leftmost virgin. The virgins are informed of all of this, and also told that the sacrificial virgin will not know she is the sacrifice before being tossed in.

A visitor to the island objects that the ceremony cannot take place. Any virgin is either (i) the rightmost, (ii) a middle or (iii) the leftmost virgin. (i) If the sacrificial virgin is the rightmost, then she realizes she is the rightmost since her right hand is free. Thus if she is offered, she goes to the volcano knowing she is the last alternative, and therefore is able to infer that she is the sacrifice. So she cannot be the sacrificial virgin. Realizing this, the rightmost virgin will signal by squeezing the hand of the virgin on her left, who is either a middle or the leftmost virgin. (ii) If the virgin to the immediate left of the rightmost virgin is a middle virgin, then, if she is offered, she is aware beforehand that no one to her left has been sacrificed. And, since she has received the signal on her right hand, she is entitled to infer that she is the sacrifice. So she cannot be the sacrifice. Realizing this, she squeezes the hand on her left. Similarly for all the middle virgins. (iii) If the sacrificial virgin is the leftmost virgin, then, since she has received the signal, she realizes she is the only remaining virgin and is therefore the sacrifice. So she cannot be the sacrifice and the ceremony is impossible.

What degree of iteration of knowledge is required in the sacrificial virgin paradox? The visitor to the island first argues that the rightmost virgin cannot be the sacrifice. His argument is based, in part, on assumptions that she knows certain facts about the ceremony and also knows that her right hand is free. But he then goes on to argue that *she knows that she is not the sacrifice*. Hence, he has to credit her with *knowing that she knows* the relevant facts. Thus one iteration of knowledge is required for the rightmost virgin. Similarly for any middle virgin. She must know that she cannot be the sacrifice, hence she must know certain premises about what she knows. The leftmost virgin, of course, is not required to know that she cannot be the sacrificial virgin. Thus, one iteration of knowledge is required for every participant other than the last. This is the case no matter how many virgins – how many potential sacrifices – there are.

Surely it cannot plausibly be argued that this single iteration is impossible. Hence, focusing on iterations of knowledge, and versions of (KK) will not provide the key to resolving the many variations of the prediction paradox.

The epistemic approach
The solutions canvassed up to this point have all been found wanting. In this section, I offer my own analysis for critical inspection. It is in the same general tradition as Quine's proposal in that the

central issues are taken to be epistemic, and the student is (in a limited way) denied knowledge of the announcement.[17] But Quine offers no positive explanation of the student's ignorance, and, as a consequence, his account seems open to the charge of scepticism either with regard to the future or with regard to testimony. The present proposal rectifies these deficiencies, and shows that the prediction paradox has considerable philosophical significance in the realm of epistemology.

First, the set-up. "Surprise" is interpreted in terms of "justified belief": to say that the exam will be a surprise is to say that the student S will not be justified in believing, before the day of the exam, that the exam will be on that day. To give the argument its due, we do not want S to fail to have justified belief for *accidental* reasons; we want him to be something akin to an ideal believer. So the four factual premises set out earlier (in the first section) must be assumed. As well as these assumptions concerning the details of the situation, the argument also relies on certain epistemological principles, which may be stated as:

(A_5) If T is justified in believing $P_1, \ldots, P_n, P_1, \ldots, P_n$ jointly imply Q and T sees this, then T is justified in believing Q.

(A_6) If T is justified in believing $P_1, \ldots, P_n, P_1, \ldots, P_n$ strongly confirm Q, T sees this and has no other evidence relevant to Q, then T is justified in believing Q.

Finally, as we saw earlier, the student must be credited with a certain degree of epistemic self-awareness. One way to spell this out is as follows. If there are k other premises required for the argument, then (A_{k+1}) will specify that throughout the week, the student is justified in believing (A_1), ..., (A_k); (A_{k+2}) will say that, throughout the week, the student is justified in believing (A_{k+1}); and so on.[18] For a period of n possible test days, after the initial k premises, a further $n - 1$ premises will be necessary.

Even though S has been credited with ideal reasoning skills and memory, it is surely possible for the teacher's announcement to be true. Where, then, is the flaw in the argument? The first stage of the argument is just:

(1) If the only exam of the week is held on Friday, then on Thurs-

day evening the student will be justified in believing that an exam will be held on Friday.

No doubt this first step of the argument looks inescapable. We reason that on Thursday evening the student will be justified in believing that it is now Thursday evening, and that an exam has not been held on this or any previous day of the week; and he will also be justified in believing, based on the teacher's announcement, that an exam will be held on exactly one of the days Monday to Friday. Hence, the student will be justified in concluding, on Thursday evening, that an exam will be given on Friday.

But this reasoning depends on our ignoring part of the student's total available evidence. Grant that on Thursday night the student remembers that the teacher is generally reliable and said:

(A) There will be an exam on exactly one of the days Monday to Friday.

We make use of this fact about S's evidence to conclude that S will be justified in believing (A) on Thursday evening. But, in so doing, *we overlook another part of the student's evidence.* He is also supposed to remember that the teacher, who is generally reliable, asserted:

(B) If an exam is held on day D then you will not be justified in believing this before that day.

Will the student be justified in believing (A) on Thursday evening? I think not. For suppose he is so justified. Now surely he will be justified in believing (A) only if he is also justified in believing (B), for there is no epistemically relevant difference for him between the two statements. He has exactly the same evidence for each: the fact of the teacher's announcement. However, if S is justified in believing both (A) and (B), then, realizing that it is now Thursday night and an exam has not been held on this or any previous day, he is also justified in believing:

There will be an exam on Friday and I am not now justified in believing that there will be an exam on Friday.

But surely this is impossible. It can never be reasonable to believe a statement of the form "P and I am not now justified in believing P". For if a person T is justified in believing a statement, then he is not (epistemically) blameworthy for believing it. But if T is justified in believing that he is not justified in believing P, then he would be at fault in believing P. Hence, if T is justified in believing that he is not justified in believing P, then he is *not* justified in believing P.

The upshot is that the student is not justified in accepting both (A) and (B) on Thursday night. And since his evidence concerning (A) is no better than his evidence concerning (B), he is not entitled to accept just (A).

Let me emphasize. It is not being maintained that the student can *never* accept the teacher's testimony;[19] the claim is only that he cannot believe it *on Thursday evening if no exam has yet been given*. And bystanders who happen to overhear the announcement, but to whom it is not addressed, can believe it even under these circumstances. There is no reason why someone other than S may not justifiably believe "There will be an exam on Friday and S is not now justified in believing there will be an exam on Friday."

Thus we see that the seemingly airtight argument can be stopped at the very first step, and a surprise exam is therefore possible on any day of the week. Of the premises needed for the first step of the argument, (A_1)–(A_4) simply specify the student's relevant intellectual abilities and evidence; and (A_5) and (A_6) seem, on the face of it, to be highly plausible principles. This is just as it should be, for an argument that we all find seductive is not likely to be based on obviously false premises. Now, however, it can be seen that (A_6) must be rejected. Even though on Thursday night the student has evidence that strongly confirms (A), sees this, and has no other relevant evidence, he is not justified in believing (A). For he cannot be warranted in believing (A) without also being justified in believing a statement of the form "P and I am not now justified in believing P".

This analysis rests, of course, on the assumption that the student has equally good evidence for (A) and (B).[20] So one might think the paradox would break out again if we simply made a slight revision. Let us suppose the teacher makes the same announcement, but, as well, the student has strong independent evidence that an exam will be given on exactly one of Monday to Friday. (For example, an

automatic and irreversible process has been set in motion that guarantees that an exam will be held on exactly one of Monday to
Friday.) In this revised situation, the objection to the first step of the
argument is no longer open to us. The student cannot believe both
(A) and (B) on Thursday evening, but now he has reason to retain
his belief in (A) and reject (B). But even if we therefore grant that a
Friday exam will not be a surprise, we can still stop the argument at
a later stage. The second step of the argument reads:

(2) If the only exam of the week is held on Thursday, then on
    Wednesday evening the student will be justified in believing (1),
    and therefore also justified in believing that an exam will be
    held on Thursday.

Now suppose that we grant that S will be justified in believing (1)
on Wednesday evening. Still, we cannot reach the desired conclusion. The difficulty is that in order to be justified in believing that
an exam will be held on Thursday, S will have to be justified in
believing both (A) and (B); for he can rule out a Friday exam only
on the basis of (B). But the student cannot be justified in believing
both (A) and (B), since this would result in his being justified in
believing:

> An exam will be held on Thursday and I am not now justified in
> believing that an exam will be held on Thursday.

Thus, under the revised conditions, the surprise exam can be held
on any day but the last.

In general, however we revise the situation, we must claim at
each stage of the argument that the student is justified in using (A)
to predict the date of the exam; and at *some* point we also assume
that he is justified in using (B) to rule out certain days. But the joint
use of (A) and (B) in this way is impossible, and the paradoxical
argument must therefore fail.

The starkest form of the paradox is the one-day version, in
which the announcement is just "There will be a surprise exam
tomorrow". The proposed analysis has it that, even under these
circumstances, an exam will be a surprise. For the student cannot be
justified in believing:

> There will be an exam tomorrow and I am not now justified in believing there will be an exam tomorrow.

If he has no reason to prefer either conjunct of this conjunction, then he cannot believe either, and a surprise exam is thus possible. On the other hand, if we consider a revised version of this abbreviated form, the result is quite different. If the student has strong independent evidence that an exam will be given tomorrow, then he is justified in believing that an exam will be given tomorrow and a surprise is not possible.

The analysis proposed here also has the virtue that it is able to deal with Sorensen's ingenious variations. To see how it applies, we must construe each situation in terms of a statement analogous to (A), which describes the basic set-up, and one analogous to (B), which states that the outcome will be a surprise. For simplicity, assume that there is no relevant epistemic difference between the subject's evidence for the two propositions. (Where there is such a difference, the analysis will proceed as above.)

Consider the designated student variation. (A*) gives the information concerning the set-up: five students are lined up in alphabetical order, a gold star is placed on the back of one of them and the student thus designated will be examined. (B*) states that the designated student will not be justified in believing that he is the designated student until after the students break formation. The argument for the designated student variation breaks down at the very first step:

(1) If Eric is the designated student, then he will be justified in believing this before the students break formation.

Eric's belief will, presumably, be based on (A*). But (A*) and (B*) are epistemically indistinguishable for him. So he can believe (A*) only if he is also entitled to accept (B*), in which case, he will also be justified in believing:

> I am the designated student and I am not now justified in believing that I am the designated student.

This is surely impossible. The upshot is that Eric cannot believe the teacher's announcement *if* he is in fact the designated student.

Thus, the argument collapses. The reader may verify that the sacrificial virgin paradox is also stopped at the first step: the rightmost virgin cannot be eliminated.[21]

The analysis thus provides a comprehensive solution to the prediction paradox, and the paradox itself appears to have considerable philosophical punch. What we learn from its resolution is that (A_6), although entirely plausible on the face of it, is in fact a flawed epistemic principle. For on Thursday evening, given no prior exam, the student is not entitled to believe the teacher's announcement despite the fact that he has good evidence for it (the testimony of a reliable person). As we shall see in Chapter 5, some would claim that the lottery paradox teaches us essentially the same lesson: roughly put, good evidence is not sufficient for justified belief. If this view of the lottery paradox is correct, then it is a close cousin of the prediction paradox.

This analysis of the paradox, and the rejection of (A_6), rest on two substantive assumptions:

(I)   It is impossible to be justified in believing a pair of statements of the form "P, I am not now justified in believing P".

(II) If it is impossible to be justified in believing each member of the set $P_1, \ldots, P_n$, and there is no proper subset of $P_1, \ldots, P_n$ of which this is true, and you have equally good reason to believe each of $P_1, \ldots, P_n$, then you are not justified in believing any one of these statements.

The reasoning underlying (I) was indicated earlier. Assumption (II), which rests on the non-arbitrary nature of justified belief, is also essential to the analysis of the paradox. Without it, we cannot ensure that S is not justified, on Thursday night, in expecting an exam the next day.

The analysis depends, then, on these two epistemological assumptions, and succeeds only if they are correct. If they are, then those of us who are no longer students may stop worrying about surprise exams.

Postscript

One might grant that the reasoning of the paradox is effectively undermined by this analysis, that the paradox has been resolved, and yet deny that the analysis has general epistemic significance. For one might deny that the analysis provides a counter-example to the highly intuitive (A_6). Although there is strong evidence for each of (A) and (B) on Thursday night, there is another condition to be met in order to satisfy the antecedent of (A_6), namely, that the student has no other evidence that is relevant to either (A) or (B). Unless this condition is satisfied, there is no counter-example to (A_6). But, it might be argued, the student knows that no exam has been given on any of the previous days, and this is surely relevant to the truth of both (A) and (B).[22]

There are two considerations that make it clear that (A_6) has indeed been overturned. First, (A_6) says, in effect, that if a proposition Q is strongly confirmed by your *total* relevant evidence, then you are justified in believing it. But it seems clear that S's total evidence on Thursday evening strongly confirms both (A) and (B). For suppose there is a bystander who has also heard the announcement, is aware that no exam has yet been given, and so on. As noted earlier, the bystander would be justified in believing (A) and (B) on Thursday night. (The possibility of a Friday surprise exam is no longer in dispute.) Hence his total evidence must strongly support each of (A) and (B). But the bystander's total relevant evidence is exactly the same as S's. It follows that S's total evidence on Thursday night must also strongly confirm both (A) and (B); yet S is not justified in believing these statements.

The second consideration is as follows. Fairly clearly, the student has strong *positive* evidence on Thursday evening for the truth of each of (A) and (B). (He remembers that the teacher is generally reliable and announced (A) and (B).) Hence, in order to save (A_6), it must be maintained that the previous non-occurrence of an exam is *negatively* relevant to the announcement and, as a consequence, S's total evidence does not strongly confirm either (A) or (B). But this is simply not the case. The absence of an exam on the first four days is not negatively relevant to (A), for (A) says that there will be an exam on *exactly* one of the five days. That is, (A) says, in part, that there will be an exam on no more than one of the five days. Neither, on the other hand, is it counter-evidence for (B). For we have seen that a Friday surprise exam is possible.

Thus, the analysis of the prediction paradox reveals that (A_6), a familiar and highly intuitive epistemic principle, is flawed. The same sort of reasoning overturns the following related principles:

(A_6^*) If T is justified in believing P at t_1, and T has exactly the same evidence for and against P at t_2, and assesses it in the same way, then T is justified in believing P at t_2.

(A_6^{**}) If T is justified in believing P, and U has exactly the same evidence for and against P, and assesses it in the same way, then U is justified in believing P.

The analysis thus increases the conceptual distance between evidence and justification.

Game theory

The most prominent approaches to the prediction paradox over the past several decades have now been canvassed. But one further line of attack advanced by some philosophers should be at least briefly considered.

The prediction paradox is sometimes conceptualized as a problem in game theory, in which the teacher's announcement is taken not just as a statement of fact, but as a statement of intention.[23] In the paradoxical situation as thus construed, there are two ideally rational agents whose rationality is a matter of common knowledge: the teacher and the student. The teacher's goal is to give a surprise exam during a certain period of time; the student's goal is to avoid being surprised. So the situation is now seen as a game or contest between the two players. The task, it is thought, is to decide on the best strategy for the teacher to use in choosing the day of the exam, and to determine whether this strategy will guarantee success, that is, will guarantee that the exam will be a surprise.

The problem, as Cargile conceives it, is that the teacher is trying to make a rational choice that cannot be predicted by the student, even though both are ideally rational and both have the same relevant information. In order for the teacher to surprise the student, they must disagree about something. But how is this possible if both are rational agents with the same information?

Within the game-theoretic approach to the prediction paradox there is no single dominant analysis, so I will comment only on the general approach. The notion of a rational agent who wants or intends a certain event to be a surprise is, on this line of attack, an essential ingredient of the paradox. No doubt this understanding of the paradox is plausible enough, given the versions that have been advanced. But there are variations in which an agent who wants a certain event to be a surprise plays no role.

Consider. A teacher intends to give one exam during the term. She will make no prior announcement to the class and, further, is indifferent as to whether or not the exam is a surprise. Now add to the mix a person M, whose track record of correct predictions concerning academic events is outstanding: he has made many such predictions, and is almost invariably correct. The basis on which he makes his predictions is unknown, but it is recognized that M tells the truth as he sees it. One day M announces to the student, "There will be exactly one exam next week and it will be a surprise." M knows nothing more about the exam, and has no control over it.

Note that the paradoxical argument has as much force here as in the original version. But the announcement on which the student relies is now clearly not a statement of intent, but a disinterested prediction. The power behind the exam has no stake in its being a surprise. Clearly, there is no unique rational choice for the teacher, and hence neither room nor reason to invoke game-theoretic principles.

As an alternative to M, the super-predictor, we might imagine that the student acquires all his evidence concerning the exam by reading a well-regarded history of the school, according to which every year since the beginning of the school, exactly one exam has been given to this class during week n, and every year it has been a surprise. The student makes the obvious inductive inference, and this provides his justification for believing that there will be a surprise exam next week. Again, the paradoxical argument gets a grip.

The key point is that the relevance of the teacher as a rational agent with the goal of surprising her student is now removed. So it is difficult to see how the game-theoretic approach might prove useful in resolving these variations. Resolution can be achieved, however, by the epistemic approach of the previous section. The prediction paradox is an epistemological problem.

The preface paradox,
4 fallibility and probability

The virtue of consistency

Is consistency always an epistemic virtue?[1] The traditional view has been that consistency is essential to rationality, that it is something to be aimed at in all our beliefs.[2] Inconsistent beliefs, it is maintained, are always unreasonable. Call this "the conservative position". The central issue of this and the following chapter is whether the conservative stance on consistency is correct.

First, some terminology. A set of statements is inconsistent if it is logically impossible for all the statements in the set to be true. For instance, the statements

(i) Pierre is a politician.
(ii) All politicians sometimes lie.
(iii) Pierre never lies.

cannot all be true. Inconsistency is to be distinguished from contradiction. Two statements are contradictory if they are of the form:

$$P, \sim P$$

Clearly, no two statements in the above set contradict each other. All contradictory statements are inconsistent, but not conversely.

Recently, there has been a flurry of discussion on inconsistent belief as philosophers have felt the need to rethink the traditional view of consistency. The focus of this and the next chapter is a group of paradoxes that are responsible for the controversy. What these paradoxes have in common is that each apparently offers a demonstration that inconsistent beliefs may be epistemically fault-less, that they may be perfectly reasonable. Each is a type I paradox, and each is controversial.

The consistency paradoxes are particularly disturbing. If it is conceded that inconsistent beliefs may be rational, some of the *apparent* consequences are: that belief in contradictory statements can be warranted, for an inconsistent set of statements implies a contradiction; that *reductio ad absurdum* arguments need have no implications for the revision of beliefs; and that any coherence theory of justification is misguided, since coherence presupposes consistency. Nonetheless, several prominent philosophers have taken the lesson of the consistency paradoxes to be that inconsist-ency in our beliefs is sometimes rational. Call this "the radical position".[3]

The challenge posed by the paradoxes, for those who take the radical approach, is to minimize the damage, to take the sting out of the paradoxical conclusion. They will argue that the counter-intuitive consequences outlined above are either apparent only, not real consequences, or can and should be accommodated. It is clear that certain commonly accepted epistemological principles have to be abandoned if the possibility of rational inconsistent beliefs is admitted; but the radicals will maintain that these principles are untenable on independent grounds, and should be rejected. The discussion of these more general issues will be left to Chapter 5, after each of the three consistency paradoxes has been presented. For the moment, we need only note that among those who have discussed these paradoxes, there is a consensus that belief in contra-dictory statements can never be warranted.

Before turning to the first consistency paradox, it is easy to see that at least one qualification of the conservative view will be necessary. If a physics professor assures Sam of the truth of certain statements in theoretical physics, and, quite understandably, Sam fails to grasp their inconsistency, he may be entirely reasonable in believing everything the professor asserts. The conservative agrees: his thesis must be understood as restricted to recognized inconsist-ency. It is only if Sam clearly apprehends the inconsistency that he is open to criticism; for if he is aware that his beliefs are inconsist-ent, he realizes that he is guaranteed to have made a mistake. For simplicity, I assume, in what follows, that we are dealing only with recognized inconsistency.

The paradox of the preface

You have just written a book of which you are enormously proud. You have been diligent in your research, scrupulously careful in your reasoning and have had several respected colleagues read drafts of the manuscript. Since you are at the moment steeped in the details, you can confidently reel off every statement in the book: B_1, $B_2, \ldots, B_n$. Given the extreme care you have lavished on this project, you are justified in believing each of these statements. While proofreading the manuscript for the last time, however, an uncomfortable thought occurs to you. You remember that errors were detected after publication in previous books of yours, books of which you were at the time equally confident; in fact, mistakes were found after publication in the majority of similar books published by other authors. Does this past experience not strongly suggest that there are errors in your present book? Your feelings of pride slightly deflated, you prepare to add a disclaimer to your preface indicating that there is likely some error in the body of the book, error for which you are, of course, entirely responsible. Discomfort turns to dismay, however, when you realize that since it is reasonable to believe there is error in the body of the book, it is also reasonable to believe $\sim(B_1 \& B_2 \ldots \& B_n)$. Putting this together with the fact that you are justified in accepting every statement in the book, it follows that you are entitled to accept inconsistent statements:

$$B_1, B_2, \ldots, B_n, \ \sim(B_1 \& B_2 \& \ldots \& B_n)$$

This is the well-known paradox of the preface in its original form.[4] Since its introduction, considerable effort has been expended in an attempt to avoid the troubling conclusion. One early suggestion builds reference to probabilities into the content of the author's beliefs. Since the author is not absolutely certain of the statements in her book, she should, strictly speaking, assert only "probably B_1", "probably B_2" and so on.[5] (We normally omit reference to probability, according to this suggestion, just in order to avoid pedantry.) And modesty surely demands no more in a preface than "probably there are errors in the body of the book". So, strictly speaking, what the author is warranted in believing is:

probably B_1, ..., probably B_n, probably $\sim(B_1 \& \ldots \& B_n)$

But this set of statements is not logically inconsistent. Thus, we avoid the paradoxical conclusion that the author is entitled to inconsistent beliefs.

This strategy seems doomed to failure on two counts. First, it might be argued that we have apparently blocked one paradoxical conclusion only to replace it by another, namely, that one can be warranted in believing, of each of a number of inconsistent statements, that it is probable. Some will find even this weaker conclusion quite untenable. Second, and more significant, we buy our way out of the paradox only at enormous cost. We have to maintain that most of our beliefs (those of which we are not absolutely certain) are about probabilities. Nor can we identify the belief that P with the belief that it is probable that P. The truth of my belief that my car is currently in the driveway depends on the present location of my car; whereas the truth of my belief that it is probable that my car is in the driveway depends on the total available evidence. Indeed, the solution *requires* that the belief that P not be equated with the belief that P is probable. For if they are equated, then the original paradoxical conclusion stands.

Another suggestion in a similar vein, put forward by Sharon Ryan, is that if the author is genuinely justified in believing each statement in her book, then she is justified in believing, *at most*, that she *might* have made a mistake, not that she actually has.[6] However, this would mean the author is justified in believing:

B_1, ..., B_n, possibly $\sim(B_1 \& \ldots \& B_n)$

While not inconsistent, this is still highly implausible as a set of justified beliefs.

Ryan also makes the point that authors are influenced not just by the quest for truth, but by deadlines, wishful thinking, a desire for recognition and so on. Since these motivations often conflict, Ryan infers that, in any realistic case, the author is not actually justified in believing each statement in her book. Perhaps this pessimistic outlook is the result of focusing largely on philosophical works. But is it entirely unrealistic to expect that the author of, say, a calculus textbook, or a medical textbook, might well be justified in believing every statement in her book? Fortunately, we can avoid having to evaluate the epistemic scruples and integrity of authors by turning, in the next section, to a generalized version of the preface paradox.

One last comment. If the argument of the preface paradox is correct, then it follows that one can gain a rather curious sort of knowledge by reading books. Readers, as well as authors, can employ the inductive inference based on past errors. If I know that the statements in David's book are $D_1, \ldots, D_n$, then I can argue, based on the past fallibility of David and other authors, that $\sim(D_1 \& \ldots \& D_n)$; if I know that the statements in Jennifer's book are $J_1, \ldots, J_n$, then I can justifiably infer that $\sim(J_1 \& \ldots \& J_n)$; and so on. This is not the sort of information one would normally expect to acquire from reading careful and serious books.

The fallibility argument

The fallibility argument is a more global version of the preface paradox. It deals with the entire body of our justified beliefs, whatever they may be, thus allowing us to avoid issues such as whether an author is ever justified in believing every statement in her book. Because the focus is less restricted, some take the argument to show that all "knowledgeable" people (not just authors) are entitled to accept inconsistent beliefs.[7] Although these are two variations of the same paradox, it will be convenient to refer to the first as "the preface paradox" and the second as "the fallibility argument".

As a preliminary, recall the example, introduced in Chapter 1, in which there seems to be good evidence for two inconsistent propositions. It is given that 90 per cent of Texans are affluent, while 90 per cent of philosophers are poor. Jones is both a Texan and a philosopher. Here there seems to be a good reason for each of (i) Jones is rich and (ii) Jones is poor. Why is it that this sort of example has never tempted anyone to argue for the rationality of inconsistent beliefs? The answer seems clear and straightforward. Grant that the evidence concerning Texans is, in its own right, good reason to believe that Jones is rich. Nonetheless, this reason is not adequate in the light of

the total available evidence: it is defeated by the data concerning philosophers and poverty. But justified belief in *P* requires (i) that there
be good reason to believe P and (ii) that this reason not be defeated.
This means that the following requirement must be met by any attempt to overturn the conservative view of consistency:

(R) An argument for the rationality of inconsistency is not successful unless, for each statement in the inconsistent set, there is
good reason to believe it that stands up in the light of the total
available evidence.

Requirement (R) provides a standard against which arguments for
rational inconsistent belief can be assessed.

Now for the fallibility argument. It is intended as an intuitive,
non-technical argument for the compatibility of rationality and
inconsistency. In contrast to later arguments for this conclusion, no
appeal is made here to any formal or technical apparatus. The
central assumption on which the argument is based is that we sometimes have perfectly justified beliefs that are nevertheless false.
Even when we are impeccably rational, we are sometimes led into
error; we are fallible in just this sense.

The core of the argument runs as follows. In the past, *T* has often
discovered error in her beliefs, not just in careless or irresponsible
beliefs, but in beliefs that were, at the time, perfectly justified, that
were based on adequate data of perception, memory and so on.
Since the body of *T*'s justified beliefs contained error in the past,
there are good empirical reasons to think that *T*'s present justified
beliefs also contain error.[8]

Let us expand on this capsule version. If the fallibility argument
is to demonstrate the rationality of inconsistent belief, it must
consist in two sub-arguments. First, there is an inference to the
conclusion that some of *T*'s present justified beliefs are false. This
inference is inductive; what is being projected is the tendency to
error when *T*'s beliefs are formed in the rational manner. This
section of the argument may be expressed as:

(1) In the past, the body of other reasonable beliefs *T* formed by
method *S* (perception, memory, induction and so on) frequently contained some error.

(2) Hence, the body of other reasonable beliefs T has now formed by method S contains some error.[9]

This first section of the argument is obviously not sufficient to yield any conclusion concerning inconsistency. What is needed now is a further premise specifying the other beliefs T has on the basis of S. The second part of the argument continues:

(3) T's other present reasonable beliefs formed by method S are: $B_1, \ldots, B_n$.
(4) Hence, $\sim(B_1 \ \& \ \ldots \ \& \ B_n)$.

Given that T is justified in accepting each step of the argument, and that premise (3) is correct, it follows that T is justified in accepting inconsistent beliefs, namely:

$$B_1, \ldots, B_n, \ \sim(B_1 \ \& \ \ldots \ \& \ B_n)$$

Note that in order for T to be justified in believing an inconsistency, she must be able to work through the four steps just set out.[10] In particular, T must be justified in believing (3); she must have a justified belief concerning all her other present justified beliefs. That the fallibility argument places such a strong and unrealistic requirement on the believer, however, is not usually appreciated.[11] This may explain why Klein can confidently assert that the argument shows that every "knowledgeable person", every person aware of his own fallibility, is entitled to believe an inconsistency. The fact is, of course, that most of us do not have a justified belief corresponding to (3); indeed, it is arguable that none of us does. So the argument cannot be used to show that it is *in fact* rational for each of us to believe an inconsistency. However, this by no means deprives the fallibility argument of its philosophical interest. For it seems possible for a rational being (perhaps an ideally rational being) to have such a belief. So the argument may succeed in establishing that it is *possible* for inconsistent beliefs to be justified. Although weaker, this conclusion still has considerable philosophical punch, and is quite unacceptable to those who hold the conservative view of consistency.

Is the fallibility argument adequate to establish that rationality does not preclude inconsistency, that rational inconsistent belief is possible? One point at which the argument is vulnerable, I shall suggest, is in the move from (1) to (2). In this inference, error is projected from the past to the present. On the face of it, this is just a standard inductive move. In this case, however, the inference is more than a little odd; I shall argue that it is in fact illegitimate.

A different but analogous example may serve to highlight the problem here. Consider a set of statements $R_1, \ldots, R_n$, where each R_i is a statement about the future; and suppose there is no epistemic reason to prefer any R_i to its negation. More specifically, there is, at the moment, no epistemically relevant difference between the set of R_is and, say, the set consisting of the negations of the R_is. Now suppose some tea-leaves are read, and a standard method of interpreting the leaves leads to $R_1, \ldots, R_n$. Certainly, tea-leaf reading, as a method of forming beliefs, has led to error in the past. But do we want to say that this fact provides us with a good reason for thinking there is error in the set of R_is?

Consider. Apart from the tea-leaf reading, the set $R_1, \ldots, R_n$ is epistemically indistinguishable from the set of the negations of the R_is. Thus, if the tea-leaf reading provides good reason to think there is error in the set of R_is, then there should be *better reason* to think there is falsity in the set $R_1, \ldots, R_n$ than in the set consisting of the negation of each R_i.[12] But this seems completely counter-intuitive and implausible. Surely tea-leaf reading cannot give us any reason to prefer one set of statements about the future to another; surely the fact of the reading does not mean that the set of the negations of the R_is is now better supported by the evidence than the set of R_is. The obvious conclusion, then, seems to be that the tea-leaf reading does not provide reason for thinking there is error in the set of R_is. But if this is so, then it is difficult to see how one might defend the inference from (1) to (2) in the fallibility argument. The onus of proof is surely on the advocate of the fallibility argument to show why her argument is completely acceptable, while the tea-leaf argument is absurd.

The tea-leaf example seems to provide an analogous argument that is patently illegitimate, and thus serves to discredit the inference from (1) to (2). Supposing it granted that (1) does not provide a good reason for (2), it is not entirely clear how to explain why the reasoning fails, or what the exact nature of the flaw is. A sketch of a possible analysis goes as follows. That a method of belief formation has led to error in the past indicates that the evidence employed is not perfectly reliable: it fails to guarantee the truth of the statement for which it is evidence. Imperfectly reliable evidence entails the *absence* of an airtight connection with truth; but it obviously does not follow from this that there is a reliable, projectible connection between such evidence and *falsity*. Invalid arguments with true premises, for example, have no tight connection with truth, but neither do they have a reliable connection with falsity. At best, imperfectly reliable evidence is connected with lack of certainty (or, in extreme cases, lack of justified belief). So the most that can be proved, based on our past fallibility, is that our justified beliefs are not all certain.

The absurdity of the analogous tea-leaf argument is sufficient to cast doubt on the assumption that (1) is, in its own right, a good reason for (2). But if we approach the inference now from a different vantage point, from a more global perspective, we find another serious difficulty for the fallibility argument. Premise (3), you will recall, requires that T be warranted in believing each of $B_1, \ldots, B_n$. Assume, then, that there is good reason provided by the data of perception, memory and so on for each of these beliefs. Now, according to the fallibility argument, there is *another* evidential datum that concerns past errors in the body of A's beliefs; this is supposed to provide good reason for (2), which, in conjunction with (3), entails "The set of beliefs $B_1, \ldots, B_n$ contains some error". This leads us to the critical problem facing the fallibility argument – the argument proceeds as if there were (at least) two distinct bodies of evidence to be considered.

Requirement (R), elicited earlier, says that in order to have a convincing argument for the rationality of inconsistency, there must be, for each statement, a good reason to believe it that stands up in the light of the total evidence. The fallibility argument proceeds as if there were good reason to believe each of $B_1, \ldots, B_n$ (this is assumed in (3)), and then, also, independent reason for believing "The set of beliefs $B_1, \ldots, B_n$ contains some error" (consisting of the errors found in the past). Suppose for a moment that this is so. The obvious suggestion is that, before embracing an inconsistency, we should consider how well the different reasons stand up in the light of the total evidence. It may be that each strand of justifying reasons (the positive data of perception, memory and so on, and the record of past errors) cancels out the evidential worth of the other, as in the Texan philosopher example. If so, then we must suspend judgement in each of the statements involved in the inconsistency. Alternatively, it may be that one line of justification is clearly overridden or defeated by other portions of the evidence. If this is the case, then some beliefs may be retained. What is clear is that we have not yet been presented with a definitive case for the rationality of inconsistency, for we are not dealing with a case in which each statement is *clearly* backed by a good reason that stands up in the light of the total evidence. Attention to requirement (R) thus suffices to reveal the inadequacy of the fallibility argument in anything like its present form.

It might be suggested that this last difficulty can be overcome by appealing to the probability calculus, in particular to the conjunction and negation rules of the calculus, in order to show that each member of the inconsistent set is indeed strongly supported by the total evidence. But, in fact, introducing the classical probability calculus here serves not so much to flesh out the fallibility argument as to move to *another* well-known argument for the rationality of inconsistency. The fallibility argument, as I understand it, is intended as a common-sense, intuitive argument that does not invoke technical or formal apparatus. So it should be distinguished from any technical argument that rests on probability considerations and the calculus. Further, there are crucial premises of the fallibility argument to the effect that *these are my present justified beliefs* and that *I have been mistaken in the past*. Once we appeal to the traditional calculus, we have a much simpler argument for inconsistency that renders these premises, as well as the problematic inductive inference, irrelevant. It is to this argument that we now turn.

The epistemic probability argument

The strength of one's evidence is surely a critical factor in assessing warranted belief. So the notion of the epistemic probability of a proposition, understood as *the degree of confirmation or support provided by the total available evidence*, must play a central role in epistemology. Epistemic probability is to be sharply distinguished from other types of probability, in particular from statistical probability (understood as the relative frequency with which a given property or event occurs within a certain reference class), and also from subjective probability (understood as degree of belief). Clearly, epistemic probability, or degree of confirmation, has direct bearing on issues of warranted belief.

The epistemic probability adequate for warranted belief is commonly thought to be high, but less than certainty. Indeed, an assumption essential to the paradoxical argument examined in this section is:

(E) There is a degree of epistemic probability less than 1 that is sufficient for justified belief.[13]

(E) ensures that something less than maximal probability (less than certainty) is sufficient for justified belief. The rationale for the principle lies in the fact that, since the evidence on which we rely is imperfectly reliable, to require absolute certainty is to fall into scepticism. If the bar is set that high, most of our common-sense beliefs will fail to qualify as justified.

The paradoxical argument that is the focus of this section, put informally, runs as follows. Consider a large set of statements that I am justified in believing. My evidence for each, let us suppose, is very strong, but short of certainty. So for each of these beliefs, there is some risk of error, however minute. If a number of these statements are conjoined, the probability of error associated with the conjunction is still greater than that associated with any individual belief, for the falsity of any conjunct suffices to make the conjunction false. Given a sufficiently lengthy conjunction, then, the probability of error increases to the point that I am justified in believing that the conjunction is false. So I am justified in believing each member of the original set, as well as the negation of their conjunction. Thus, I am justified in believing inconsistent statements.

A more formal, and more precise, statement of the argument appeals explicitly to the rules of the probability calculus. First, the multiplication rule for the probability of a conjunction of independent statements is:[14]

$$\Pr(P \ \& \ Q) = \Pr(P) \times \Pr(Q)$$

Consider now a set of my justified probabilistically independent contingent beliefs $A_1, \ldots, A_n$.[15] The degree of confirmation of each belief is high but less than 1, since maximal probability is reserved for necessary statements. The probability of the conjunction of A_is thus decreases with the addition of each further conjunct. Given that the set of justified beliefs is extremely large, it follows that the probability of the conjunction of the A_is is bound to be low. But according to the rule of negation, the probability of a statement and its negation are complementary:

$$\Pr(\sim P) = 1 - \Pr(P)$$

Thus the probability of the negation of the conjunction of the A_is is bound to be high. Given a sufficiently large number of A_is, it is high enough to warrant belief. So each of the A_is, as well as the negation of their conjunction, is highly probable, and I am justified in believing each of these statements. That is, I am justified in holding inconsistent beliefs.[16]

Reaction to the epistemic probability argument (EPA) is mixed: some take it as a definitive disproof of the conservative view of consistency; others regard it as a *reductio* of one or more of the premises. In what follows, I shall argue that, at the very least, the EPA is untenable as it stands. One of the strategies employed is to construct an analogous argument that leads to an utterly preposterous conclusion, a conclusion no one can accept. If successful, this strategy shows the argument to be flawed, but does not in itself enable us to pinpoint or diagnose the error in reasoning. Thus it cannot constitute a complete resolution of the paradox.

The first difficulty facing the EPA is that, even if the probability of the conjunction of the A_is declines with the addition of each conjunct, it does not strictly follow that, given sufficient conjuncts, the probability is extremely low. For despite the fact that the probability continues to decrease, it may not get arbitrarily close to 0. In fact, it may never get below some threshold x, where $x > 0$. This can be illustrated by considering the following sequence:

$$a + \frac{1}{2}, \quad \frac{a + \frac{1}{3}}{a + \frac{1}{2}}, \quad \frac{a + \frac{1}{4}}{a + \frac{1}{3}}, \quad \frac{a + \frac{1}{5}}{a + \frac{1}{4}}, \quad \ldots$$

Suppose $a = 4/10$. Then each number in the sequence is less than 1 and greater than 0. The product of the numbers clearly becomes smaller as the sequence grows, but it does not get arbitrarily close to 0. In fact, it is never less than 4/10, the value of a. (To see this, first cancel numerators and denominators appropriately. The product of the numbers in the sequence as thus far stated (the first four numbers) can then be seen to be $a + 1/5$. Similarly, the product of the first five numbers in the sequence is $a + 1/6$; the product of the first six numbers is $a + 1/7$ and so on.)

There is at least an initial problem here for the EPA. For the argument to go through, it is not enough that the probability of the conjunction of the A_is continues to decrease as the number of conjuncts increases; rather, it must become sufficiently low that the degree of confirmation of its negation is high enough to warrant belief. The first, as it turns out, does not ensure the second. This difficulty will be overcome, however, if it can be shown that the probability of the conjunction of the A_is becomes arbitrarily close to 0, approaches 0, as the number of conjuncts becomes indefinitely large. For that would mean that the probability of the conjunction eventually becomes as close to 0 as you like (although always greater than 0).

How can it be ascertained if this in fact happens as the number of A_is in the conjunction increases? The mathematics of the situation is complex. However, it can be determined that the product of an indefinitely large sequence of x_is ($0 < x < 1$) will approach 0 when the x_is are equal; this should be of use to the EPA.[17]

To force the EPA through to its conclusion, then, further restrictions on the A_is are required. But taking, as the set of A_is, an adequately large set of probabilistically independent contingent justified beliefs, *all of which have the same probability*, seems to meet the current difficulty. Of course, one might question whether we in fact have a sufficiently large set of justified beliefs that satisfies this requirement. Still, it seems as least epistemically *possible* that we should. And this should be enough for the advocate of the EPA to maintain that it is at least *possible in principle* to have justified inconsistent beliefs, and thereby to overturn the conservative view of consistency.

I maintain, however, that even this revision does not suffice to salvage the EPA. Two arguments to this effect are advanced below.

In the first, the strategy is to apply analogous probabilistic reasoning to a carefully tailored example. The plausibility of the EPA rests, in part, on the fact that the conclusion that is supposedly justified, the negation of the conjunction of the A_is, does not strike us as particularly informative or significant. But the corresponding statement that emerges in the analogous argument is substantive, informative and utterly implausible. Thus the EPA, according to this line of reasoning, leads to patent absurdity. The second objection attempts to show that the EPA is, at the very least, seriously incomplete. If *either objection* is successful, the EPA fails.

Argument I

A presupposition of the first argument is that Nelson Goodman's curious term "grue" is not a projectible predicate: that is, finding one item to be grue does not confirm that the next is grue, nor that all items are grue. Similarly for any other Goodman-style predicate modelled on "grue".[18]

An argument analogous to the EPA can now be constructed as follows. Consider a large number of therapies or regimens that we believe do not cure AIDS: drinking eight glasses of water a day, taking aspirin, wearing copper bracelets, taking AZT, and so on. Suppose we have a long list of such therapies: $x_1, \ldots, x_n$. The Goodman-style predicate relevant here is "aica", which is defined as follows: an item is aica if and only if it is tested before t and is a cure for AIDS, or is not tested before t and is a cure for cancer. Let A_i be the claim that x_i is not aica. The A_is are independent given that "aica" is not a projectible predicate; one A_i does not confirm any other. Suppose now that each x_i is tested before time t and found not to cure AIDS, and thus not to be aica. The probabilities of each A_i, let us further suppose, are equal; and we are justified in believing each A_i.

It follows from the now familiar reasoning that, given sufficient A_is, the degree of confirmation of the negation of the conjunction of the A_is is sufficient for warranted belief and we are justified in accepting it. Note, however, that the negation of the conjunction of the A_is logically implies:

(A) At least one of $x_1, \ldots, x_n$ is aica.

(A) in turn logically implies:

(A*) At least one of $x_1, \ldots, x_n$ is either a cure for AIDS or a cure for cancer.

It follows that the degree of confirmation of (A*) is at least as high as that of the negation of the conjunction of the A_is; if we are warranted in believing the latter, then we are also warranted in believing (A*).

But these results are absurd. Surely we are not prepared to grant that belief in (A*), belief that there is a cure for either AIDS or cancer, *could ever be warranted on this basis*. Further, it seems completely untenable to suggest that the A_is could, in principle, provide strong confirmation that there is a cure for either AIDS or cancer. Thus, reasoning analogous to the EPA leads to utterly incredible conclusions.

If this is so, then the EPA must be flawed or fallacious in some way. The nature and location of the error, of course, are still entirely open. So even if correct, the argument thus far certainly does not provide a full resolution of the paradox. Some suggestions made at the end of this section may help to locate the substantive error in the EPA.

Argument II

The second argument is more modest, and does not make use of a Goodman-style predicate. Consider certain of our justified beliefs. We are justified in believing that drinking eight glasses of water a day is not a cure for AIDS, nor is taking aspirin, nor is wearing copper bracelets, nor is taking AZT. We have a large set of justified beliefs, about a host of unrelated items, to the effect that each is not a cure for AIDS. Suppose we have a list of such items: $x_1, \ldots, x_n$. A_i will be the claim that x_i is not a cure for AIDS.

One might be inclined to think that the A_is are independent, on the grounds that the items on the list are unrelated; in which case, if they are also equally probable, we may simply repeat argument I and thereby again reach preposterous results. But suppose, on the other hand, that the A_is are not independent. In that case, argument I does not apply; now to calculate the probability of the conjunction of the A_is, we must appeal to the general rule for the probability of a conjunction:

$$\Pr(P_1 \mathrel{\&} P_2) = \Pr(P_1) \times \Pr(P_2/P_1)$$

Clearly, the probability of the conjunction of the A_is decreases as the number of conjuncts increases, for each conditional probability is less than 1. But does the probability of the negation of the conjunction become sufficiently high to warrant belief? If so, the consequence is disastrous: we are justified in believing that there is a cure for AIDS (since this is implied by the negation of the conjunction of the A_is) *on the basis of our justified belief in the* A_is. The advocate of the EPA, therefore, must maintain that the probability of the negation of the conjunction of the A_is in this and similar cases *does not become sufficiently high* to warrant belief. But how can this be established?

Earlier, we isolated a sufficient condition for the probability of the conjunction to become arbitrarily close to 0 as the number of conjuncts becomes indefinitely large: the A_is must be contingent, independent and their probability equal. Showing that this sufficient condition is *not* satisfied in this case is, of course, not adequate to prove that the probability of the conjunction does not approach 0, for the condition is not also necessary.

Assuming that the A_is are not independent, the probability of their conjunction is calculated as follows:

$$\Pr(A_1) \times \Pr(A_2/A_1) \times \Pr(A_3/A_1 \mathrel{\&} A_2) \ldots$$

Each conditional probability in the sequence, it might be pointed out, will be slightly higher than its predecessors. But this is of no help in establishing that the probability of the conjunction does not approach 0, for even when the x_is steadily increase in size, the product of an indefinitely large sequence may approach 0. To see this, note the sequence:

$$1/2, 2/3, 3/4, 4/5, \ldots$$

Here the product of an indefinitely large sequence will come as close as you like to 0, as can be seen by cancelling numerators and denominators appropriately. The product of the first four numbers is 1/5; the product of the first five numbers is 1/6 and so on.

The upshot is this. The advocate of the EPA must maintain that the probability of the negation of the conjunction of the A_is in the AIDS case and related cases does not become sufficiently high to warrant belief. This issue has never been addressed by those who endorse the EPA; and it is difficult to see how they can establish that the relevant probabilities do not become sufficiently high. Thus, as it stands, the EPA is incomplete.

What chiefly distinguishes arguments I and II is a matter of whether or not the independence of the A_is is built into the situation.[19] The predicate "aica" was introduced in argument I precisely in order to guarantee such independence. Still, if the reader balks at Goodman-style predicates, then he can reserve judgement on argument I, and on the issue of independence, and fall back on the more modest argument II.

The main conclusion of this section, then, is that the EPA does not succeed as an argument for the rationality of inconsistency. At best, it is seriously incomplete (objection II); at worst, it leads to utter absurdity (objection I).

To close, let us consider what seems to be a further significant consequence of argument I. Epistemic probability, degree of confirmation, does not appear to conform to the axioms of the classical calculus. For surely it is completely untenable to suppose that (A*) is strongly confirmed in the situation described. Specifically, the degree of confirmation of the conjunction of the A_is does not appear to follow the conjunction rule. Others, of course, have challenged the fit between the principles of the calculus and degree of support or confirmation.[20] But the argument advanced here seems more compelling than previous discussions; the implications of the classical calculus that have been revealed in argument I are simply absurd.

There are, of course, possible manoeuvres to salvage the conjunction rule of the calculus. Two objections to argument I would have this effect, and should be considered here. First, it might be suggested that each A_i in the analogous argument should be assigned a probability of 1 on the grounds that we are entitled to be confident that each A_i is true. Such an assignment would ensure that the probability of the conjunction does not decrease. This result would be achieved, of course, only at the cost of abandoning another standard convention of probability theory, namely, that the value of 1 be reserved for statements that have maximal probability – typically, necessary statements. This in turn would mean that there is no longer any way to distinguish the degree of confirmation of justified contingent beliefs such as the A_is from that of necessary truths. Finally, the effect of such an assignment would also be the complete collapse of the EPA.

A second suggestion is that it is the rule of negation that must be rejected. More specifically, it might be proposed that the probability of a statement plus that of its negation need not equal 1.[21] This move would also clearly stop argument I, for we could not infer a high probability for the negation of the conjunction from the low probability of the conjunction. Of course, for this very reason, the EPA would also fail.

Each of these manoeuvres, it appears, blocks argument I only to the extent that it also defeats the EPA. So neither is effective as a means to rescue the EPA. Further, each objection involves rejecting *some* aspect of the traditional calculus. Thus, the upshot of the analogous argument seems to be that epistemic probability cannot conform to the calculus as a whole. A plausible diagnosis, although not the only one possible, is that the rule of conjunction is, at least in part, the source of the problem.[22]

In this chapter, the arguments of two of the consistency paradoxes – the fallibility argument (in restricted as well as generalized form) and the epistemic probability argument – have been shown to be untenable. Thus, two threats to the conservative view of consistency have now been defused.

5 The lottery paradox

The paradox

The lottery paradox is the most powerful of the consistency paradoxes, and the greatest threat to the traditional view of consistency. It draws us into a tangle of thorny issues in epistemology, in particular, issues concerning knowledge and justified belief. But the paradox itself is simple and elegant. It depends on one key philosophical premise, the principle of high probability, which can be stated as:

(HP) There is a number n ($0.5 < n < 1$) such that if P has probability n for S, then S is justified in believing P.

(HP) is motivated largely by the threat of scepticism. The moral many contemporary philosophers have drawn from the Cartesian exploration of the foundations of knowledge is that to insist on evidence that confers absolute certainty is to ensure, as an inevitable consequence, a thoroughgoing scepticism concerning the world around us. For any empirical belief admits of the *possibility* of error. (Although I believe I am now typing on a keyboard, for instance, it is possible, given my evidence, that I am merely a brain in a vat, being stimulated to have certain sensations.) If requiring certainty for justified belief is setting the bar too high, then it seems the only alternative is a retreat to high probability; and since a probability of 1 is associated with complete certainty, there must be some degree of probability less than 1 that is sufficient to warrant belief – which brings us to (HP). Note that those who take high probability to be central to warranted belief normally regard it as both a necessary and a sufficient condition. However, as stated above, (HP) expresses only a sufficient condition for warranted belief; this is all that the lottery paradox requires.

Now for the paradox.[1] Imagine a fair lottery with 1,000 tickets, numbered consecutively from 1 to 1,000. Exactly one ticket is to be drawn, and the owner of that ticket will win a fabulous sum. (HP) guarantees that there is some degree of probability less than 1 that is sufficient to warrant belief, and it seems reasonable to think that a probability of 0.999 is high enough. (If it is not, we may simply consider a larger lottery, say, one with 10,000 tickets.) Let

T_i = Ticket i will lose the lottery

The probability of T_1 is 999/1,000 or 0.999, and we are thus entitled to believe T_1. Similarly for T_2, T_3, and so on. We are justified in believing each T_i, since each has a probability of 0.999. Now we also know that the lottery has exactly one winner, that is:

$$\sim(T_1 \,\&\, T_2 \,\&\, \ldots \,\&\, T_{1,000})$$

So we are justified in believing each of the following:

$$T_1, T_2, \ldots, T_{1,000}, \ \sim(T_1 \,\&\, T_2 \,\&\, \ldots \,\&\, T_{1,000})$$

But this is an inconsistent set of statements. Thus we are justified in believing an inconsistency.[2]

In this classic version of the lottery paradox, it is a given, a datum, that exactly one of the T_is is false. It is worth noting that there are other variations that lack this feature. For instance, it might be inferred from random sampling that 99 per cent of the 10,000 blood samples currently available in the blood bank are free of HIV infection, and 1% are infected. Given this statistical hypothesis, it is highly probable that sample 1 is HIV free (H_1); similarly for sample 2 (H_2); and so on. But if we are justified in believing, of each sample, that it does not contain the HIV virus, we are justified in believing a set of statements that are jointly inconsistent with the statistical hypothesis on which they are based. That is,

$H_1, H_2, \ldots, H_{10,000}$, 1 per cent of the 10,000 blood samples are infected with HIV

is an inconsistent set of statements.[3]

Like the other consistency paradoxes, the lottery paradox is a type I paradox, and is controversial. As in the other consistency paradoxes, the set of apparently justified inconsistent beliefs can be presented in the form:

$P_1, P_2, \ldots, P_n, \sim(P_1 \& P_2 \ldots P_n)$

The HIV example above may not appear to fit this pattern, since the set of inconsistent statements specified is not of this form. But there is another set of apparently justified inconsistent beliefs here, for the negation of the conjunction of the H_is, which says that at least one sample is infected with HIV, is also clearly warranted. So this version of the lottery paradox can also be seen to fit the mould.

Response to the argument of the lottery paradox is divided: some take it to be impeccable (the radical response), while others reject the conclusion (the conservative position).[4] But it is virtually unanimous that the *logic* of the paradoxical argument is airtight. If the conclusion is not established by the argument, then, the fault must lie with what is apparently the only substantive philosophical premise, (HP). Accordingly, a good part of the discussion of the paradox focuses, directly or indirectly, on this premise.

One possible objection to the reasoning of the paradox, however, should be forestalled before going further. Suppose we first consider T_1, recognize that it is highly probable, and therefore believe it. Once T_1 is added to our beliefs, we may count it as part of the evidence; so the probability of T_2, given the new evidential base, is 998/999 (since ticket 2 is now one of 999 tickets, exactly one of which will win). This is less than 999/1,000, but may still be high enough to warrant belief in T_2. If so, then T_2 can also be regarded as evidence; and thus the probability of T_3 is 997/998, which is less than the probability of T_2. As we continue this process, adding one belief at a time, the probabilities continue to decline and eventually we reach some statement T_k, whose probability is not sufficient to warrant belief. So we are not entitled to believe each T_i, and the conclusion of the paradox cannot be reached.[5]

This way of evading the paradox, however, won't work. For one thing, it has the consequence that which statements you are justified in believing depends on the order in which they are considered. Or, to put the point a little differently, two people who have the same initial evidence concerning a lottery may be warranted in believing quite different T_is. In short, this approach to the paradox introduces an element of arbitrariness into our conception of justified belief that seems entirely unacceptable.

As a final preliminary, let us consider whether requirement (R), introduced in Chapter 4, can be of any help in handling the paradox. Essentially, (R) claims that the evidential status of a statement must be evaluated in the light of the total available evidence. Within the framework of probability considerations and (HP), (R) can be understood as requiring that a statement be highly probable relative to the total evidence in order to be warranted. But in the lottery, the evidence for each T_i is that exactly one of the 1,000 tickets will win; and this is the *only* evidence relevant to each T_i. Unlike the case of the fallibility argument, then, there is no problem of combining different lines of evidence here, for the evidence for each T_i consists in *one and the same fact*. Clearly, in the lottery each T_i is highly probable relative to the total evidence. At a minimum, then, one thing we learn from the lottery paradox is that it is *possible* for each member of an inconsistent set of statements to be highly probable on the total evidence. No doubt this is a rather surprising result.

The moral thus far is that there is no quick and easy way out of this paradox.

The cost of inconsistency

The apparent implications of abandoning the conservative position on consistency are troubling. In particular:

(i) Since any set of inconsistent statements logically implies a contradiction, granting the rationality of inconsistent beliefs seems to force us to grant the rationality of contradictory beliefs.

(ii) A *reductio ad absurdum* argument works by demonstrating that a given set of statements logically implies inconsistent statements; this is then taken to show that one must give up belief in some of the original set. But if inconsistent beliefs are countenanced, then the *reductio* apparently has no force.

The challenge posed by the consistency paradoxes, for those who take the radical line, is to minimize the damage. It will be argued that the consequences outlined above are apparent only, not real consequences. To do so will require rejecting certain well-entrenched epistemological principles; but the radical will contend that these principles can be seen, on independent grounds, to be mistaken.

The issue of the consequences of granting the rationality of inconsistency was postponed at the beginning of Chapter 4, but it is now time to address it. What is the cost of inconsistency?

(i) Contradictory beliefs will be rational

The logic underlying this charge is clear-cut. Any set of inconsistent statements implies a contradiction. Suppose $P_1, \ldots, P_n$ is an inconsistent set. Clearly, the set implies P_1. But since it cannot be the case that all members of the set are true, it cannot be the case that $P_2, \ldots, P_n$ are all true while $\sim P_1$ is false. Thus, $P_2, \ldots, P_n$ jointly imply $\sim P_1$. So the inconsistent set implies $P_1, \sim P_1$. Further, a contradiction implies any statement whatsoever: $P_1, \sim P_1$ jointly imply P_1, which in turn implies $P_1 \vee Q$; but $P_1 \vee Q, \sim P_1$ jointly imply Q.

Now add to these logical truths the following epistemic principle:

> *Deductive closure principle (DCP)*: If you are justified in believing $P_1, \ldots, P_n$, and $P_1, \ldots, P_n$ jointly imply Q and you see this, then you are justified in believing Q.[6]

What (DCP) tells us is that we are justified in believing what we can see to follow from our other justified beliefs; that is, we can expand our stock of justified beliefs by deductive reasoning. Combining (DCP) with the logical truths above provides powerful ammunition against the view that rational belief may be inconsistent, for the radical position is now apparently saddled with wildly implausible consequences: you may be justified in believing contradictions and, indeed, justified in believing any arbitrary statement.

All who have discussed the consistency paradoxes agree: rational belief in a contradiction is impossible. The radical response, therefore, is to avert disaster by rejecting the highly intuitive (DCP). What is incontrovertible and worth retaining in this principle, it is maintained, is just:

> *Weak deductive closure principle (WDCP)*: If you are justified in believing P, and P implies Q and you see this, then you are justified in believing Q.

By abandoning (DCP), and replacing it only with (WDCP), the radical appears to evade the first implausible consequence.

But the cost of inconsistency is not limited to (DCP). To complete the survey of the epistemological terrain, consider another, more modest, principle:

> *Conjunction principle (CP)*: If you are justified in believing P and you are justified in believing Q, then you are justified in believing P & Q.

It would be an understatement to say that (CP) is also a venerable epistemic principle. If combined with (WDCP), however, it has the logical force of (DCP). To see this, suppose that $P_1, \ldots, P_n$ is a set of statements you are justified in believing. Repeated applications of (CP) yield the result that you are justified in believing the conjunction P_1 & $\ldots$ & P_n; and then, by (WDCP), you are entitled to believe whatever statements are implied by the conjunction – which are exactly those implied by the original set of statements. Thus the radical must also reject (CP).

The cost of inconsistency thus far is that two highly intuitive and compelling principles, (DCP) and (CP), must be abandoned.[7]

How plausible is the radical response? Is there any *independent* reason to reject these principles? Let us focus on the weaker principle, (CP); any argument against it will automatically weigh against (DCP).

The argument standardly invoked against (CP) is as follows.

> Suppose we have a large set of contingent, logically independent propositions. In general, the probability that any two

propositions are true is reasonably taken to be the prior probability of the first multiplied ... [by] the conditional probability
of the second given the first. Since the propositions in the set
are contingent, each has a prior probability of less than unity;
but then, by the rule just given, the probability that the conjunction of any two is true is still less, since the conditional
probability of the second conjunct, given the first, is also less
than unity on the assumption of logical independence. ... If the
set is large enough, the probability of the conjunction of all the
members in the original set will have to be very small, no
matter how high the prior probability of each member taken
individually. It is reasonable to conclude, therefore, that we
cannot be completely justified in believing that this conjunction
is true, even if we are completely justified in believing each of
its conjuncts.[8]

A presupposition of this argument, of course, is that high probability is *necessary* for justified belief. (In contrast, (HP) claims only
that it is sufficient.) No doubt this presupposition has considerable
intuitive appeal, but there is no reason to think that it is more
impregnable than (CP). More significantly, the argument against
(CP) bears a striking resemblance to the epistemic probability argument of Chapter 4 and, as a consequence, is subject to the same
difficulties. Very briefly, even if the probability of a conjunction
decreases with the addition of further conjuncts, it cannot be
assumed that it will become arbitrarily small; it may approach some
threshold that is still fairly high. Further, in exploring the EPA we
saw reason to doubt that epistemic probability conforms to the
axioms of the classical calculus; the multiplication rule for conjunction, in particular, was suspect. These difficulties with the EPA are
transmitted to the argument against (CP).

Note also that a plausible alternative model for the probability of
a conjunction has been suggested in the literature, namely, that
the probability of a conjunction is equal to that of its least probable conjunct.[9] On this model, there is no basis for an argument
against (CP).

At the moment, then, there is no independent compelling case
for rejecting either (DCP) or (CP). But these issues will be reconsid-
ered in the last section of this chapter.

(ii) *Reductio ad absurdum* loses its force

A serious worry for the radical position concerns the role that considerations of consistency seem to play in determining what we ought to believe. One of our most powerful tools of rational criticism is *reductio ad absurdum*, in which a set of statements is shown to imply an inconsistency. But if inconsistent beliefs are countenanced, it seems that one might acknowledge the validity of a particular *reductio* while insisting that it need have no impact on belief. A properly executed *reductio* will have no epistemic force.

How can a significant role for *reductios* be preserved if inconsistent beliefs can be acceptable? The only option is to maintain that while any *reductio* establishes that its premises cannot all be true, only some provide decisive reason for rejecting one or more of those premises. Only certain *reductios*, that is, have epistemic implications for belief. A *reductio* based on lottery statements (T_is) would presumably be taken not to provide a compelling reason for rejection of any of its premises.

But on what basis can those *reductios* that have epistemic force plausibly be distinguished from those that do not? Richard Foley suggests one way to draw the line.[10] First, if the premises of the *reductio* are so theoretically interdependent that they are probably all true or all false, then the *reductio* provides a strong argument against each. Secondly, if one premise is distinctly weaker than the others and the other premises are relatively few in number, then a *reductio* will provide a decisive argument against this weakest premise. Only in these two cases does the discovery of inconsistency have epistemic impact.

Since the statements in the lottery are not theoretically interdependent, are large in number and are all strongly supported, none of them need be rejected on Foley's account. But Foley's criteria seem somewhat arbitrary: it is unclear why the *reductios* he specifies should have epistemic significance, while others do not. Moreover, this way of drawing the distinction does not always accord with our intuitions. Suppose, for instance, that several reliable and trustworthy witnesses testify at a trial. The total set of statements offered in testimony is large, and deals with a wide variety of details: how many times a car horn was sounded, when a train left a certain station, what television programme was on when the door-bell rang, and so on. So the statements are not theoretically intertwined, and, we may suppose, are all equally well supported. Nonetheless, if, in conjunction with background knowledge, the statements offered in evidence can be shown to imply an inconsistency, the testimony of the witnesses cannot be accepted in its entirety – contrary to Foley's account. Suspension of belief appears to be the only rational response here.

There is, however, a more promising route for distinguishing those *reductios* that are epistemically significant. The inconsistent statements in the lottery, as noted earlier, are all highly probable on the total evidence. It is only when the inconsistent statements have this feature, the radical might contend, that *reductios* have no epistemic clout. For surely if a statement is strongly confirmed by the total evidence, you are justified in believing it; that is the essence of (HP). The radical can concede that when a number of apparently justified beliefs are demonstrated to imply an inconsistency, we do normally think that at least some of these beliefs must be renounced. But the explanation for this is that in the typical case, discovery of the inconsistency forces us to *re-evaluate the evidence*; it brings to light the fact that at least some of the beliefs in question are not highly probable on the total evidence. *Reductios* standardly have epistemic force because, for the most part, they require a revision of the evidential status of some of the statements in the inconsistent set, which in turn requires an adjustment in our beliefs. On this account, (HP) is both the source and the solution of the problem.

The fact that each member of a set of inconsistent statements may be highly probable on the total evidence thus provides a promising route for distinguishing those *reductios* that are epistemically relevant from those that are not. The radical position on consistency may not require wholesale rejection of *reductio ad absurdum*.

Belief in the T_is is unwarranted

The previous section dealt with general issues relevant to each of the consistency paradoxes. This section shifts the focus back to the lottery.

Is belief in the T_is warranted? Clearly, opinions differ here. But one argument in support of a negative response is based on the intuition, shared by both the conservative and the radical, that even if I believe that my ticket will lose, and my belief is true, I *do not know* that my ticket will lose. Knowledge of the T_is, it seems, must be based on more than just information about the size of the lottery. But knowledge, it is claimed, is a matter of true belief that is justified, where the justification is not defective (as in the Gettier cases).[11] Now the lottery is not another Gettier case: the evidence for the T_is does not seem to be defective in the typical Gettier style. It follows that if I truly believe that my ticket will lose, and my belief is justified, then I know that my ticket will lose. Since it is agreed by all that I do not have such knowledge, it must be concluded that my true belief that my ticket will lose is not justified. Call this the "not-knowledge" argument.[12]

The argument has considerable weight, assuming the traditional framework for the analysis of knowledge, according to which knowledge is a matter of (i) truth, (ii) belief, (iii) justification and (iv) some further condition to ensure the justification is non-defective.[13] However, two alternative theories of knowledge that have gained some currency in recent years make available different explanations of why the T_is are not known, explanations that have no implications for the issue of justification. One such account is the relevant alternatives approach: S knows that P just in case S's evidence rules out every relevant alternative in which $\sim P$. For example, if I see one of the Baker twins in the library, I may know that it is either Tom or Ted I see. In order to know that it is Tom, my evidence must be sufficient to rule out the relevant alternative that it is his twin, Ted. But I do not have to be able to eliminate the possibility that the person is a friend who has undergone plastic surgery in order to look just like his idol, Tom. For that, presumably, is not a relevant alternative. How to specify what counts as a relevant alternative is clearly a critical issue for those who endorse this theory. But if it is granted that the possibility that ticket i wins is a relevant alternative to T_i, as seems entirely plausible, then the consequence is that I do not have knowledge that T_i, for my evidence clearly does not suffice to rule out the possibility that ticket i wins.[14] Thus the relevant alternatives approach can easily explain the lack of knowledge in lottery cases.

Another current explication of knowledge relies on subjunctive conditionals. It requires, as a necessary condition for S knows that P, the truth of:

If P were false, S would not believe P.[15]

Of course, knowledge that P also requires true belief, and possibly other subjunctive conditionals, but for present purposes all that is relevant is this one conditional. Now suppose I believe, based on the fact that there are 1,000 tickets in the lottery, that my ticket will lose, and that my belief is true. Given the nature of my evidence, even if my ticket were going to win, I would still believe that it is a losing ticket; for if my ticket were going to win, my evidence would be exactly the same as it is now. So the failure to satisfy the subjunctive conditional that is necessary for knowledge provides a straightforward explanation of why I don't know, in the lottery, that my ticket will lose.

The success of the not-knowledge argument is closely tied to the traditional framework for the analysis of knowledge. So the argument can hardly be taken as conclusive without an evaluation of the merits of alternative theories of knowledge. But a second reason for denying that the T_is are warranted, by contrast, is not tied to any theoretical framework, and thus offers a more direct route to the desired conclusion. Suppose the following. A rational person, Judith, knows of a fair lottery to be held in Glasgow in which there are n tickets, exactly one of which will win. The probability of the statement

(G) Ticket j is a losing ticket in the Glasgow lottery

is $(n-1)/n$, which is very high. But there is also another lottery in Edinburgh, in which the drawing has already occurred. Judith sees the results of that lottery in her morning newspaper, which reports that some ticket k $(k \neq j)$ won in the Edinburgh lottery. We may suppose that, based on the report in the newspaper, and on the newspaper's reliability, the probability of

(E) Ticket j is a losing ticket in the Edinburgh lottery

is also $(n-1)/n$. Now it seems intuitively clear that there is, and should be, a difference in Judith's cognitive attitude to (G) and (E).[16] But in what does this difference consist? It cannot be a matter of regarding (E) as more probable than (G), for the example has been constructed to ensure that the two probabilities are the same. Indeed, the size of the Glasgow lottery may be increased, if necessary, without significantly altering the example. The most plausible explanation of the difference in attitude, it seems, is in terms of the difference between believing a statement (in the case of the Edinburgh lottery), as opposed to regarding a statement as highly probable (in the case of the Glasgow lottery). So it seems that a rational person in this situation would believe only (E), and would regard (G) as highly probable.[17] If this is so, then, in general, belief that a given ticket will lose in a lottery is not warranted just on the basis of the size of the lottery.

This argument has considerable appeal, and merits further exploration. That there is a difference in cognitive attitude to (G) and (E) seems clear. The only point open to debate is whether the best explanation of the difference is in terms of the distinction between believing a statement and regarding it as highly probable.

Revising (HP)

The villain in the lottery paradox, if there is one, is usually thought to be (HP). But probability is surely not altogether irrelevant to issues of warranted belief; we do not want to eliminate the concept entirely from our epistemic theory. The question that concerns us in this section is whether there is any revision of (HP) that avoids the lottery paradox, and yet allows some significant role for probability in the theory of rational belief.

Competition

There is considerable intuitive appeal in the idea that whether a given hypothesis is acceptable is, at least in part, a matter of how it compares to alternative hypotheses. Laura's frosty behaviour towards John may, in context, be evidence that she is jealous. But we are not warranted in accepting the jealousy hypothesis if her cool, distant manner is better explained by her having become interested in someone else.

One possible revision of (HP), then, is to build in a comparative element. Keith Lehrer's proposal is roughly:

(C) *S* is justified in believing *P* when *P* is more probable for *S* than any of its competitors.[18]

According to Lehrer, in a lottery situation, each T_i competes with all the others. Since they are all equally probable, none of them may be believed. Of course, the individual statements in the lottery do not logically conflict; a given T_i and T_j may both be true. But this just makes clear the need to construe "competition" broadly. Lehrer's explication of the concept is:

> A statement P competes with a statement Q provided that Q is negatively relevant to P (the likelihood that P is true on the assumption that Q is true is lower than otherwise).

On this understanding, it is clear that each T_i competes with all the others.

The comparative probability principle, (C), yields a welcome result in the standard lottery situation: none of the T_is is warranted, and the paradoxical conclusion is thus avoided. Difficulties and anomalies begin to emerge, however, when lotteries in which the probabilities are unequal are considered. For one thing, it seems that very slight differences in probability may make a significant difference in what should be believed. Imagine a situation in which, for some reason, ticket 1 in a 1,000-ticket lottery is slightly more likely to win than other tickets (it is a "sticky" ticket). It is apparently reasonable, according to (C), to believe that ticket 1 will win, even though the differences in probabilities may be minimal. Further, the probability that ticket 1 wins may be only minutely higher than 1/1,000 – which means that a statement may be warranted despite exceedingly low probability.

These consequences of (C) are, at the least, counter-intuitive, and suggest that the principle is too permissive. Even more telling, however, are the examples that indicate that it is too restrictive. We have seen that the notion of a competitor has to be construed broadly if it is to be of help in the lottery paradox. The T_is are competitors only in the sense that each is negatively relevant to the others. But surely it is far too stringent to require, for warranted belief in P, that P be more probable than any statement that is negatively relevant to it. If Q is warranted and is negatively relevant to P, then there must be further evidence that overrides or defeats the evidential significance of Q. There is, however, no reason to suppose that P must be more probable than Q. For instance, let

> E = A normally reliable witness asserts sincerely that Rebecca is at the library

> H = Rebecca is at her apartment

E is negatively relevant to H. But you may be warranted in believing both E and H, provided that you have further evidence that defeats (or overrides) E. (Perhaps you find out that the witness has confused Rebecca with Reesa.) It is not necessary that H be more probable than E.

Given the above, principle (C) is both too permissive and too strict, and cannot be considered a promising replacement for (HP).

Prima facie reason and collective defeat

(HP) takes high probability as definitive grounds for belief. But a more modest and promising variation regards high probability as providing only a prima facie reason for belief. A prima facie reason is understood as a reason that guarantees warrant provided that there are no conflicting considerations. It is defeasible: in the absence of other relevant information, it may warrant a conclusion, but if certain additional information is acquired (a "defeater"), it may no longer justify that conclusion. That a reliable witness asserted P is a prima facie reason for believing P; but it is defeated by the information that another reliable witness denied P.

How can this revision of (HP) deal with the lottery paradox? The idea is roughly as follows. We have equally good prima facie reason for each T_i based on the statistical information concerning the lottery. But because the T_is cannot all be true, there are also grounds for rejecting a given T_i, consisting of the grounds for accepting all the other T_is. (Note that the conjunction of all the T_is but one logically implies the negation of that one.[19]) The lottery is a situation in which the prima facie reasons, in effect, cancel out, or collectively defeat, one another.

To make this intuitive idea more precise, the thesis that high probability is a prima facie reason for belief is supplemented by the principle of collective defeat:

(CD) If we are warranted in believing R and we have equally good prima facie reasons for each member of a minimal set of propositions deductively inconsistent with R, and none of these prima facie reasons is defeated in any other way, then none of the propositions in the set is warranted on the basis of these prima facie reasons.[20]

Let us see how (CD) handles the lottery. The set of T_is is inconsistent with the statement that one of the 1,000 tickets will win (R). There is equally good prima facie reason for each T_i, and none of these reasons is defeated in any other way. Hence, none of the T_is is warranted.

(CD) has considerable initial appeal, and deals well with the standard version of the lottery. But it does not fare as well with certain variations. Consider a possibly-no-winner variation: a fair lottery of 1,000 tickets in which there will be *at most* one winner. Whether or not a ticket is drawn depends on the whim of the Queen, or on some random process. It is likely that there will be a winner, but not sufficiently likely to warrant belief. And since we are not entitled to believe that there is a winner, there is no warranted statement that is inconsistent with the T_is; (CD) thus does not rule out warranted belief in the T_is. But to maintain that we are warranted in believing the T_is in this variation, although not in the original version, is surely counter-intuitive. The cases are just too similar. Further, if we are warranted, in the variation, in believing

$T_1, \ldots, T_n$, There are 1,000 tickets

then, given (DCP), we are also warranted in believing that no ticket wins. But this clearly is a matter on which we should suspend belief.

Not only is (CD) too permissive, as we have just seen, but it is also too stringent: it rules out statements we want to believe. Consider an *n*-ticket fair lottery in which there is one winner. Let:

W_i = Ticket i wins

W_{1-x} = One of tickets 1, 2, ..., x wins

S = It will snow in Toronto tomorrow, 22 July

Suppose that the probability of the following statements is equal, and very low:

$$S \mathrel{\&} W_{1-x}, \quad S \mathrel{\&} W_{x+1-n}, \quad {\sim}S \mathrel{\&} W_1, \quad {\sim}S \mathrel{\&} W_2, \quad \ldots, \quad {\sim}S \mathrel{\&} W_n$$

(The size of the lottery, the partition of the possible outcomes, and the statement S, we may assume, have been selected to ensure this result. Note that ${\sim}S$ is more probable than S, while W_{1-x} is more probable than W_1.) Now consider the set of statements Z whose members are the negations of the conjunctions:

$$\begin{aligned}&{\sim}(S \mathrel{\&} W_{1-x}), \quad {\sim}(S \mathrel{\&} W_{x+1-n}), \quad {\sim}({\sim}S \mathrel{\&} W_1), \quad {\sim}({\sim}S \mathrel{\&} W_2), \quad \ldots, \\ &{\sim}({\sim}S \mathrel{\&} W_n)\end{aligned}$$

The members of Z are also equally probable, and the probability of each is high.[21]

It is a consequence of (CD) that belief in any member of Z is prohibited, for Z is a minimal set inconsistent with the claim that one ticket will win (R). Perhaps this consequence does not at first seem too troubling; in fact, it is disastrous for the theory. Presumably I am justified in believing that it will not snow in Toronto tomorrow, 22 July ($\sim S$). But from $\sim S$, it follows that $\sim(S \mathrel{\&} W_{1-x})$. Thus, if I cannot believe $\sim(S \mathrel{\&} W_{1-x})$, then I cannot believe $\sim S$. So (CD) does more than prohibit beliefs about lotteries, and it does more than prohibit weather forecasts. For any warranted empirical statement can be matched with an appropriate lottery, and the possible outcomes of the lottery can be suitably partitioned so as to create a set of statements corresponding to Z.

Clearly, taking high probability as a prima facie reason for belief that can be defeated according to (CD) offers no improvement on an unrevised (HP).

Scepticism and the lottery

To accept (HP), it appears, is to grant the rationality of inconsistency. But the implications of rejecting (HP) may be even more calamitous. According to some, to reject (HP) is to be defenceless against the sceptic.

Richard Foley, for one, insists that rejecting (HP), and denying that the T_is are warranted, leads straight to scepticism.[22] If I am not justified in believing T_1, he contends, then it must be admitted that statements for which a person has extremely strong evidence are nevertheless not rational for him. Suppose, for example, that the lottery is extremely large – say, a billion tickets. Surely the evidence for T_1 would be at least as strong as the evidence I have for most of my common-sense beliefs. Surely it would be at least as strong as the evidence I have that the room I just left still has furniture in it, and at least as strong as the evidence I have that it will not snow in Chicago next August. Thus, if my evidence is not strong enough to warrant T_1, then it is not strong enough to warrant these other beliefs. The upshot, then, is scepticism concerning most of our empirical beliefs.

Does the lottery paradox force on us the dilemma of rational inconsistency or scepticism? In light of the previous section, can anything of substance be salvaged from (HP) that would enable us to side-step the apparent dilemma? The key term "probable" has thus far been used uncritically in this chapter, as it is in most treatments of the lottery paradox. To explore these questions, however, it is necessary to ask exactly what is meant by "probable" in this context. To what kind of probability does (HP) refer? In so far as it functions as a general epistemic principle designed to guide belief, and to protect us from the excessive demands of the sceptic, it seems clear that (HP) refers, at least, to epistemic probability, understood as degree of support or confirmation. On this reading, (HP) assures us that something less than maximal degree of support is sufficient for rational belief. Turning to the argument of the lottery paradox, note that it appeals to statistical probabilities (relative frequencies). There can be no doubt, in lottery-style cases, that the statistical probability of each T_i is high, given the data. Hence, in order for there to be a conflict between (HP) and consistency in the lottery situation, we must assume either that:

(A) (HP) makes reference, in part, to statistical probability.

or:

(B) A high statistical probability ensures a high epistemic probability.

To avoid a conflict between (HP) and consistency, then, it is sufficient to maintain that:

(A*) (HP) makes reference only to epistemic probability.

and:

(B*) A high statistical probability does not ensure a high epistemic probability.

With regard to (A*), a version of (HP) that refers only to epistemic probability seems sufficient to combat the sceptical threat posed by the Cartesian; absolute certainty, or a guarantee of truth, is not necessary for warrant if strong support by the evidence is sufficient. If (B*) is correct, there is not a direct, straightforward link between statistical and epistemic probability. That is, high statistical probability is not, *in itself*, a source of good evidence or warranted belief.[23] But there is reassurance in the fact that there are other sources of evidence (perception and memory, for instance) whose evidential worth is presumably independent of considerations of statistical probability. And (B*) leaves room for statistical data to play some role in theories of justified belief.

So the lottery paradox appeals to two different senses of "probability". (HP) is most transparently true when construed in terms of epistemic probability. On the other hand, it is clear that the T_is have high probability in the statistical sense. The critical issue now is the link between the two types of probability. Of course, to develop a theory of justification in which high statistical probability does not, in itself, confer warrant will prove a considerable undertaking.[24] But if both (A*) and (B*) are tenable, then it is possible to endorse a version of (HP) that avoids a wide-ranging scepticism based on the demand for certainty, while at the same time insisting on the consistency of rational belief.

Still, the spectre of scepticism hangs over the conservative. His position on consistency may not necessitate a thoroughgoing scepticism concerning empirical beliefs. But it has recently been suggested by Jonathan Vogel that it may lead to semi-scepticism – that is, to a sceptical stance concerning some (although not most or all) of our empirical beliefs. For instance, suppose you own a car that you parked last night on a street in Toronto. It seems reasonable for you now to believe that your car is where you left it, that it has not been stolen. But you know that there is usually at least one car theft every night in Toronto. Vogel says:

> Now, in certain important ways, one's epistemic situation with respect to the lottery is like one's epistemic situation in the Car Theft case. In effect, when you park your car in an area with an appreciable rate of auto theft, you enter a lottery in which cars are picked, essentially at random, to be stolen and driven away. Having your car stolen is the unfortunate counterpart to winning the lottery.[25]

How exactly is your epistemic situation with respect to the lottery like your epistemic situation in the car theft case? Let

Q_1 = Your car has not been stolen.

Q_1 is one of a set of statements each of which says, of a particular car parked in Toronto last night, that it has not been stolen. The analogy with the lottery case, for Vogel, apparently consists in at least the following: (i) you know, or have good reason to believe, that at least one of the Q_is is false; and (ii) you have no non-arbitrary reason for preferring Q_1 to any other Q_i, that is, for believing Q_1 rather than any other Q_i. If the analogy holds, then it seems that the conservative stance on consistency, coupled with the recognition that rational belief cannot be arbitrary, dictates that Q_1 is not warranted.[26]

Similarly, it can be argued that you are not justified in believing that George W. Bush has not had a fatal heart attack in the past five minutes on the grounds that: (i) you have reason to believe at least one man in his fifties in the United States has had a heart attack in the past five minutes; and (ii) your reason for believing that Bush has not been stricken is no better than your reason for believing this of any other American male in his fifties. Nor, it appears, could you be warranted in believing that your house has not burned down during your absence, since there is presumably reason to think that at least one house has burned down in the UK during the period of your absence. And so on. Denying the possibility of rational inconsistent belief appears to have this semi-scepticism as a consequence.

The conservative's first reaction might be to minimize the significance of the argument, to suggest that semi-scepticism is something we can live with. But this would be a short-sighted response. Surely we all have a justified belief that George W. Bush is the President of the United States. But that belief implies that Bush is alive, that he hasn't just had a fatal heart attack. If we aren't justified in believing that, how can we be entitled to believe that Bush is President? Similarly, it seems that you cannot have a justified belief concerning the location of your car if you are not entitled to believe that it hasn't been stolen. The conservative, and indeed, anyone committed to even the weak version of the closure principle (If S is justified in believing P, P implies Q and S sees this, then he is justified in believing Q) cannot deny the impact of this semi-scepticism.

But is the argument for semi-scepticism successful? Is the epistemic situation in the lottery really closely analogous to the epistemic situation in the examples given? Let us focus on the car theft case. One significant *disanalogy* is that in the lottery, all that can be offered as evidence for T_1 is that exactly one ticket will win; and the same is true for any T_i. By contrast, in the car theft case, the evidence you have for Q_1 includes the fact that your car is parked in a reasonably safe neighbourhood in Toronto, is an old car with considerable rust on the body, has a security system and so on. The evidence for Q_1 does not consist (just) in the fact that one of the Q_is is false. Whether it is based, even in part, on statistical data is far from clear.

For closely related reasons, the two-pronged analogy Vogel claims to find between the lottery and the car theft case does not in fact hold. Specifically, it is not the case that the Q_is have equal epistemic status, that there is equal reason to believe any Q_i. Cars are not generally "picked, essentially at random, to be stolen and driven away". Unlike the selection of a winning ticket in a lottery, car theft is not a random process. A BMW, new, unlocked and with no security system, is considerably more attractive to a thief than an ancient Toyota with security devices and significant rust.

Thus, in the *normal* or *typical* situation in which you reasonably believe that your car has not been stolen, there does not appear to be a strong analogy with the lottery. But we can doctor the standard situation so that there is a stronger resemblance. What seems particularly relevant is that there should be no non-arbitrary reason for preferring Q_1 to any other Q_i. Here is such a case. Suppose the police are in league with organized crime. The city is so completely under their control that only the police steal cars (independent car thieves are a vanished breed). Every night, the police steal exactly one car, which is chosen by a purely random process. (Perhaps the licence number of every car parked in the city is entered in a computer, and a computer program randomly selects a number.) Now there is transparently equal epistemic status for each Q_i. But now it seems dubious that you are warranted in believing your car has not been stolen. In this situation, there is no great difficulty in granting that the Q_is and the T_is are epistemically on a par.

To construct a car theft that strongly resembles the lottery, what is required is a scenario in which there is no better reason to believe Q_1 than any other Q_i. This is nothing like the typical situation. The challenge, for Vogel's argument, is to construct a case in which the strong resemblance to the lottery is built in, and yet it is clear that you may justifiably believe Q_1. If such a case can be found, the conservative stance on consistency is untenable.

Closure and the lottery

Here is an example that might be used as the basis for an argument that the T_is are warranted and the radical position therefore correct. Suppose that George has a sizeable mortgage on his home. Having calculated his income and expenses for the coming year, he justifiably believes that he will not be able to pay off the mortgage this year. (Surely we all frequently have justified beliefs of this sort.) George has not forgotten that he has a ticket in next week's Super-Lotto, and, of course, he realizes that he would be able to pay off the mortgage if he were to win the Super-Lotto.[27] Losing in the lottery is a necessary condition for being unable to pay off the mortgage, as George knows; yet he justifiably believes that he will be unable to pay off the mortgage. Does it not follow that George is justified in believing that he will not win the lottery? But if he is, then surely the T_is in *any* lottery are warranted.

This example might seem to clinch the case for the radical, for it is unquestionable that there are situations in which you may justifiably believe that you will not be able to pay off the mortgage (not be able to afford a Porsche or a trip to Martinique), despite the fact that you own a ticket in a lottery in which the drawing has not yet occurred. But persuasive though the example is, it would be premature to concede the point, for there is a similar strategy available to the conservative.

Suppose, for example, that the head of an underground resistance unit decides that a certain government official must be assassinated. One member of the unit is to do the deed, but there are compelling reasons why the killer should be selected randomly from within the unit. Which person is assigned the task is therefore to be determined by a lottery, whose results will be secret; the person holding the "winning" ticket will get the assignment. The assassination, we may suppose, takes place according to plan. Now consider Max, a typical member of the unit. Surely we are not entitled to believe, in the absence of independent evidence, that he is not the assassin. But we know that if he lost the lottery, then he did not kill the official. Losing the lottery is a sufficient condition for not being the assassin. Does it not follow that we are not entitled to believe that Max lost the lottery? But if so, then surely the T_is in *any* given lottery are not warranted.

This is baffling: two highly intuitive, structurally similar arguments for opposing conclusions. Are we, or are we not, warranted in believing a given T_i based just on the statistical evidence? Does either argument make the case that belief in the T_is is (is not) warranted? Let us look more closely.

The key statements in the radical's argument are:

(A) (1) George will not be able to pay off his mortgage this year.
    (2) If George wins the lottery, he will be able to pay off his mortgage this year.
    (3) George will not win the lottery.

The argument of the conservative makes use of:

(B) (1*) Max did not win the lottery.
    (2*) If Max did not win the lottery, then he was not the assassin.
    (3*) Max was not the assassin.

The radical maintains that since George is entitled to accept (1) and (2), he must also be entitled to accept (3). On the other hand, the conservative argues that since (3*) is not warranted and (2*) clearly is, it must be the case that (1*) is not.

A presupposition essential to both arguments is the closure principle, stated earlier as:

(DCP) If S is justified in believing each of $P_1, \ldots, P_n$, and $P_1, \ldots, P_n$ jointly imply Q and S sees this, then S is justified in believing Q.

Consider (A) and (B) as arguments, with (3) and (3*), respectively, as conclusions. The radical maintains that since (A) is valid, and the premises are warranted, then so must be the conclusion. But this of course presupposes (DCP). (It is assumed throughout that the individuals in question are aware of the relevant logical relations.) Similarly, the conservative argues that since (B) is valid, and (2*) is warranted while (3*) is not, it must be the case that (1*) is not warranted; again (DCP) is assumed.

But it cannot be that both are right. It cannot be that (3) is warranted while (1*) is not, for there is exactly the same sort of statistical evidence available in each case (we may even assume the lotteries are the same size). So either (3) and (1*) are *both* justified, or *neither* is.

Let us consider each side of this dilemma. Suppose (3) and (1*) are both warranted. In this case, it seems that the only way to make room for the fact that (3*) is not warranted is to deny (DCP). Suppose, on the other hand, that neither (3) nor (1*) is warranted. Then, in order to accommodate the fact that (3) is not warranted, (DCP) must again be denied. The conclusion that (DCP) does not hold seems inescapable. Either (A) or (B) appears to provide a counter-example, depending on whether or not the lottery statements in the two cases are warranted.

A new problem has surfaced: *whatever* stance is taken on the lottery paradox, the home-owner and the assassin cases jointly present a disturbing challenge to the closure principle for justification.[28] Of course, if (DCP) cannot be assumed, both the argument put forward by the radical in this section and that offered by the conservative must fail in their present form. Thus nothing is established by either argument concerning the correct position on the lottery paradox.

A critical step in the argument against (DCP) is the dilemma:

Either (3) and (1*) are both justified, or neither is.

This disjunctive claim is based on the fact that there is exactly the same evidence for (3) and (1*) (assuming the lotteries are of equal size). But it may be possible to escape the dilemma if justification is not solely a function of the strength of the evidence, but is, in certain ways, context-sensitive. One possibility worth considering is that the standards of justification are necessarily different in the two cases. The radical might argue that stronger evidence, a higher degree of confirmation, is required in the case of (1*), because the question of whether Max won the lottery is directly relevant, and known to be directly relevant, to whether Max is the assassin – a matter of the utmost gravity and seriousness. Justification is, in this sense, context-dependent: the strength of the evidence required for warrant is a function of the significance of the statement.

There are several difficulties with this attempt to evade the dilemma. First, it is clear that particularly strong evidence is required before we can justifiably base significant action on a belief; we should, for instance, have compelling evidence for the belief that a person has committed a particular crime before imposing a prison sentence on him. But this may signify only that we need more than mere reasonable belief to justify the appropriate *action* when the stakes are high. It is far from clear that the *belief* in question requires a higher degree of confirmation in order to be justified. Further, to maintain that (3) is warranted and (1*) is not, it has to be granted that statistical information alone constitutes good evidence and can warrant belief, in which case increasing the size of the lottery should increase the strength of the evidence. But increasing the size of the lottery in the case of Max has no significant impact on the example; it remains clear that (3*) is not warranted. Finally, the Max example can be revised so that the issues are not as momentous. Suppose Max belongs to a gang of teenage boys who are keen to establish a reputation for being cool. They decide to commit some petty act of vandalism: scratching a car door with a key. A lottery is held to determine who will be the vandal. Again, we are not warranted in believing that Max is not the person who scratched the car.

So appeal to the relative stringency of differing standards of justification does not seem to enable us to escape the dilemma. The gravity of the issues in the original example serves only to make clearer, to highlight, what may justifiably be believed.[29]

The conclusion that seems to emerge from the dilemma, that there are cases in which the closure principle for justification does not hold, is troubling. Still, it may be that the failure of (DCP) is not pervasive, but is limited to a narrow range of cases. Of particular concern in this connection is the following. Suppose it is granted that the argument above shows that there are exceptions to the closure principle construed in its most general form, as (DCP). Is it nevertheless possible to maintain that (WDCP) is unscathed? Consider again the dilemma: either (3) and (1*) are both justified, or neither is. Suppose first that neither (3) nor (1*) is justified. Now, in argument (A), (1) and (2) are individually justified. If the conjunction of (1) and (2) is also warranted, then argument (A) can be restated as a one-premise argument. We then have a one-premise valid argument in which the premise is warranted, but the conclusion is not. Hence, (WDCP) fails if the conjunction of (1) and (2) is justified. Suppose, on the other hand, that both (3) and (1*) are justified. Clearly, (2*) is also justified. If the conjunction of (1*) and (2*) is warranted, then argument (B) can be restated as a one-premise argument. And so on.

The outlook for (WDCP) depends on the plausibility of maintaining, with regard to one of these conjunctions, that it is not warranted even though each individual conjunct is. Clearly, this is not guaranteed by the failure of the conjunction principle ((CP)). The most plausible counter-examples to (CP), we saw earlier, are lengthy, highly detailed and informative conjunctions whose (epistemic) probability might be regarded as very low. But for (WDCP) to remain undisturbed now will require that a very *modest* conjunction, either (1) & (2) (if (3) is not warranted) or (1*) & (2*) (if (1*) is warranted), is not justified despite each conjunct being justified. It is difficult, to say the least, to see why this should be so. The upshot is that even (WDCP) may be vulnerable to the argument of this section.

The lottery paradox is the most threatening and intriguing of the consistency paradoxes. To resolve it will require a deeper understanding of the tangle of difficult epistemic issues that surround it.

Reflection on the lottery has also revealed a new concern: there is a disturbing case that can be made against the highly intuitive (DCP), a case that threatens even (WDCP). The lottery paradox may offer a significant lesson without itself being resolved.

6 Newcomb's problem

The paradox

You have been presented with an exciting opportunity.[1] Before you on the table are two boxes, B_1 and B_2. B_1 is transparent; you can see that it contains $1,000. B_2, which is opaque, contains either $1,000,000 or nothing.

B_1: $1,000 B_2: $1,000,000 or nothing

You have a choice between two actions: taking what is in both boxes or taking only what is in the second box. Before you make your choice, the following background information is carefully explained. The content of the second box is determined by a superlative predictor who has successfully predicted the choice of all (almost all) those who were previously placed in this situation. His prediction is based on an in-depth psychological study of the individual; you have already been examined by him, and a detailed profile of your basic personality and character traits has been constructed. After making his prediction, the predictor acts as follows:

- If he predicts that you will take what is in both boxes, he puts nothing in the second box.
- If he predicts that you will take just the second box, he puts $1,000,000 in the second box.

Now it is your turn. You have five minutes to reflect. What should you do?

One line of reasoning that seems utterly compelling goes as follows. The predictor has already consulted your psychological profile, made his prediction, and either placed $1,000,000 in B_2 or left it empty. Nothing you do now can affect his prior decision. The content of B_2 is fixed and determined. Consider the two possibilities: either there is $1,000,000 in B_2 or there is $0 in B_2. In the first case, you will get $1,001,000 if you take both boxes, whereas you will get (only) $1,000,000 if you take just B_2. In the second case, you will get $1,000 if you take both boxes, but nothing if you take just B_2. In either case, you are $1,000 richer if you take both boxes. So clearly taking both boxes is the rational thing to do.

But another argument seems equally forceful. Given the predictor's astonishing past record of predictive success, it is virtually certain that he will correctly predict your choice. Thus, if you take both boxes, almost certainly he will have predicted this, will have left B_2 empty, and you will get only $1,000. Similarly, if you take just B_2, almost certainly he will have predicted this, will have placed $1,000,000 in B_2, and you will get $1,000,000. The choice is between $1,000 and $1,000,000. Clearly, taking just B_2 is the rational thing to do.

Newcomb's problem thus provides the makings of a paradox: two highly intuitive arguments, each with apparently impeccable reasoning and premises, for two incompatible conclusions. Plainly this is a type II paradox, and equally plainly it is falsidical; for the conclusions (taking just one box is the rational act, taking both boxes is the rational act) are unquestionably incompatible, and cannot both be true. It is also a controversial paradox, for there is no consensus as to which argument is defective. To many, it is obvious that the first argument is compelling, and the choice of B_2 is silly. However, to many others, it is just as obvious that the second argument is incontrovertible, and choosing both boxes is completely irrational.

The force of each of the two key arguments can be brought out by considering two back-up arguments, each of which takes the point of view of an observer of the game.

First, there is the *well-wisher argument*. Imagine that the predictor has already made his prediction, and placed $1,000,000 in B_2 or not. A good friend of yours, who has your best interests at heart, can see into B_2 from where she sits (it is transparent on one side). If she sees the money in B_2, it will be there whatever you choose; if she is looking at an empty box, then it will remain empty whatever you choose. (It is assumed that backward causation is not a possibility in this problem.) So whether she sees the money in B_2 or not, surely she is hoping that you will take both boxes. Can it be rational to act contrary to what you know a sincere well-wisher with superior knowledge hopes you will do?

The *betting argument* makes the case for taking just one box. You know that in the past all those who chose only B_2 received $1,000,000, while all the "smarties", people who took both boxes, got only $1,000. You have no reason to think that you are any less predictable than previous players. If you were to commit yourself to taking just B_2, would it not be rational for an onlooker to make a bet that you will get $1,000,000? And if you were to choose both boxes, would it not be rational for that onlooker to bet that you will get only $1,000? But surely it cannot be rational to act against what it is rational to bet on.

Newcomb's problem and decision theory

Newcomb's problem was devised by Dr William Newcomb, an American physicist, and first presented to the philosophical world by Robert Nozick.[2] In his initial, seminal study, Nozick sets the problem in the framework of contemporary decision theory, where it is shown to raise vexing problems concerning the fundamental principles of rational action. To understand and appreciate these problems, let us ignore the paradox for the moment and take a quick tour of the basic elements of decision theory.

Decision theory is concerned with the question of what it is rational to do when there is less than complete information concerning the outcomes or consequences of your actions. For even if the actual outcome of a given act is not known, there may still be a determinately rational act. A central concept in decision theory is the desirability or utility of a possible outcome of an act. The desirability of an outcome encompasses any type of value (disvalue) *the agent finds in it*: the value may be self-regarding (you win a prestigious scholarship) or, if you are altruistic, other-regarding (your best friend wins a scholarship). The utility of an outcome *for you* is entirely a matter of how much you value it.

A fundamental principle of decision theory is the expected utility principle. The motivation underlying this principle is simply the idea that the agent wants to maximize the desirability of the situation that her action achieves. If you know the consequences of each alternative action, then, clearly, you should perform the act that yields the most desirable consequences; you have no need of decision theory. But if you do not know what the outcomes of your actions will be, you must take into account probabilities, as well as utilities. Suppose, for instance, that you are invited for dinner, and you know the hosts will serve wine with dinner only if you bring a wine that, in their view, complements the main course; otherwise there will be only mineral water. You also know that the hosts will serve either beef tenderloin or fish, and that they consider only a red wine to be acceptable with beef, and only a white with fish. The choice you face is whether to bring red or white wine. If there is a rational decision here, it must take into account the *likelihood* of each main course, as well as your own *preferences* concerning wine.[3]

Although the basic idea is simple and intuitive, its execution is rather technical and complex. First, the statement of the expected utility principle presupposes that it is possible to assign numerical values to the desirability of the possible outcomes of an act; but this is intended only to indicate the *relative strength* of the desirability of each possible outcome, that is, to indicate how the different utilities may be compared. Now suppose the (exclusive and exhaustive) outcomes an act may yield are O_1, ..., O_n;[4] the conditional probability of O_i given act A is p_i; and the utility of O_i is $u(O_i)$. To take into account both the utilities and the probabilities, the notion of the expected utility of an act A is defined as follows:

EU(A): $p_1 \times u(O_1) + p_2 \times u(O_2) + \ldots + p_n \times u(O_n)$

The principle of expected utility then says simply:

(MEU) You ought to do the action that has maximal expected utility.

To illustrate, consider a horse race. S_1 = Horse 1 wins; S_2 = Horse 2 wins; A = I bet on horse 1; B = I bet on horse 2. The utility of each outcome is represented in the matrix:

	S_1	S_2
A	50	−5
B	−6	49

(Positive numbers represent positive value while negative numbers represent disvalue; an outcome with a utility of −6 is worse than an outcome with a utility of −5.) Given only this information, any decision might seem arbitrary. But suppose horse 2 is much more likely to win. The probability of S_1, let us say, is 0.2, and the probability of S_2 is 0.8.[5] Then the expected utility of each of the two acts is:

$$\mathrm{EU}(A) = (0.2 \times 50) + (0.8 \times -5) = 6$$

$$\mathrm{EU}(B) = (0.2 \times -6) + (0.8 \times 49) = 38$$

Hence, (MEU) recommends act B.

(MEU) relies on the highly technical conception of the expected utility of an act, which results from the attempt to combine appropriately the relevant features of utility and probability. A second fundamental principle of decision theory, however, is more easily grasped. Even with incomplete information concerning the outcomes, there can be cases in which it is known how the consequences of the possible acts compare. It may be known, for instance, on the basis of knowledge of *possible outcomes*, that you will be better off doing A rather than B. In still other cases, it can be determined that, no matter what the actual outcomes, you will be at least as well off doing A rather than B, and possibly better off. In the first sort of case, we say that A *strongly dominates* B; in the second, that A *weakly dominates* B.

More precisely, the outcome of an act depends on background conditions, on "the state of the world". We may be ignorant of the outcome of an act because which possible state of the world holds is unknown to us. Now suppose that $S_1, \ldots, S_n$ is a set of the (exclusive and exhaustive) possible states of the world. If for every S_i, the value of the outcome of A, given S_i, is greater than the value of the outcome of B, given S_i, then A strongly dominates B. If for every S_i, the value of the outcome of A, given S_i, is at least as great as the value of the outcome of B, given S_i, and for some S_i, the value of the outcome of A, given S_i, is greater than the value of the outcome of B, given S_i, then A weakly dominates B.[6] The dominance principle then states:

(DP) If A dominates B (either weakly or strongly), then A should be preferred to B.

The appeal of the dominance principle is not difficult to fathom. If A strongly dominates B, you are certain to be better off by doing A. If A weakly dominates B, you are certain to be at least as well off by doing A rather than B, and possibly better off. Consider a decision situation that can be represented as follows:

	S_1	S_2
A	10	3
B	8	3

Surely it seems clear that the rational course, as (DP) recommends, is to do A.

Now to return to Newcomb's problem. Can any progress be made by appealing to either of these two principles? The situation in Newcomb's problem can be represented by the following matrix:

	$1,000,000 in the second box	$0 in the second box
Take both boxes	$1,001,000	$1,000
Take only second box	$1,000,000	$0

What is immediately apparent is that taking both boxes (strongly) dominates taking just the second, and is thus the rational choice, according to (DP). Note also that argument I, outlined above, essentially points out that taking both boxes is the dominant act.

Before the "two-boxers" among us claim vindication, however, it would be wise to consult (MEU). Let us modestly assign a probability of only 0.9 to the predictor's correctly predicting your act, and suppose that the value of an outcome for you is proportional to the money received. Let S_1 = The predictor placed $1,000,000 in the second box; S_2 = The predictor left the second box empty; A = You take both boxes; B = You take only the second box. Then:

$$EU(A) = Pr(S_1/A) \times 1,001,000 + Pr(S_2/A) \times 1,000$$
$$= 0.1 \times 1,001,000 + 0.9 \times 1,000 = 101,000$$

$$EU(B) = Pr(S_1/B) \times 1,000,000 + Pr(S_2/B) \times 0$$
$$= 0.9 \times 1,000,000 + 0.1 \times 0 = 900,000$$

Since the expected utility of B is greater than that of A, (MEU) recommends act B, taking just the second box.

So it turns out that (DP) and (MEU) conflict in the Newcomb situation: each identifies a different act as rational. Indeed, one reason why Newcomb's problem has generated such intense interest is that it illustrates, in a particularly forceful manner, the conflict between the two principles, and the difficulty in determining the proper scope of each. The rational strategy in Newcomb's problem can be determined, it seems, if the conflict between the principles can be successfully adjudicated.

We began with a fairly specific question: what is the rational course of action in Newcomb's problem? This has now blossomed into the more general question: how is the conflict between (DP) and (MEU) to be resolved? Exploring this broader issue, it appears, first, that (DP) must be restricted, for we are not willing to apply (DP) to *any* set of states of the world. Consider again the horse-race example described earlier, where the probability of the first horse (H_1) winning is 0.8. The following matrix accurately represents the situation:

	I win my bet	I lose my bet
I bet on H_1	50	–5
I bet on H_2	49	–6

An unrestricted (DP) would recommend betting on H_1, even though H_2 is highly likely to win – a result that is clearly wrong. It follows that the application of (DP) must be limited in some way.

Note that in this situation the states are not probabilistically independent of the acts.[7] For Pr(I win my bet/I bet on H_1) = 0.2, while Pr(I win my bet/I bet on H_2) = 0.8. A classic view, endorsed by

Richard Jeffrey, is that probabilistic independence is the critical factor; dominance can be legitimately appealed to, he claims, only when the states are probabilistically independent of the actions.[8] Where the states are not thus independent of the actions, according to this view, (MEU) prevails. (It can easily be demonstrated that, when the states are probabilistically independent of the actions, the recommendations of (DP) and (MEU) will not conflict.) Although this position has considerable intuitive appeal, there is reason to think it is not ultimately satisfactory.

The difficulty with the Jeffrey proposal for the legitimate scope of dominance has to do with "common cause" examples. Here is one such example. King Solomon wants another man's wife. She adores him; if he sends for her, she will come. As a student of psychology, Solomon knows that kings have two basic personality types: charismatic and uncharismatic. Whether or not a king is charismatic depends entirely on his genetic endowment. Charismatic kings have a strong tendency to act justly, and uncharismatic kings unjustly. Solomon does not know whether or not he is charismatic, but he does know that it is unjust to send for another man's wife. As a student of political science, Solomon has also learned that charismatic kings rarely face successful revolts, whereas uncharismatic kings frequently do. The connection between lack of charisma and successful revolts is not explained by the unjust acts, but rather by the lack of confidence and ease projected by uncharismatic kings.[9] Schematically we have:

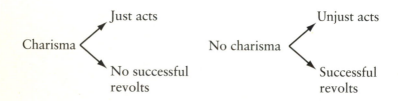

Let A = Solomon calls for the woman he wants; B = Solomon refrains from calling for the woman he wants; S_1 = There is no successful revolt against Solomon; and S_2 = There is a successful revolt against Solomon. The matrix, we may suppose, is as follows:

	S_1	S_2
A	100	–20
B	80	–30

Dominance reasoning seems entirely natural here, for Solomon can have no impact on his basic personality type and, therefore, no impact on whether or not his subjects will successfully rebel against him. Whatever his political future may be, he will be happier with the woman he loves.

But according to the classic position we have been considering, dominance cannot be invoked here, for the states are not probabilistically independent of the actions. Solomon's calling for another man's wife is a sign that he is unjust, and thus uncharismatic, and thus revolt-prone; while refraining from his desire is evidence that he is just, charismatic and not revolt-prone. Specifically, let us say that $Pr(S_1/A) = 0.1$, $Pr(S_1/B) = 0.9$, $Pr(S_2/A) = 0.9$ and $Pr(S_2/B) = 0.1$. Thus:

$$EU(A) = 0.1 \times 100 + 0.9 \times -20 = -8$$

$$EU(B) = 0.9 \times 80 + 0.1 \times -30 = 69$$

So (MEU) prescribes that Solomon not call for the woman he loves.

For Nozick, the result of applying (MEU) in this sort of case is patently absurd. Whether or not Solomon is charismatic is fixed and determined. Nothing he does now can have any effect either on his degree of charisma, or on his being revolt-prone. Surely his action should be directed toward what he can achieve: life with the woman he desires.

Since Nozick takes it that the proper response to cases like that of King Solomon is transparently clear, he rejects the classic view of Jeffrey concerning proper appeal to dominance. What is critical, he maintains, is not that the states be probabilistically independent of the actions, but rather that they be causally independent of the actions. That is, dominance is legitimately applied as long as the actions do not affect or causally influence which states obtain. Since Solomon's action can have no impact on whether or not he will face a successful revolt, the dominance principle is properly invoked, and prescribes Solomon's calling for the other man's wife.

Now to shift the focus back to Newcomb's problem. What is the upshot of Nozick's conclusions concerning dominance? Let us take it as a given that there is no backwards causality: what choice you make now does not affect what the predictor did in the past. Then, given Nozick's criterion, dominance is properly applied here, and the rational course of action is thus to take both boxes.

This is Nozick's considered view; but he remains uneasy, for he admits that the case in which the predictor is infallible is troubling. If you know or are certain that the prediction will be correct, then you naturally argue:

> If I take both boxes, I will get $1,000. If I take just the second box, then I will get $1,000,000. So I should take only the second box.

This line of argument surely seems eminently reasonable. But how can the one-box decision in the case of an infallible predictor be squared with the above account of the legitimate scope of dominance? Even if the predictor is infallible, the states are still causally independent of the actions. And is there any plausibility to advocating a one-box strategy in the case of infallibility, but a two-box strategy otherwise? Can the fact that there is a minute probability that the predictor is mistaken make that much difference?

Nozick admits he finds these issues mind-boggling.

Incoherence and under-determination

Faced with this impasse, some philosophers have attempted to escape the clutches of the paradox by arguing that there is no (unique) rational solution. There are two principal escape routes here: one maintains that the description of the paradoxical situation is incoherent; the other, which is diametrically opposed, has it that the description of the paradox is under-determined, and that the correct answer will depend on exactly the details that are fleshed out.

First, let us consider the view that the Newcomb story is incoherent or involves a contradiction. G. Schlesinger has argued as follows.[10] Given the predictor's success rate in the past, it seems entirely justified to conclude that he has successfully predicted my action. But then I have an incontrovertible argument for taking the second box: if I take both boxes, I get $1,000; if I take just the second box, I get $1,000,000. So I should take just the second box.

But suppose, Schlesinger continues, that Smith, who is perfectly intelligent and a perfect well-wisher of mine, is so positioned that he can see inside the second box. Whatever he sees in that box, surely he is advising me in his heart to take both boxes. Even though he does not communicate with me, I can be certain he would advise taking both boxes. The previous argument, however, has shown that it is not in my interest to follow this advice. Here, says Schlesinger, we reach a contradiction. It is contradictory to maintain that it is not in my best interest to follow the advice of an intelligent, well-informed, perfect well-wisher; such a claim is necessarily false.

Grant, as part of the description of Newcomb's problem, that the predictor has always been correct in the past. Still, Schlesinger maintains, a contradiction is reached *only if* we assume (what is clearly intended) that his past success can be inductively extrapolated to the present; that is, that it is highly probable that he will predict correctly in my case. A description that implies that the predictor's past success is not just an enormous coincidence, but is based on a genuine connection between predictions and subsequent choices, will thus be incoherent.

From this analysis, Schlesinger draws a moral with far-reaching impact: our voluntary choices must be unpredictable; therefore they are not determined beforehand; therefore they are free in a very strong sense.

Schlesinger's argument that the Newcomb story is incoherent comes perilously close to simply giving in to the paradox. True enough, in the standard version, the informal argument for one box appears impeccable, as does the well-wisher argument for both boxes. *But that is just to say we have a paradox.* Before concluding that the Newcomb story instantiates a conceptual conflict, it has to be determined whether, despite appearances, one of the two arguments is fallacious.

In this regard, it is essential to recognize that the assumption that the predictor will be correct in my case does not suffice to generate the argument for the second box (a point that also applies to Nozick's previous discussion of the infallible predictor). That assumption guarantees the truth of the following material conditionals (where A is the act of taking both boxes and B is the act of taking just one):

(1) I do $A \supset$ The predictor predicted I would do A
(2) I do $B \supset$ The predictor predicted I would do B

But *these* conditionals are not strong enough to provide the basis of an argument for preferring B. For it is sufficient for the truth of (1) and (2) that I will in fact do A and the predictor has predicted that I will do A. These facts, however, are quite compatible with the subjunctive conditional:

(3) If I were to do B, the predictor would (still) have predicted that I would do A.

But if (3) is true, the standard argument for taking just one box collapses. What is necessary for that argument is the truth of the *subjunctive conditionals* corresponding to (1) and (2). And the truth of these conditionals is not guaranteed by the assumption that the predictor will predict correctly. I may predict correctly that my friend will have coffee rather than tea after lunch, but it may nevertheless be true that if she were to choose tea, I would have predicted incorrectly.

So Schlesinger has hardly made his case. A radically different approach has it that, whether or not the predictor's success can be inductively extrapolated, the Newcomb story is under-determined: there is insufficient information to determine which course of action is rational. Given that the predictor is highly likely to be correct, we have:

(1) $\Pr(A/\text{predictor predicted } A) \approx 1$
(2) $\Pr(B/\text{predictor predicted } B) \approx 1$

But in order for there to be an argument for B (in order for (MEU) to recommend B), we need:

(3) $\Pr(\text{predictor predicted } A/A) \approx 1$
(4) $\Pr(\text{predictor predicted } B/B) \approx 1$

It is fallacious, however, to infer (3) and (4) from (1) and (2), as Isaac Levi has pointed out.[11] Consider three different cases where the statistics concerning the predictor's past success are as follows:

Case 1		Predicts B	Predicts A
	Chooses B	900,000	10
	Chooses A	100,000	90

Case 2		Predicts B	Predicts A
	Chooses B	495,045	55,005
	Chooses A	55,005	495,045

Case 3		Predicts B	Predicts A
	Chooses B	90	100,000
	Chooses A	10	900,000

All three cases are situations in which the predictor is highly likely to predict correctly. Yet while (1) and (2) hold in all cases, (3) and (4) are both true only in Case 2. In Case 1, Pr(predictor predicted A/A) = 0.0008991; while in Case 3, Pr(predictor predicted B/B) = 0.0008991. However, to calculate the expected utilities of the two actions as we did above, it must be assumed that both (3) and (4) hold. Whether (MEU) in fact prescribes B, Levi argues, cannot be determined without filling in more details than Nozick has given us. Each of the three cases is compatible with the Newcomb story as thus far specified.

Levi is unquestionably correct in arguing that (3) and (4) are not guaranteed by the predictor's high success rate. The difficulty, in Cases 1 and 3, is that the probability of the predictor's predicting correctly is not independent of which action is chosen. In Case 1, for instance, if A is chosen, the probability of correct prediction is low. But all that is necessary to guarantee (3) and (4), and thus ensure that (MEU) recommends act B, is that the predictor be highly likely to predict correctly *regardless of which action is chosen*. There seems no reason why it cannot simply be further specified that the predictor's success rate is independent of the choice of action, and thus (3) and (4) are both true. Indeed, there is evidence that this is how Nozick understood the problem.[12] The fallacy in reasoning that Levi points out seems easily repaired.

J. L. Mackie considers another possible source of under-determination, which has to do with how the predictor's amazing predictive success is to be explained.[13] Mackie canvasses many possibilities, and suggests that the rational solution is not the same in every case. One scenario is that the predictor initially places the money in the second box, and then, by sleight of hand, manages to remove it if you pick both boxes. Another is that backward causation is operative, and your present choice brings about the predictor's past prediction. In either of these cases, the rational course is to take only the second box. But clearly neither of these alternatives is part of the intended interpretation of the Newcomb story. What Mackie wants to show is that the Newcomb situation, when understood *with all the features of its intended interpretation*, is impossible or incoherent. Two scenarios that come close to the intended interpretation are particularly relevant.

In the first case, the predictor is a brilliant psychologist who assesses the player's character in order to make his prediction. The player's choice flows with strict regularity from his character, thus permitting prediction with certainty. Here Mackie objects that the question "What is it rational to do?" is now idle, for it presumes, mistakenly, that the player's choice is still open. In fact, it is as fixed and determined as the content of the second box. The agent's choice, Mackie contends, cannot be assessed either as rational or as irrational in this case. But the obvious response is that if free action and causal determinism are compatible, there seems no reason why the player's choice could not qualify either as rational or irrational. Suppose, for instance, that the aspect of "character" that determines the choice is the player's preference, based on delving into the foundations of decision theory, for dominance reasoning when there is causal independence. Is it clear that his choice would be neither rational nor irrational?

The second scenario is even less problematic. Here character "strongly influences" choice, but does not rigidly determine it. We may imagine that the predictions are based on observed dispositions to act in certain ways. A player can act contrary to the disposition he manifests, but this hardly ever happens. This ensures that the predictor will almost invariably predict correctly. To this interpretation, Mackie objects that a *perfect* past record of prediction would now owe something to luck, which is not an intended part of the Newcomb story. But it is by no means *essential* to the story that the predictor is always correct (is infallible); it is sufficient for the paradox that the predictor is almost always correct, and is therefore highly likely to be correct in the future.

There is as yet no compelling reason to suppose that the Newcomb situation does not admit a unique rational choice. The paradox stands.

Causal distinctions in decision theory

Despite early efforts to represent standard versions of Newcomb's problem as somehow illegitimate, and therefore not requiring a solution, most of the later discussion continues within the framework of Nozick's seminal paper, according to which (i) there is a unique rational action, and (ii) the problem embodies a conflict between two different decision principles.

Nozick, recall, favours the two-box solution. What gives the problem its bite, in his view, is that it illustrates in a particularly troubling way the potential for conflict between (DP) and (MEU). To adjudicate the conflict, he insists, it is necessary to introduce causal concepts into decision theory; probability and desirability will not suffice. Dominance is legitimately appealed to when the states are *causally independent* of the action; if, in such a case, there is a conflict with the prescription of (MEU), then (MEU) is over-ridden. The moral of Newcomb's problem is the need for causal concepts in decision theory.

A key factor, in creating the Newcomb problem, is the divergence of probabilistic and causal independence. The probability of S_1 (there is \$1,000,000 in the second box) is high on the assumption that I do B (take just the second box), and low on the assumption that I do A (take both boxes). But doing B plays absolutely no role in *bringing it about* that S_1 holds. If I do B, that is *evidence* that S_1 holds and I will get \$1,000,000; it is thus good news. Whereas if I do A, that is *evidence* that S_2 holds and I will get only \$1,000; that is not such good news. The *news value* of B is greater than that of A. And that is precisely what expected utility measures: the news value of an act. The view that the recommendations of (MEU) always prevail, and that the fundamental concepts of decision theory need include only probability and desirability, has thus come to be known as *evidential decision theory*; according to it, you act so as to create good news about events over which you may have no control. Opposed to it is *causal decision theory*, which maintains that it is the desirable outcomes an act may help to bring about that determine rationality.

The perception that causal concepts are essential in decision theory stems from the judgement that the two-box strategy is correct. But critics have attacked this strategy vociferously. The favourite way of stirring up trouble for the two-boxer is to raise the question of what should be done in the case of an infallible predictor.[14] If it is a given that the predictor is always correct, then you are certain he will predict your action. So if you take just one box, you are guaranteed $1,000,000; if you take both boxes, you are guaranteed $1,000. What could be clearer? And surely it would be utterly *ad hoc* to suggest that the difference between an infallible predictor, and a predictor who is wrong once in a million cases, could make a difference in rational strategy, could yield opposite solutions.

The fallacy in this argument for the one-box solution has already been exposed in the discussion of Schlesinger in the previous section. Briefly, the fact that the predictor will predict my action correctly guarantees the truth of the material conditionals:

(1) I do $A \supset$ The predictor predicted I would do A
(2) I do $B \supset$ The predictor predicted I would do B

The truth of these material conditionals, however, is not an adequate basis for preferring B. What we want is to be able to make the *comparative* judgement that I would be better off if I were to do B than if I were to do A. This does seem an overwhelming reason for preferring B. But the comparative conclusion is warranted only if we are assured of the subjunctive conditionals corresponding to (1) and (2); and more is necessary to yield the truth of these stronger conditionals.[15]

The view that dominance trumps expected utility in the Newcomb situation has also been challenged by appeal to mind-bending instability cases.[16] Consider the famous story of a traveller who meets Death on his way to Damascus. Death looks surprised, but remarks only, "I have an appointment with you tonight." Terrified, the man hires a camel and flees to Aleppo; sadly, he finds Death awaiting him there. As he reaches out to the traveller, Death observes, "I was surprised to see you earlier on your way to Damascus, since I knew my appointment with you was in Aleppo."

The classic story is fleshed out as follows. Death's schedule is fixed weeks in advance on the basis of almost certainly correct predictions about the location of his victim. The victim dies if and only if he meets Death at the appropriate time and place. Assume also that the only choices are between Aleppo and Damascus. The traveller knows that his decision as to where to be that evening does not causally bring it about that Death is at that location, but it is nonetheless strong evidence that Death will also be there.

According to Reed Richter, a principle essential to the defence of the two-box option, and jeopardized by the Death case, is:

(P) If options A and B are both available to an agent x and if x knows that were he to do A he would be better off in every respect than if he were to do B, then in the strictest sense of rational self-interest rationality requires x to do A over doing B.[17]

Assuming (P), the traveller's dilemma in the Death case may be put this way. Suppose he decides to go to Damascus. This provides excellent evidence that his appointment with Death is in Damascus, which in turn means that he would be better off going to Aleppo. But precisely the same reasoning dictates that if he were to head for Aleppo, he could infer that he would be better off going to Damascus. Thus, given (P), the traveller's decision is unstable because each decision provides evidence that the other alternative is rationally preferable.

At first glance, this may seem all right – just an odd consequence of a mind-boggling situation. But what is being claimed is not merely that there is no unique rational choice for the traveller; that would perhaps be acceptable. What is being claimed is that *every choice is irrational* in the Death case – that the traveller will necessarily act irrationally. To avoid the conclusion that a decision problem may ensure inevitable irrationality, Richter argues, we must reject (P), and with it, the basis of the two-box strategy.[18]

We appear to be faced with the dilemma that either (P) is false, or there are decision problems in which every option is irrational. Assuming the disjunction holds, it is not entirely clear that the first alternative is more palatable. Fortunately, however, it is not necessary to accept the dilemma.

The core of the reasoning that is attributed to the traveller, and underlies the claim of instability, is essentially:

(A) (1) I now choose to go to Damascus.
    (2) Death will be in Damascus tonight.   from (1)
    (3) If I were now not to choose to go to Damascus,
        then I would not meet Death tonight.   from (2)

This sort of reasoning initially seems innocuous; but once brought under scrutiny, it is highly suspect. Consider two analogous arguments:

(B) (1) The patient's blood tests are not positive for
        HIV.
    (2) The patient does not have HIV.   from (1)
    (3) If the patient's blood tests were positive for
        HIV, then the tests would be inaccurate.   from (2)

(C) (1) Russell is married to Elaine.
    (2) Russell is not a bachelor.   from (1)
    (3) If Russell were not married to Elaine, then
        Russell would be married to someone else.   from (2)

These three arguments are apparently analogous. In each case, (1) is the only reason offered for (2), (2) is the only reason offered for (3), and the antecedent of (3) is the negation of (1). But are we clearly entitled to hold (2) constant, or fixed, when envisaging the possibility that (1) is false? I think not. The issue of what can be held constant when a false statement is considered as the antecedent of a subjunctive conditional is difficult, as the next section makes clear. For the moment, however, it suffices to point out that, *as far as we know*, it may be that

$$\sim(1) \rightarrow \sim(2)$$

That is, as far as we know, it may be that (2) would not be true if (1) were not. Given this, it can hardly be legitimate to take (2) as fixed when assessing the truth of a conditional with ~(1) as antecedent. The issue, it should be noted, is not whether or not (3) is true. Rather, it is whether we are entitled to maintain (3) based *only* on the preceding reasoning. To suppose that we are is to be committed to the absurdity of arguments (B) and (C).

I suggest that each of the three arguments is defective for the same reason, and that Richter's instability defence of (MEU) therefore fails.

Still, in order to defend unrestricted appeal to (MEU), it may not be necessary to deny the rationality of the two-box choice. Even granting the rationality of the dominant option in cases of Newcomb's problem, the appearance of a counter-example to (MEU), it has been argued, is an illusion.[19] Consider a situation that many find an even more intuitive counter-example to (MEU). Statistical data indicate a high correlation between smoking and lung cancer. Let us suppose that the correlation results from some common genetic factor that causes both lung cancer and a tendency to smoke. So it is not smoking that causes lung cancer, but the bad gene. Given that smoking is enjoyable, and that you have no control over whether or not you have the gene, it seems absurd to forego the pleasure of smoking. Smoking dominates not smoking. But not smoking, given plausible utilities for the different outcomes, seems to be dictated by (MEU); for the probability that you have the bad gene is very high given that you smoke, and very low given that you do not smoke.

The aim of the "tickle defence" of (MEU) is to show that the evidential principle does *not* dictate abstaining from smoking (and, in general, does not recommend the non-dominant option in Newcomb-style situations). Since the acts are voluntary, the correlation between the gene and smoking must be the result of, or mediated by, a strong correlation between the gene and having the *inclination* to smoke. This means that the probability that you have the bad gene is dependent on your inclination to smoke. If you are aware of being inclined to smoke, then it is highly likely you have the genetic cause of cancer. But this probability does not increase if you *actually* decide to smoke (nor decrease if you refrain).

The picture is this. The gene tends to cause the inclination to smoke, which in turn tends to cause smoking; and the gene also tends to cause cancer. Knowledge that you have the inclination to smoke makes it probable that you have the gene; and that probability is unaffected by further information as to whether or not you smoke. The inclination, the "tickle", screens off the evidential implications of the act. Feeling the tickle is already the bad news; finding yourself smoking adds nothing to that news. Thus (MEU) does not prescribe not smoking.

The essence of the defence of (MEU), then, is that in the alleged counter-examples, there is always a tickle (a disposition or inclination) of which the agent is introspectively aware, and this tickle screens off the evidential impact of the act itself. The issues raised by this defence are complex, and it seems fair to say that it has not attracted many advocates. Let me mention just two concerns. First, many acts involve indecision, change of mind and lengthy deliberation. In such cases, it seems most plausible to expect that the correlation would have to be between the prior event or state (the bad gene) and your *final* inclination. But can your final inclination be known independently of knowing *how you will act*? If not, then it seems it cannot serve as a screen for the evidential significance of the act. Secondly, the question "What *should* I be inclined to do?" seems entirely legitimate, and it is reasonable to expect that the principles of decision theory will yield an appropriate answer. Now, if in the smoking example we attempt to answer the question by calculating the expected utility of the *actions* of smoking and not smoking, and employ the information screen as suggested by the tickle defence, then the question "What *should* I be inclined to do?" will be answered on the basis of information concerning what I am *in fact* inclined to do. But that surely seems inappropriate. On the other hand, if, in attempting to answer the question, (MEU) is applied by calculating the expected utility of the *inclinations* to smoke and not to smoke, then since the inclination not to smoke will have the highest news value, it will be rational, according to (MEU), to be inclined not to smoke.

Despite the tickle defence, the standard conception remains that dominance and expected utility yield conflicting prescriptions in Newcomb-style cases. Advocates of the two-box strategy and of causal decision theory have attempted to formulate a broadly applicable decision principle to replace (MEU), a principle that acknowledges the relevance of causal considerations. One version of causal decision theory that has received considerable attention is due to A. Gibbard and W. Harper.[20] Instead of maximizing expected utility as previously defined, the new principle advocates maximizing *causal expected utility*, defined as follows:

$$\mathrm{CEU}(A) = \mathrm{Pr}(A \rightarrow O_{A_1}) \times u(O_{A_1}) + \mathrm{Pr}(A \rightarrow O_{A_2}) \times u(A_{A_2}) \ldots$$

where "$A \rightarrow O_{A_i}$" is to be read as a counterfactual conditional, and "O_{A_i}" denotes the outcome of doing A when S_i obtains. Thus the *probability of counterfactual conditionals* replaces conditional probabilities. However, in order for this version of causal decision theory to get the expected results in Newcomb-style cases, the counterfactual conditional must be interpreted in a particular way: $P \rightarrow Q$ is to be regarded as true only if (i) P would bring about Q or (ii) Q holds regardless of whether or not P holds. Whether a satisfactory theory of conditionals will yield this interpretation is a matter of some dispute.[21]

Conditionals, we have now seen, surface repeatedly in the discussion of the Newcomb scenario. It is time to examine more directly the exact role they play in the problem.

Newcomb's problem and conditionals

To begin, let us revisit the question of the proper scope of (DP). Nozick and later writers typically try to deal with this question by, first, citing cases in which it seems absolutely clear to them that dominance does (does not) apply, and then trying to abstract the relevant features of the cases in virtue of which dominance is (is not) legitimately invoked. This approach faces several pitfalls. For one thing, our intuitions on the particular cases cited may not agree; or they may be no clearer than in the original Newcomb case.[22] More significantly, even if our judgements concerning individual cases are perfectly correct, we may fail to identify the *relevant* features in virtue of which (DP) does (does not) apply.

The best approach, I believe, is more direct. I shall try to deal with the question of the scope of (DP) in a way that does not rest on our intuitions about particular cases, and that also enables us to understand *why* it is fallacious, in certain circumstances, to argue that an act ought to be done because of dominance considerations.

The first step is to consider why it is that if (DP) is properly applied and recommends *A*, this provides good reason for doing *A*. Restricting attention for the moment to cases in which *A* strongly dominates *B*, one could point out the following. First, supposing I did *A* and got *x* units of utility, I would then be assured that if I had done *B*, I would have got less than *x*. So there will never be room for regret if I do *A*. More generally, prior to acting, I could say, "No matter what state obtains (obtained, will obtain), if I were to do *A* I would be better off than if I were to do *B*." Such a statement must be true if application of (DP) is justified; and if it is true, it seems indisputable that I ought to do *A*.

Suppose now that the matrix for a given situation is as follows.

	S_1	S_2
A	10	4
B	8	2

To establish the truth of "No matter what state obtains, if I were to do *A* I would be better off than if I were to do *B*", one would naturally resort to the following argument.

(1) Either S_1 obtains or S_2 obtains.
(2) Suppose S_1 obtains.
(3) If I were to do *A*, I would get 10.
(4) If I were to do *B*, I would get 8.
(5) Suppose S_2 obtains.
(6) If I were to do *A*, I would get 4.
(7) If I were to do *B*, I would get 2.
(8) Therefore, no matter what state obtains, if I were to do *A*, I would be better off than if I were to do *B*.

What is crucial, and might be overlooked, is that (3) and (4) must be true on the supposition of S_1, and (6) and (7) must be true on the supposition of S_2. Having recognized this, it is now relatively easy to see *why* appeal to dominance considerations is fallacious in certain circumstances. More specifically, we can now see why there should be general agreement that the dominance principle cannot be correctly applied here if doing *A* would cause S_2 and doing *B* would cause S_1. Note first that the appropriate tense for (1), (2) and (5) may vary, depending on the details of the particular case. (I assume throughout that backwards causality is impossible.) The key point is this. If doing A would cause S_2, then we cannot argue as follows:

(2) Suppose S_1 will obtain.
(3) If I were to do A, I would get 10.

The reason we cannot infer (3) from (2) is that if doing A would cause S_2, then *even if* S_1 will obtain, the following is still true:

(*) If I were to do A, S_2 would obtain and I would get 4.

But (*) is incompatible with (3): the two statements are contraries. Hence, we cannot grant that, in this situation, (3) is true on the supposition of S_1, and the dominance argument consequently does not go through.

An example may help clarify the logic of the above. Suppose that the result of my jumping from an aeroplane at 5,000 feet with no protective devices at time t and being dead shortly after t would be –20 units of utility. Now *even if* I will in fact be alive shortly after t, the following is still true:

(**) If I were to jump from an aeroplane at 5,000 feet with no protective devices at t, I would be dead shortly after t and would get –20 units of utility.

My being alive shortly after t corresponds to S_1, and (**) corresponds to (*). I take it that (**) is unquestionably true, despite the fact that I will be alive after t.

The dominance principle can now be restated so as to incorporate the necessary conditions.

> *Dominance principle*: Let $a_1, \ldots, a_n$ and $b_1, \ldots, b_n$ be utility numbers. Suppose there is a set of exclusive and exhaustive states of the world $S_1, \ldots, S_n$, such that for every i, on the assumption that S_i obtains (obtained, will obtain) it is true that: (i) If I were to do A, I would get a_i; and (ii) If I were to do B, I would get b_i. Then if for every i, $a_i \geq b_i$ and for some i, $a_i > b_i$,

A should be preferred to B.

(To add just one point of clarification, note that "If I were to do A, I would get a_i" is true on the assumption of S_i just in case if "S_i obtains" were true, then "If I were to do A, I would get a_i" would also be true.)

What exactly is the difference between having this version of (DP) satisfied, and simply having a matrix in which one action is dominant? The information provided by a payoff matrix concerns the *joint* occurrence of a certain state and a certain action. Thus the matrix just considered tells us that the result of the occurrence of both S_1 and A would be 10 units of utility. But, and this is the essential point, from this fact alone it does not follow that if "S_1 will obtain" were true, then "If I were to do A, I would get 10" would also be true. A slight variation of an earlier example may help to make it clearer that this is not a valid pattern of inference. The result of the joint occurrence of my living 10 years after t and jumping from an aeroplane at 5,000 feet (with no protective devices) at t would be, say, to become a medical phenomenon. But even though I will in fact live 10 years after t, we surely would not grant "If I were to jump from an airplane at 5,000 feet (with no protective devices) at t, I would become a medical phenomenon."

What this means for the logic of conditionals is that the principle of exportation does not hold for subjunctive conditionals. That principle asserts that a conditional of the form

$$(P \, \& \, Q) \rightarrow R$$

logically implies a conditional of the form

$$P \rightarrow (Q \rightarrow R)$$

But the example just cited makes it clear that the implication does not hold. To see this, replace "P" by "I am alive 10 years after t", "Q" by "I jump from an aeroplane at 5,000 feet (with no protective devices) at t" and "R" by "I become a medical phenomenon".

Thus a general problem in decision theory raised by the Newcomb case is now resolved. The approach to the question of the proper application of dominance was direct: we considered what the appeal to dominance is supposed to show, and how this can be established. Once the problem is framed in this way, the answer seems to fall out clearly and easily. What is required is the truth of certain complex subjunctive conditionals.

The question remains whether the dominance principle can be applied to the Newcomb case. Certainly, the argument below looks impeccable at first sight.

(I) (1) Either the predictor placed $1,000,000 in B_2 or he left it empty.
     (2) Suppose the predictor placed $1,000,000 in B_2.
     (3) If I were to do A (take both boxes), I would get $1,001,000.
     (4) If I were to do B (take just one box), I would get $1,000,000.
     (5) Suppose the predictor left B_2 empty.
     (6) If I were to do A, I would get $1,000.
     (7) If I were to do B, I would get $0.
     (8) Therefore, no matter what state obtained, if I were to do A, I would be better off than if I were to do B.

But the advocate of the one-box strategy will claim he has excellent evidence for the premises of the argument below.

(II) (1*) If I were to do A, the predictor would have predicted this, would have left B_2 empty, and I would get only $1,000.
      (2*) If I were to do B, the predictor would have predicted this, would have put $1,000,000 in B_2, and I would get $1,000,000.
      (3*) Therefore, if I were to do B, I would be better off than if I were to do A.

Once stated explicitly, it is evident that the conclusions of the two arguments are logically inconsistent: specifically, they are contraries. Let us try to understand why the two arguments yield logically incompatible conclusions. In order for argument (I) to be correct, (3) and (4) must be true on the assumption of (2), and (6) and (7) must be true on the assumption of (5). If this is in fact the case, then since either (2) or (5) is true, either (3) and (4) are true or (6) and (7) are true. But the conjunction of (3) and (4) is incompatible with (1*), for (3) and (1*) are contraries; similarly the conjunction of (6) and (7) is incompatible with (2*). (If we preface the premises and conclusion of (II) with "It is almost certain that ...", the two arguments will no longer conflict in this way. But we can still say that one cannot reasonably accept both. For if P and Q are logically incompatible, it cannot be reasonable to believe that P is true *and* that it is almost certain that Q is true.[23] Alternatively, if we rewrite (1*) and (2*) as material conditionals, there will be no conflict with argument (I); but we cannot conclude, from these new premises, anything that provides a reason for preferring B.)

It is, I think, the plausibility of both arguments (I) and (II) that serves to create the conflict in the Newcomb case. Of course, neither argument represents anything novel to discussions of Newcomb's problem: each is a more explicit version of the informal arguments offered on behalf of each strategy. But what is not normally discerned (perhaps because the conclusion of argument (II) is usually left implicit) is that the empirical claims made in the two arguments are not all compatible and cannot all be maintained. As a result of this oversight, there has been a natural tendency to assume that the dilemma posed by Newcomb's problem is that of deciding *which of two sets of facts provides a better reason* for performing an action. But once the inconsistency is evident, the focal point becomes: what should we take to be the facts?

Having seen that the arguments for each option make conflicting assumptions concerning the empirical facts, there is no longer any difficulty in understanding how the argument for one strategy, if correct, would disarm or destroy the force of the other. It is also possible to zero in on the key issue in determining which strategy should be preferred. To provide a complete resolution of Newcomb's problem, the critical question that must be dealt with is: given the description of the Newcomb case, is it more reasonable to believe (1*) and (2*) or to grant that (3) and (4) are true on the assumption of (2), and (6) and (7) are true on the assumption of (5)?

Unfortunately, the question of which conditionals are true in the Newcomb case admits no easy answer. It might be thought that the chief obstacle to endorsing one set of conditionals is the indeterminacy, or lack of specificity, concerning how, exactly, the predictor works. In fact, the problem goes much deeper, and has to do with fundamental problems in our understanding of conditionals, as we shall see.

Whether (1*) and (2*) ought to be accepted depends entirely on the credibility of:

(E) If I were to do A, the predictor would have predicted that I would do A.

(F) If I were to do B, the predictor would have predicted that I would do B.

Once convinced of the truth of these conditionals, there should, given the rules of the game, be no further hesitation in accepting (1*) and (2*).

Consider now a fleshed-out version of the Newcomb case, a version that provides the strongest possible case for (E) and (F). What is critically important here is the *nature of the evidence* on which the predictions are based.[24] The predictor, let us suppose, examines you one hour before you play. If he determines that you are in state C_1 one hour before you must play, he predicts that you will do A; if he finds that you are in state C_2, he predicts B. Further, the states used as evidence are strongly nomically linked to the actions. Let us make the connection as tight as possible. Suppose there is a law that guarantees that all and only those who do A are in state C_1 one hour before playing; similarly for act B and state C_2. (If we wish to make it part of the Newcomb case that the predictor is not infallible, we could add that, very infrequently, the predictor is mistaken about which state the player is in.)

Now the focus is on the truth of:

(G) If I were to do A, I would have been in state C_1 one hour before playing.

Clearly, there is no difficulty in granting the truth of:

(H) If I were to do A and to have been in state C_1 one hour before playing, the predictor would have predicted that I would do A.

Together, these conditionals guarantee the truth of (E).

What, then, can be said about (G)? Does the description above guarantee the truth of (G)? Intuitions may diverge here, or may not be firm; but current theories of the logic of conditionals may yield answers.[25]

The first well-developed theory of counterfactual conditionals, best expounded by Nelson Goodman, was metalinguistic.[26] A counterfactual is true if the antecedent, together with further suitable premises, implies the consequent. More specifically, the consequent must "follow by law" from the antecedent. That is, the truth of a counterfactual requires that there be a valid argument from the antecedent (A^*), a relevant law or laws (L^*), and possibly certain other true statements describing the relevant conditions (S^*), to the consequent (C^*). It is easy to see that, in a typical case in which a counterfactual is deemed to be true, there will be need of premises describing the relevant conditions in order to have the appropriate valid argument. When we say:

If that match had been scratched, it would have lighted.

we are assuming, among other things, that the match is well made, is dry enough, sufficient oxygen is present and so on. The inference from antecedent to consequent will be valid only if, as well as the relevant law, there are additional true premises asserting that these conditions hold.

The major hurdle for the metalinguistic approach lies in specifying what truths can properly be included in S^*. Not any true statement will do, for, if the antecedent A^* is false, then $\sim A^*$ is true; but from $A^* \& \sim A^*$ *any* statement follows. Nor will it suffice to require that A^* and S^* be logically compatible. In the match case above, suppose that both antecedent and consequent are false; then $\sim C^*$ is true. But if we may include $\sim C^*$ in the relevant conditions, then as the total $A^* \& S^*$ we may have:

The match was scratched. It did not light. It was well made. Sufficient oxygen was present.

And from this, and the appropriate law, we may infer:

The match was not dry.

Ultimately, Goodman concludes, the best that can be said is that S^*

must be *cotenable* with A^*: A^* and S^* are cotenable provided that it is not the case that if A^* were true, then S^* would not be true.

The circularity here is evident. The truth-conditions of counterfactuals are specified in terms of cotenability, but the notion of cotenability is defined in terms of counterfactuals. Until a non-circular account of cotenability is provided, the theory is incomplete. Still, the theory, as far as it goes, can provide insight into the logic of conditionals. The restrictions on S^* remind us that not just *any* true statement may be held constant in evaluating a counterfactual.[27] And I would maintain that, in general, which truths may be taken as fixed is a function of cotenability (as Goodman defines the term) with the antecedent.

Despite its deficiencies, the metalinguistic theory is sufficiently developed to yield an unequivocal verdict on the truth of (G). The relevant law asserts an unmediated connection between doing A and being in state C_1: all and only those who do A are in C_1 one hour before playing. Hence the conjunction of just the law and the antecedent logically implies the consequent of (G); there is no need to worry about a cotenable set of conditions. According to the metalinguistic theory, then, (G) is true, and the one-box argument is therefore sound.

The major alternative to the metalinguistic analysis, and the currently dominant theory, makes use of the machinery of possible worlds. This approach posits possible worlds that are more or less similar to the actual world. According to David Lewis, a counterfactual $A^* \rightarrow C^*$ is true if and only if there is some possible world in which (i) A^* and C^* are both true and (ii) that world is more similar, overall, to the actual world than is any world at which A^* is true and C^* is false.[28] What is critical, of course, is how similarity is to be understood. The notion of overall similarity among worlds is admittedly vague; our intuitive judgements may differ depending on the importance we attach to particular similarities. So the analysis must be fleshed out with an account of the appropriate similarity relation; that is, there must be a system of weights or priorities assigned to types of similarity.

Lewis develops his account of the appropriate similarity relation on the basis of an apparent counter-example to his analysis due to Kit Fine. Fine states the difficulty as follows:

The counterfactual "If Nixon had pressed the button there would have been a nuclear holocaust" is true or can be imagined to be so. Now suppose that there never will be a nuclear holocaust. Then that counterfactual is, on Lewis's analysis, very likely false. For given any world in which antecedent and consequent are both true it will be easy to imagine a closer world in which the antecedent is true and the consequent is false. For we need only imagine a change that prevents the holocaust but that does not require such a great divergence from reality.[29]

Lewis responds that the notion of similarity employed in the analysis of counterfactuals is subject to the following priorities:

(1) It is of the first importance to avoid big, widespread diverse violations of law.
(2) It is of second importance to maximize the spatio-temporal region through which perfect match of particular fact prevails.
(3) It is of third importance to avoid even small, localized, simple violations of law.
(4) It is of little or no importance to secure approximate similarity of particular fact, even in matters that concern us greatly.[30]

Consider a counterfactual $A^* \to C^*$, where A^* is about the state of affairs at time t, and is false in the actual world. Any possible world w in which A^* is true will be most similar to the actual world only if: (i) there is a perfect match of particular fact between w and the actual world until just before t; and (ii) there is a small, localized violation of actual world law in w just before t, just enough of a miracle to make A^* true in w. Since the past (until just before t) must be held absolutely fixed in any most similar possible world, it is true that if Nixon had pressed the button, there would have been a nuclear holocaust. For any situation in which pressing the button did not produce a holocaust would require some change in the past: a defect in wiring, the missiles having been deactivated, and so on.

How does this apply to the strengthened version of Newcomb's problem in which there is a nomic connection between the evidence and the actions? The premises necessary for the one-box solution are:

(G) If I were to do A, I would have been in state C_1 one hour before playing.

(H) If I were to do B, I would have been in state C_2 one hour before playing.

Given Lewis's account of similarity, it is clear that (G) and (H) cannot both be true. If I was *in fact* in C_1 one hour before playing, then H is false, for a possible world in which the antecedent is true is most similar to the actual world only if they have a common past until just before the time referred to in the antecedent. But the consequent of (H) will be false in any such possible world. Similarly, if I was in fact in C_2, then (G) is false. According to Lewis's possible worlds analysis, then, the argument for the one-box strategy is unsound.

Thus, the two most influential theories of counterfactuals give contradictory answers in Newcomb's problem. Perhaps it is not surprising, then, that we are torn between the two key arguments in the paradox; each can be seen to reflect a different view of the truth-conditions of counterfactuals.

A final comment. The reader will, of course, have noticed that conditionals such as (E), (F), (G) and (H) have a common feature: the antecedent is entirely about a present state of affairs, and the consequent is entirely about an earlier state of affairs. Conditionals that have this structure, and whose antecedent and consequent are both false, are commonly referred to as "backtracking" conditionals; a backtracking conditional says how the past would have been different if the present were different. Lewis's position on the proper resolution of the vagueness of overall similarity among possible worlds, we have seen, ensures that no backtracking conditionals can be true on this resolution. But Lewis concedes that certain special, unusual contexts favour a different, non-standard resolution, one in which backtrackers have a chance of truth. Picking up on this concession, it has been proposed that the need for a non-standard resolution is not restricted to a few unusual contexts, but in fact extends to the context of practical decision-making.[31] To make this proposal viable, it must be shown, first, that practical inference creates a context in which the truth-conditions for counterfactuals differ from those in most other ordinary contexts. (Certainly, our intuitions in Newcomb's problem provide no help here for, to many of us, *both* the backtracking conditionals and the conditionals associated with the dominance argument seem plausible.) Further, the resolution appropriate to practical decision-making must be such as to render the conditionals of the dominance argument true in many decision contexts, for there are undoubtedly cases in which the dominance principle is legitimately invoked.

What has been established thus far is that the critical issue that confronts us in determining which strategy is rational is not the legitimate application of the dominance principle. Nor does the dispute centre on whether one set of empirical facts provides a better reason for performing an act than does another. Rather, the problem is simply to decide what the empirical facts are (alternatively what, given the evidence, it is reasonable to believe them to be). This may appear to replace one knotty problem with another, but that is often the way of philosophical progress.

7 | The prisoner's dilemma

The paradox

You and a colleague have been arrested and charged with committing a crime. You are isolated in separate cells, unable to communicate. The prosecutor, aware of the shakiness of his case, offers a deal in order to elicit a confession. If you both remain silent, he informs you, there is enough evidence to convict you of a lesser charge, and you will consequently each receive a year in prison. However, if you provide details of the crime and your partner remains silent, you will get off scot-free and he will face a sentence of ten years. Similarly if he confesses and you remain silent. But if you both confess, you will each be sentenced to five years. The dilemma can be summed up in the following matrix.

	He confesses	He does not confess
You confess	5, 5	0, 10
You do not confess	10, 0	1, 1

The entries represent years in prison: the first number represents the length of your sentence, the second his.

It is a given that your choice is causally independent of your colleague's, and that it has no impact on your welfare other than the severity of your sentence (no one is lying in wait for those who "rat"). Your only concern is to minimize your time in jail; in particular, what happens to your accomplice is a matter of indifference to you. It is common knowledge that the prisoners are in exactly symmetrical situations, and that both players are fully rational.

What should you do? The answer seems obvious and inescapable. Either the other prisoner is going to confess or he is not. Suppose he will confess. Then you will get five years in prison if you confess, compared to ten years if you remain silent. On the other hand, suppose the other prisoner is going to remain silent. Then you will go free if you confess, while remaining silent will carry a penalty of one year in prison. Clearly, confessing is the rational strategy: you are bound to be better off by confessing no matter what your colleague does.

This is the dominance argument for confessing, which of course applies equally to the other prisoner. For each of you, it appears that confessing strongly dominates remaining silent.

Now the paradox begins to emerge. If both prisoners act rationally, each will receive a five-year sentence. But if both act irrationally (remain silent), each will face only one year in jail. In short, two players who act rationally will be worse off than two players who act irrationally.

But is this really paradoxical? After all, acting rationally need not always guarantee the best outcome, for you may have less than complete information, and the improbable may happen. The paradox, however, lies in the fact that the result of both agents acting rationally in the prisoner's dilemma is not a matter of luck, or fluke, but an inevitable consequence, which can be known in advance by the players. How can it be rational to confess if the players can foresee that they will be worse off if both confess than if both remain silent?

This is the prisoner's dilemma in its simplest form. It is a type I paradox and, I would claim, is veridical. Since there is general (although not universal) agreement on this last point, the dilemma is properly classed as uncontroversial.

The prisoner's dilemma is a classic problem in game theory. Decision theory, discussed in Chapter 5, deals with rational choice in situations in which the outcome of your choice depends on which of the possible states of affairs obtains. Game theory, however, is more narrowly construed: it deals with *competitive* decision situations, where the outcome of your choice is dependent on the decisions of another agent whose interests conflict with your own, and who may therefore take your decision strategy into account.

Certain elements of game theory are of particular relevance for understanding the dilemma. In classical game theory, a game is defined in terms of its utility payoffs. Utility, or desirability, as we noted earlier, is a measure of preference: one outcome has a higher utility than another just in case the player prefers it to the other. *Why* the player prefers it is irrelevant. Our desires and goals are not subject to rational criticism, on this conception. It does not matter whether the agent is an egoist or altruist, philistine or aesthete, conservative or liberal: rationality is a matter of attempting to obtain maximal satisfaction of one's preferences.

One assumption of classical game theory, which is essential to certain versions of the paradox, is that the structure of the game is *common knowledge* between the players. This means more than just that both players know how the game works. Common knowledge, as here understood, is an iterative concept. P is common knowledge between A and B provided that both A and B know that P, A knows that B knows that P, B knows that A knows that P, A knows that B knows that A knows that P, and so on. Similarly, it is assumed that it is a matter of common knowledge that both players are perfectly rational.

Now to return to the prisoner's dilemma. Is the paradox of any practical significance? The classic formulation in terms of two prisoners facing sentence can create the appearance that the dilemma is too fantastic to have much practical relevance. But this is appearance only. In fact, the necessary ingredients for a version of the prisoner's dilemma are minimal. Consider this matrix:

		Y's strategy	
		C	D
X's strategy	C	b	d
	D	a	c

Suppose X ranks the outcomes, in order of preference: a, b, c, d. Y, however, ranks them in the order: d, b, c, a. That the two players agree on which outcomes rank second and third and disagree on the best and worst outcomes suffices to create a prisoner's dilemma. (Note that it is only the ranking, and not the exact measure of utility, that is relevant.) Dominance reasoning shows that whatever Y does, X is bound to be better off doing D (a is better than b, and c is better than d). Similarly for Y. Thus, D is rational for both players, even though they would be better off if both were to do C.

Now for a "real-life" example. Competitive consumerism, a familiar phenomenon, creates a prisoner's dilemma. It is regrettable, but true, that the sorts of consumer choices you make contribute to your social status, and social status essentially involves competition: you only achieve status by having *more* of some good than most of your peers. Now suppose that two neighbours both drive Honda Civics. By working harder and putting in overtime each could afford a more prestigious car, say a BMW. For each, the gain in status associated with being the *only* one to own such a car more than compensates for reduced leisure time; on the other hand, the social embarrassment associated with being the *only* one not to own such a car is worse than the loss of leisure. The rankings for each neighbour are:

1. You get a BMW, your neighbour does not. (Status high, work demanding.)
2. You do not get a BMW, nor does your neighbour. (Status middling, work relaxed.)
3. You both get a BMW. (Status middling, work demanding.)
4. You do not get a BMW, your neighbour does. (Status low, work relaxed.)

If rational, each neighbour will apparently opt to work harder and buy the luxury car, thereby ending up with the third outcome and making his own life worse.[1]

Another example concerns more vital issues. Suppose two major powers sign a nuclear disarmament pact. Sadly, the provisions for inspection are far from foolproof; there is thus a real possibility that either side could violate the pact and secretly rearm. If one side rearmed, and the other did not, the unarmed power could be completely dominated by the armed power. Such vulnerability is regarded by each as the worst outcome, worse even than the risk of war posed by two armed powers. So we have:

	They honour the pact	They violate the pact
You honour the pact	No risk of war (*b*)	We are at their mercy (*d*)
You violate the pact	They are at our mercy (*a*)	Risk of war (*c*)

Your preference ordering is *a*, *b*, *c*, *d*; theirs is *d*, *b*, *c*, *a*. By the familiar dominance reasoning, if both sides act rationally, they will continue to suffer the risk of war; for there will be mutual violation of the pact.

At this stage, one may be inclined to try to explain away the paradox. A counter-intuitive conclusion is reached, it might be suggested, only because unrealistic restrictions have been placed on the agents. In the example of the prisoners, cooperation cannot come about without mutual understanding and trust, which in turn is impossible without communication. The way to escape the outcome of joint confession is to allow communication, and to have each player make a commitment (explicitly or implicitly) to remain silent. The standard version of the dilemma is unrealistic precisely because it allows no room for the making of promises and commitments.

But suppose that the prisoners are allowed to communicate, and promise each other to remain silent. How does this change things? The prisoners, after all, can break promises; and as long as the choice matrix remains the same, there is still the same argument for confessing. More precisely, all that is necessary is that one's *preferences among the possible outcomes* remain the same.

Now the focus has shifted to utilities and preferences. If the cooperative act involves keeping a promise, wouldn't that give it a moral value that would be relevant to most agents? Isn't the example of the two prisoners unrealistic because the agents are assumed to be concerned only with their own welfare (that is, minimizing their own sentences)?

Again, the proper response is that the paradox requires only a certain preference ranking of the possible outcomes. The utility a prisoner attaches to a given outcome may reflect his moral values, his concern for his family or any other factor; it need not be narrowly limited to considerations of his own welfare. Provided the *ranking* that the two players attach to the different outcomes remains the same, however, the paradox will not be dispelled. This is the short answer to the charge that all prisoner's dilemma situations are unrealistic because the players' motivation is assumed to be entirely selfish, or egoistic. But the conviction that converting the prisoners into altruists will resolve the paradox tends to be intractable. Perhaps the most effective response is to show that two purely altruistic players may face a prisoner's dilemma in a situation in which egoistic players would not.[2] Consider a game with a structure like this:

Joan

		C	D
Judy	C	$10, $10	$20, $0
	D	$0, $20	$9, $9

Judy and Joan approach this game as pure altruists: each is primarily concerned to satisfy the other's desire for money. This will lead Judy to do D, since she reasons as follows: Joan will either do C or D. Suppose she does C. Then she will get more money if I do D ($20) than if I do C ($10). Suppose, on the other hand, that she does D. Then again she will get more money if I do D ($9) than if I do C ($0). So I should do D.

Of course, the same reasoning applies to Joan. Thus, both players will do D, ensuring a less desirable outcome for each than if both had done C. This seems to quash any hope that an unrealistic egoism is the source of the paradox.

These and other attempts to explain away the paradox focus on trying to show that the examples used to illustrate it are all unrealistic, do not correspond to familiar, real-life situations, and thus have no bearing on those everyday situations. If successful, no doubt such attempts take some of the sting out of the paradox. But what remains untouched is the conclusion that there *can be* situations in which it is rational for both players to do X despite their knowledge that the outcome will be worse if both do X than if both refrain from X. This itself qualifies as a paradoxical conclusion. Hence, the paradox cannot be completely defused by appeal to lack of realism in the illustrative examples.

Thus far, the prisoner's dilemma has been presented in its simplest form, as a type I paradox, but there are several significant variations to consider. The dilemma is sometimes presented as a type II paradox, as a conflict between two compelling arguments: the dominance argument for confessing, and the symmetry argument for remaining silent. The dominance argument we have already encountered. The symmetry argument draws on the assumptions that the players know that their situations are symmetrical, and know that both are rational. Thus, each can expect that they will make the same decision; that is, either both will confess or both will remain silent. These are the only possible outcomes. Consequently, if you were to confess, then so would he, and you would receive c; while if you were to remain silent, so would he, and you would receive b. Since b is preferred to c, the rational choice for you is to remain silent; similarly for the other player. Thus, the rational choice for each is not to confess.

Presented in this way, the paradox is type II and is falsidical, since at least one of the conclusions is false. However, it is still uncontroversial, since there is general agreement as to which conclusion is true. The conflict between the symmetry and dominance arguments, and the merits of the symmetry argument, are discussed in detail later (pp. 148–54).

One choice in a prisoner's dilemma is considered to be cooperating (keeping silent in the prisoners example, honouring the agreement in the nuclear arms pact), while the other is taken as defecting (confessing, violating the agreement). Most theorists grant that in a prisoner's dilemma in which each participant chooses just once, a one-play dilemma, one ought to defect. It is possible, however, to think of a player making a series of choices in a situation that has the structure of a prisoner's dilemma. Suppose two players are certain they will play this game 100 times. In this *iterated* prisoner's dilemma, it seems even more plausible that the players will cooperate on at least some rounds, since there is now the possibility of influencing your opponent's play on later rounds. Perhaps you can influence him to consider your well-being, to cooperate, by signalling your willingness to consider his: you might, for instance, begin by cooperating, and continue to cooperate as long as he responds in kind. Such a hope is apparently thwarted, however, by what is known as *the backward induction argument*. Grant that the correct strategy in a one-play dilemma is to defect. But the situation in the last round of the series is equivalent to a one-play dilemma, for there is no hope of influencing future rounds, and thus the rational course for both players is to defect. Now given that the players know they will defect on the last round no matter what has happened in previous rounds, they should also defect on the penultimate round (the 99th), for there is no possibility of influencing an opponent's play on a later round. And given that the players know they will defect on the 99th round, they should defect on the 98th round; and so on. We are forced to the conclusion that rational players will defect on every round of an iterated dilemma.

The paradoxical argument can be expressed more succinctly as an apparently sound mathematical induction:

(1) The players will defect on round 100.
(2) If the players will defect on round n, then they will also defect on round $n - 1$.
(3) Therefore, the players will defect on every round.

The backward induction argument ("backward" because it begins with the last round) is taken by many to be the heart of the prisoner's dilemma paradox.

The iterated prisoner's dilemma is a type I paradox. But since there is much less agreement here on the truth-value of the conclusion than in the one-play case, this paradox is properly classed as controversial. The iterated dilemma is the topic of a later section (pp. 154–66).

Note that if the length of the series is not known, is indefinite, the backward induction argument cannot get a toehold. There is some reason to think that an indefinitely iterated series of plays of a game with the structure of a prisoner's dilemma corresponds most closely to the structure of everyday social conflict, and, as a result, there has been considerable empirical research on such situations. In particular, the work of Robert Axelrod suggests that a rule known as "tit-for-tat", which instructs the player to cooperate on the first play, and then do whatever the other player did on the previous move, is most successful in the indefinitely iterated game. Although important questions are raised by such cases, and by Axelrod's research, the focus in this chapter will be on attempts to resolve the *paradox* of the prisoner's dilemma.

Versions of the paradox encountered thus far all pit one player against another. But there is also, finally, the *n*-person prisoner's dilemma. Suppose your union has called a strike in order to win an adequate medical plan from the employer. If you go on strike, you will receive a small weekly stipend from the union; however, there is the possibility of continuing to work (scabbing), in which case you will receive your normal salary. Whether you go on strike is a sufficiently confidential matter that there is no fear of reprisals; and the strike will achieve its goal as long as *enough* union members participate. Since the union is very large, it is unlikely that your participating will have any impact on the effectiveness of the strike. The matrix for the situation might be as follows.

	Enough others go on strike	Not enough others go on strike
Go on strike	Health plan, small stipend	No health plan, small stipend
Continue to work	Health plan, normal pay	No health plan, normal pay

Again, dominance reasoning leads to the conclusion that it is rational for you to continue to work. Of course, if it is rational for you, it is rational for every union member. Thus a union whose members are all rational cannot conduct a successful strike![3]

Related paradoxes

The terrain of the prisoner's dilemma is particularly fertile: the paradox has several significant variations, as we have seen. As well, there are related paradoxes that have enough in common with the dilemma that there is the possibility of mutual illumination, and in some cases, the sense that they should fall to essentially the same solution.

This section sets out three other paradoxes that are strikingly similar to the iterated dilemma.

The chain store paradox

A chain store has branches in 20 different towns. Each branch is faced with an independent local store that is a potential competitor; these independent stores will be given an opportunity to compete at different times. At the appropriate time, the potential competitor may choose to compete (the IN option) or not (the OUT option). The chain store, in responding to an actual competitor, may choose to adopt a defensive or an aggressive pricing policy. All parties are fully rational, and have all the relevant information. The matrix looks like this:

		Local store	
		IN	OUT
Chain store	Defensive policy	2, 2	5, 1
	Aggressive policy	0, 0	5, 1

It seems, intuitively, that the chain store will do best by making aggressive choices early in the game in order to deter future competitors. This is the verdict of common sense. But consider the last potential competitor. If this local store chooses IN, then clearly the chain store should take the defensive option, for 2 is better than 0. Knowing this, the last competitor will surely choose IN. But then the 19th competitor should also choose IN, for it is clear that the last competitor cannot be deterred, and therefore the chain store has no incentive to do anything other than respond defensively to the 19th competitor. Since the 19th competitor cannot be deterred, the 18th competitor will also surely choose IN. And so on. Thus it seems that the chain store should respond defensively to all actual competitors.[4]

Unlike the prisoner's dilemma, the opponents in the chain store paradox (the chain store and the independent local stores) are not in symmetric situations. One player faces a succession of other players, rather than two players engaging repeatedly. There is, however, a dominance argument available that recommends the defensive response at each stage – again a highly counter-intuitive result.

The bottle imp

There is a bottle containing an imp who can grant almost any wish you might have. The bottle can be purchased; however, anyone who buys the bottle must sell it to a rational, fully informed individual for a price less than she paid. Failure to meet these conditions carries a penalty of death, and no wish will be granted until after the conditions have been met. It seems clear that some (rational) billionaire should be willing to purchase the bottle, say, in order to save his dying child. But familiar reasoning yields the conclusion that no rational person would purchase the bottle. Clearly, no one would be willing to purchase it for one penny, since that person would be unable to sell it according to the conditions, and would thus face death and have no wish granted. But since this is known, no one would be willing to purchase the bottle for two pennies, for he would be unable to sell it in accordance with the conditions. Similarly, no rational person would buy the bottle for three pennies, and so on. The bottle is worthless.[5]

Note that, in this game, there is no sense in which the players are opponents or competitors. Nor does dominance have any recommendation here.

The centipede game

Suppose A and B are offered the following opportunity. One hundred loonies (Canadian $1 coins) are heaped on the table. The players are to choose in turn whether to take one or two coins from the pile. If one is taken, the other player takes her turn, but as soon as two are taken, the game is over and the remaining coins are removed. As long as each player takes only one coin, the game continues until the pile is exhausted.

Intuitively, it seems that each player stands to gain a fair sum from this generous offer. But A and B are both rational, have common knowledge of their rationality, and common knowledge of the rules of the game. If the game reaches the point where only two coins are left on the table and it is A's turn, she will certainly take both since there is nothing to gain by leaving one for B. If the game gets to the stage where there are three coins on the table, and it is B's turn, B will take two, since if she takes only one and leaves two, A will take them both at the next turn. If there are four coins left on the table, and it is A's turn, A will take two, for if she takes only one and leaves three, by the above reasoning, B will take two. And so on. However many coins are left, a player will take two when it is her turn. Thus, on the first round, *A* will take two and end the game. Offered \$100 to share, the outcome for two rational players will be \$2 and \$0.[6]

The scenario of the centipede game is entirely straightforward and easily instantiated, which makes this perhaps the most disconcerting paradox in the group.

The one-play dilemma and the symmetry argument

Is there any solution to the prisoner's dilemma? This section will examine one way in which some have attempted to escape the paradoxical conclusion in the one-play case. The next section will deal with attempts to block the argument of the iterated dilemma.

The prevailing view is that defection is the rational strategy in the one-play dilemma. But for some this counter-intuitive result is just too much to swallow; they reject the standard view on the basis of the symmetry argument, according to which cooperation is rationally required even in the one-play dilemma.[7] Two assumptions play an important role in this argument: the rationality assumption says that each participant is fully rational, and that this is a matter of common knowledge; the symmetry assumption says that the decision situation of the participants is symmetric (given the matrix and the preference orderings), and that this is a matter of common knowledge.

The core of the symmetry argument for cooperation is:

(1s) If I were to cooperate, then he would also cooperate and I would get *b*.

(2s) If I were to defect, then he would also defect and I would get *c*.

(3s) Therefore, if I were to cooperate, I would be better off than if I were to defect.

The two assumptions provide the basis for the premises, (1s) and (2s). Because the players both know that each is fully rational, and that they are in symmetric situations, they know that they are guaranteed to choose the same action. Hence, if one were to cooperate, so would the other.

The symmetry argument, for some, suffices to put the prisoner's dilemma to rest: the argument establishes that rationality requires cooperation, and there is thus no paradox.[8] But this is surely too quick, even if the symmetry argument is impeccable. Presenting a counter-argument, however strong, against the paradoxical conclusion does not suffice for a resolution of the paradox, as we saw in Chapter 1. If cooperation is rational, then to dispel the paradox we must also find a flaw in the argument for defecting, which is:

(1d) Either the other player will cooperate or he will defect.
(2d) Suppose he will cooperate.
(3d) If I were to defect, I would get a.
(4d) If I were to cooperate, I would get b.
(5d) Suppose he will defect.
(6d) If I were to defect, I would get c.
(7d) If I were to cooperate, I would get d.
(8d) Therefore, no matter what the other player does, I would be better off if I were to defect than if I were to cooperate.

This is the dominance argument for defecting. Grant for the moment that the symmetry argument is irrefutable. Still, the paradox is not fully resolved until the flaw in the dominance argument is isolated and diagnosed. Of course, if the dominance principle is thought of in terms of a matrix in which one act is dominant, and a recommendation that whenever there is such a matrix, one ought to do the dominant act, it may seem adequate simply to dismiss dominance considerations as "inapplicable" or "irrelevant" in the face of the symmetry argument.[9] Presented with an apparently compelling dominance *argument*, however, it becomes clear that nothing is resolved until further diagnostic work is done.

Given the discussion of Chapter 5 as background, it is not difficult to see that if the symmetry argument is sound, the empirical claims of the dominance argument cannot all be true. If (3d) and (4d) are true on the assumption of (2d), and (6d) and (7d) are true on the assumption of (5d), then it is also true that:

$$[(3d) \ \& \ (4d)] \lor [(6d) \ \& \ (7d)]$$

But the disjunction is incompatible with the premises of the symmetry argument, that is, with:

(1s) & (2s)

For (1s) is incompatible with (7d), and therefore with the second disjunct; while (2s) is incompatible with (3d), and thus with the first disjunct. Thus, if the symmetry argument is sound, some of the empirical claims made in the dominance argument must be false.

With the conflict between dominance and symmetry now clearly delineated, let us inspect the symmetry argument more closely. The point of the argument is to establish (3s); it is in virtue of this comparison that cooperation is deemed rational. Since (3s) is expressed as a subjunctive conditional, the premises, it seems, must also take the form of subjunctive conditionals.

But Davis insists that his version of the symmetry argument requires only material conditionals.[10] Knowledge of (1s) and (2s), construed only as material conditionals, provides adequate ground, he maintains, for an assessment of rationality; the only further requirement he adds is that the agent know the material conditionals independently of knowing the truth-value of the antecedents. This additional constraint, however, does not obviate the sort of difficulty noted earlier. Suppose I know

(1s′) I cooperate $\supset$ I get b
(2s′) I defect $\supset$ I get c

because some reliable, trustworthy person has so informed me. Surely, this is not adequate grounds for determining that I should cooperate, for (1s′) is compatible with "I cooperate $\supset$ I do not get b", and also with "If I were to cooperate, I would not get b".[11]

The argument, then, requires subjunctive conditionals. Are (1s) and (2s) true if so understood? A quick excursion into the logic of subjunctive conditionals (henceforth just "conditionals") may help cast some light on the symmetry argument. Recall Goodman's account: The conjunction of the antecedent (A), together with some law (L), and relevant conditions (S), must logically imply the consequent (C). Further, A and S must be cotenable, that is, it must not be the case that if A were true, S would be false. Goodman builds in explicit reference to laws, likely because he thinks that the connection between A & S and C must be mediated by a generalization (All cases of A & S are cases of C), and only law-like, as opposed to accidental, generalizations suffice to yield true conditionals. For instance, the accidental generalization "All the objects in my pocket are silver", although true, does not guarantee the truth of "If this penny were in my pocket, it would be silver".

However, in many instances of a true contingent conditional, there does not seem to be any natural law that is relevant. For example:

If he were incarcerated, he would be unjustly punished.

More significantly, once the notion of cotenability is introduced, the explicit reference to law seems eliminable. To the extent that laws support subjunctive conditionals, while accidental generalizations do not, the most likely explanation is that *laws are cotenable with the relevant contrary-to-fact antecedents,* while accidental generalizations are not. What needs to be insisted on is not that all laws be held constant, but simply that all true statements cotenable with the antecedent be taken as fixed.

Goodman's account, then, can be simplified and made more broadly applicable by removing the explicit reference to laws. I would propose a revision as follows. A conditional is true provided that the conjunction of the antecedent, A, with some true statement, S, logically implies the consequent, C, and S is cotenable with A; that is, it is not the case that if A were true, S would be false.[12] (Note that S may be the conjunction of several statements, one of which may be a law.) When this condition is met, we may say that S *supports or sustains* the conditional $A \rightarrow C$. Thus, "All the objects in my pocket are silver" does not support "If this penny were in my pocket, it would be silver"; but "Any piece of butter heated to 66 °C melts" does support "If this piece of butter were heated to 66 °C, it would melt."

The symmetry argument can now be assessed against this background. It is assumed that the participants are fully rational; that this is a matter of common knowledge; that their decision situations are symmetric; and that it is common knowledge that each is fully informed concerning both their situations. The core of the argument, as stated earlier, can now be fleshed out. The full argument underlying (1s) of the initial formulation is:

(1) If I were to cooperate, it would be rational for me to cooperate.
(2) If I were to cooperate and it were rational for me to cooperate, then he would cooperate.
(3) Therefore, if I were to cooperate, then he would cooperate.[13]
(4) If I were to cooperate and he were to cooperate, I would get b.
(5) Therefore, if I were to cooperate, I would get b.

Similarly for (2s) of the original formulation:

(6) If I were to defect, it would be rational for me to defect.
(7) If I were to defect and it were rational for me to defect, then he would defect.
(8) Therefore, if I were to defect, then he would defect.
(9) If I were to defect and he were to defect, I would get c.
(10) Therefore, if I were to defect, I would get c.

Once the argument is expressed fully, the fallacious move stands out. Consider steps (1) and (6). Can *both* be maintained based just on the fact that I am rational? Analogous inferences might be:

(i)   I am a completely moral person.
(ii)   Therefore, if I were to keep my promise, I would be acting morally.
(iii) Therefore, if I were to break my promise, I would be acting morally.

Surely we would not be prepared to grant these inferences in anything like the normal case. To say that I am completely moral is not to say that I will act morally *no matter what I do*. Similarly with rationality. To maintain (1) and (6) of the symmetry argument would be tantamount to asserting that I will act rationally *whatever I do*. But this goes far beyond the given of the prisoner's dilemma, which is simply that I will act rationally.

Consider the logic of the situation in light of the revised account of conditionals. What is clear is that:

I am fully rational (S) & I cooperate (A)

logically implies

It is rational to cooperate (C)

But this is not sufficient to yield the truth of step (1) (If I were to cooperate, it would be rational for me to cooperate). The statement "I am fully rational" must not only be true, but must also be cotenable with "I cooperate" (S must be cotenable with A) in order to guarantee the truth of $A \rightarrow C$. Similarly, the truth of step (6) of the symmetry argument requires that "I am fully rational" be cotenable with "I defect". Thus, steps (1) and (6) require *the joint truth* of:

(i) If I were to cooperate, I would still be fully rational.
(ii) If I were to defect, I would still be fully rational.

But there is absolutely no reason to think that (i) and (ii) are both true in the prisoner's dilemma. Certainly they are not guaranteed by the mere fact that I am rational; for that fact does not ensure that I act rationally no matter what I do.

This analysis also highlights the fact that, as we saw earlier, exportation is not a valid logical principle for subjunctive conditionals. That principle says (where "$\Rightarrow$" designates logical implication):

$$[(P \& Q) \rightarrow R] \Rightarrow [P \rightarrow (Q \rightarrow R)]$$

However, while it is necessarily true that

(I am fully rational & I do x) $\rightarrow$ x is rational

we have seen that this does not guarantee the truth of

I am fully rational $\rightarrow$ (I do x $\rightarrow$ x is rational)

I leave to the reader the question of whether it is *possible* that steps (1) and (6) should both be true, that is, whether there is some coherent variant of the usual prisoner's dilemma situation in which I act rationally no matter what I do. My claim here is just that the assumption that is supposed to yield these premises, that I am fully rational, does not in fact do so.

One last consideration. Perhaps these difficulties can be avoided by the simple tactic of making the assumptions of the problem, the rationality assumption, R, and the symmetry assumption, S, part of the antecedent of the conditional premises. Thus:

(1′)   If R & S & I were to cooperate, then it would be rational to cooperate.

(2′)   If R & S & I were to cooperate & it were rational for me to cooperate, then he would cooperate.

(3′)   Therefore, if R & S & I were to cooperate, then he would cooperate.

(4′)   If R & S & I were to cooperate & he were to cooperate, then I would get b.

(5′)   Therefore, if R & S & I were to cooperate, I would get b.

And so the argument continues. But we are no further ahead. For now the problem is that even though R and S are true, I cannot infer

(5″)   If I were to cooperate, I would get b.

For as we have just seen, the principle of exportation is not valid for subjunctive conditionals. And (5″) is necessary in order ultimately to conclude that if I were to cooperate, I would be better off than if I were to defect.

The argument from symmetry fails to establish that cooperation is the rational strategy in the one-play prisoner's dilemma.

The iterated dilemma and the backward induction argument

The backward induction argument for a dilemma of known length is considered by many to be the heart of the prisoner's dilemma paradox. Defecting as the rational strategy in the one-play dilemma can perhaps be granted; but there is a strong intuition that a rational player in an iterated dilemma would hope to influence her opponent in future rounds by signalling her willingness to engage in a mutually advantageous strategy, and would thus cooperate in at least some rounds.

In attempting to block the argument, several commentators have been struck by an analogy with the surprise exam paradox, where the paradoxical argument can also be expressed as a backward induction. The surprise exam argument goes as follows:

(1) An exam held on day n will not be a surprise.
(2) If an exam held on day n will not be a surprise, then an exam held on day $n - 1$ will not be a surprise.
(3) Therefore, an exam held on any of days 1 to n will not be a surprise.

Further points of resemblance between the surprise exam and the iterated dilemma are that both concern highly idealized, perfectly rational subjects, and both make strong assumptions about the knowledge or justified belief such an ideally rational subject would have.

The striking similarity between the two paradoxes suggests that their solutions may also be analogous. This section examines the work of recent commentators who find the points of resemblance telling, and who locate the solution to each paradox in certain excessively strong epistemic assumptions concerning ideally rational subjects.

First, the backward induction argument of the iterated dilemma (the BIA) should be further clarified. The premises of the argument can be spelled out as:

(R)   Rational: At each round, the players are perfectly rational agents who seek to maximize their own utility.
(C)   Circumstances: The players are engaged in an iterated prisoner's dilemma of n rounds.
(E)   Epistemically ideal: At each round, the players are perfect with respect to memory and logical abilities; and they believe exactly what they are justified in believing.
(CBR)   Common belief in (R): At the outset, each player believes (R), each believes that each believes (R), and so on.
(CBC)   Common belief in (C): At the outset, each player believes (C), each believes that each believes (C), and so on.
(CBE)   Common belief in (E): At the outset, each player believes (E), each believes that each believes (E), and so on.

As well, a premise ensuring that the players retain their beliefs throughout the game is often thought to be necessary. One version of such a premise is:

(RT) Retention: (i) Each player will believe (R), (C) and (E) throughout the game.

(ii) Each player will believe (i) throughout the game.

(iii) Each player will believe (ii) throughout the game.

And so on.

Many commentators spell out premises corresponding to (CBR), (CBC), (CBE) and (RT) in terms of knowledge, rather than belief. But the proper understanding of the concept of knowledge is a matter of some controversy. In connection with the BIA, for instance, it has been argued that knowledge is unrevisable; that is, if A knows that P at t, A cannot "lose" this knowledge after t.[14] I take this position to be based on fallacious reasoning. But whatever view one has on the matter, this and other controversies pertaining to knowledge need not be considered here. The notion of belief is perfectly adequate for the BIA. We give the paradox a fair hearing, and avoid unnecessary controversy, by employing the weaker concept.

Now for the argument. The critical move in the paradoxical argument is to establish, for each round, that a player cannot hope to influence her opponent's strategy on future rounds by her action on the present round. (It is assumed that the players act simultaneously on a given round.) As in the surprise exam, the argument must begin at the end of the sequence. Thus we have:

(1) At round n, both players will believe there are no future rounds, and thus will believe that the only consequences of acting at round n are given by the payoff matrix. Since both are rational, both will defect.

Round n becomes, in effect, a one-play dilemma. Clearly, the BIA can get a toehold only if it is conceded that defecting is rational in a one-round dilemma. The argument continues:

(2) At round $n - 1$, the players will believe (1), will thus believe that each will defect in round n, and will thus believe that the only consequences of acting at round $n - 1$ are given by the payoff matrix. Since both are rational, both will defect.

Step (2) requires that the players believe the truth of (1). But (1) is based on the fact that at round n, the players are rational, believe that they are in an n-round prisoner's dilemma and are epistemically ideal.[15] Thus, step (2) requires the first iteration of belief: the players must believe at $n - 1$ that both will be rational, that both will be epistemically ideal, and that both will *believe* that they are in an n-round dilemma. In general, each step requires an attribution of belief in previous steps, which necessitates further iterations of belief. To continue:

(3) At round $n - 2$, the players will believe (1) and (2), will thus believe that each will defect in rounds n and $n - 1$, and will thus believe that the only consequences of acting at round n are given by the payoff matrix. Since both are rational, both will defect.

So now the players must believe (1) and (2). But (2) is based on the assumptions given above. It follows that the players must believe at $n - 2$ that, in future rounds: (i) both will believe (R); (ii) both will believe (E); and (iii) both will believe that both will believe (C).

It is easy to see that each subsequent step will require another iteration of belief. Hence the necessity of common belief premises that specify multiple iterations of belief. Note that the argument has been presented from the viewpoint of a bystander, since this creates less danger of confusion concerning what the participants must believe. Understood in this way, for a game of n rounds, $n - 1$ iterations of belief in (C) must be assumed, as well as $n - 2$ iterations of belief in (R) and in (E). ("*A* believes that *B* believes that *P*" is taken to express one iteration of belief.)

This, then, is the BIA. It was remarked earlier that there is an analogy between the BIA and the argument of the surprise exam. Does the resemblance between the two paradoxes indicate a similar solution? The first attempt to extend an analysis of the prediction paradox to the prisoner's dilemma was made by Russell Hardin.[16] Following Quine on the prediction paradox, Hardin's objection to the BIA is that the participants cannot be certain of the exact length of the game, and cannot be certain of what the other player will do. It is no surprise that Hardin's analysis suffers from much the same defect as Quine's: no rationale can be given for denying the participants this knowledge that does not balloon into a more thoroughgoing scepticism.

More substantial efforts to exploit the similarity between the two paradoxes can be found in the work of those who subscribe to the sort of epistemic approach to the surprise exam paradox proposed in Chapter 3. That analysis, you may recall, resolves the prediction paradox by stopping the argument at the first step. On Thursday evening, assuming the exam has not yet been given, the students can no longer believe both (i) there will be an exam on one day of this week and (ii) the exam will be a surprise. Thus the students' beliefs at the beginning of the week may not be warranted later in the week. Although the details differ, all versions of the epistemic approach focus on the issue of the *retention* of the students' belief or knowledge throughout the week.

Roy Sorensen, a leading exponent of the epistemic approach to the prediction paradox, was the first to see the possibility of extending the analysis to the iterated dilemma.[17] Sorensen reasons as follows. Although the game begins with players A and B being certain that each will be rational throughout, A's confidence may be eroded by new evidence consisting of B's previous moves. Specifically, if B were to cooperate, A could no longer believe in all the announced conditions of the game, and thus would have to revise some of her beliefs. The most likely revision would involve doubts concerning B's rationality, and would cast B as someone willing to cooperate under certain circumstances. Since such a revision of A's beliefs would increase the likelihood of A's cooperating, it is in B's interest to cooperate at some point in order to compel belief revision by A. Since B is rational, she will take advantage of the opportunity, and cooperate. The specific flaw in the argument, then, is located in the premise of the argument that asserts belief retention in rationality throughout the game.

Sorensen's proposal, that an act of cooperation by one agent might force the other into belief revision, seems to promise a way out of the BIA. There is difficulty, however, in fully understanding his analysis, for it seems necessary to grant the soundness of the paradox-generating argument in order to proceed with the solution. What reason is there to think that B's cooperating would force A to revise some of her initial beliefs? The only *obvious* reason is the apparent soundness of the backward induction argument for mutual defection. But an assumption of the soundness of the argument can hardly be part of the diagnosis of its flaw.

Sorensen's analysis, then, leaves it unclear why an act of cooperation by one player would require belief revision by the other. But others have picked up on his basic strategy. Philip Pettit and Robert Sugden share with Sorensen the conviction that the fallacy, in both the surprise exam paradox and the iterated dilemma, lies in the assumption of belief retention.[18] In their version of the BIA, it is a premise that the players have a common belief in their rationality at the outset. The key issue is whether the players are warranted in holding that this common belief in rationality will survive through the game. After all, the fact that you believe P at one time does not guarantee that you will continue to believe P at a later time, regardless of what happens in the interim. Pettit and Sugden argue not only that the players will not necessarily believe that the common belief in rationality will endure but, even more strongly, that necessarily they will not believe in its survival.

In the course of the argument, it is claimed that what is required for the soundness of the backward induction is the assumption that the common belief in rationality will survive *no matter what either player has done previously.* It is by no means entirely clear why Pettit and Sugden take the "no matter what" qualification to be necessary. But the suggestion has considerable plausibility, and merits further study. My own justification for their claim would go as follows. First, it is clear that the actions of each player depend on the beliefs she has at the time. More specifically, at any round before the last, the decision to defect rests on the player's belief that her opponent will continue to be rational. So if player A can have an impact on B's belief in her future rationality, she may influence B's actions. But the BIA aims to show that neither player can influence the other's future actions, and that, as a consequence, at each round the players will take into account only the payoff matrix, and mutual defection will be inevitable. So the soundness of the BIA requires that neither player can have an impact on the other's belief in her opponent's future rationality. Hence the need for the premise that the common belief in rationality will persist *no matter what either player does.*[19]

Let us try to pinpoint where the gap in the argument occurs if the premise is not strengthened by the "no matter what" clause. Consider, for instance, step (3) of the BIA:

(3) At round $n - 2$, each player believes that the other will defect in rounds n and $n - 1$, and thus believes that the only consequences of acting at round $n - 2$ are those given by the payoff matrix. Therefore, being rational, each will defect.

The difficulty comes in the inference to the claim "each believes that the only consequences of acting at round $n - 2$ are those given by the payoff matrix". This implies, in part, that A believes that she can now have no effect on B's actions at n and $n - 1$. According to the reasoning attributed to A, she infers the conclusion from "B will defect in rounds n and $n - 1$". But the inference is valid only if the premise is taken as "B will defect in rounds n and $n - 1$ *no matter what I do now*". And in order to establish this, the assumption that B's initial beliefs will persist *no matter what* A *does* is necessary. The reasoning attributed to each player requires strong belief retention premises.

To come back to Pettit and Sugden, the backward induction cannot be run, they maintain, unless it is assumed that the common belief in rationality will survive come what may. However, they go on to argue, any act of cooperation will cause the common belief to break down. Their argument on this score echoes, rather curiously, the argument of the paradox. Suppose A cooperates on the final round. This is an irrational act, so B would believe A irrational and the common belief would break down. Suppose instead that A cooperates on round $n - 1$. B would either believe that she has no good reason for so acting, and is thus irrational, or she would believe that A believes that B can be induced by A's cooperation at $n - 1$ to cooperate at n. But this would be an irrational act, so again the common belief does not survive.

Suppose next that A cooperates at round $n - 2$. B may believe that A is irrational. Or she may believe that A believes that, by cooperating at $n - 2$, B can be induced to cooperate at $n - 1$ or at n. But cooperating at n is irrational, so this would mean the breakdown of the common belief in rationality. And cooperating at $n - 1$ is either irrational or results from the belief that such cooperation would prompt A to (irrationally) cooperate at n. And so on.

Thus, Pettit and Sugden conclude, the common belief in rationality cannot be held to survive regardless of what either player does. This constitutes their solution to the paradox: an assumption essential to the paradoxical argument cannot be true.

Has the BIA been derailed? The solution Pettit and Sugden offer has two components: (i) the BIA requires, as a premise, that the common belief in rationality will survive no matter what; and (ii) that premise cannot be true. Let us take clause (ii) first. There may be some perplexity here. For some, the retention of the common belief in rationality, however it is to be formulated, is one of the defining properties of the iterated dilemma scenario; it has the status of a stipulation. But if this is so, how can it be rejected as false? Of course, Pettit and Sugden do not take the survival of the common belief to be part and parcel of the iterated dilemma set-up. But even if it is regarded as one of the defining elements of the iterated dilemma, there is no serious difficulty here for Pettit and Sugden's analysis. Their solution can simply be restated as the claim that the survival, come what may, of the common belief in rationality conflicts with other stipulated elements of the scenario. Put this way, the solution amounts to the claim that the script of the iterated dilemma, taken in whole, is incoherent.

Pettit and Sugden's analysis seems to have isolated a critical feature of the argument. But examination of clause (i) of their solution is best deferred until later in this section.

Extending the solution of the prediction paradox to the iterated prisoner's dilemma is also the strategy of Luc Bovens.[20] As he sets up the problem, it is assumed, for purposes of the backward induction, that there is no cooperative play in the last round, and that both players believe this at pre-game time. Another assumption, particularly significant for Bovens, is that if a player holds a certain belief at a given time, he will continue to hold it at a later time; this assumption he calls "retention".

Bovens's solution to the iterated dilemma focuses on retention; he maintains that the players are not (cannot be) justified in believing it. One substantive principle underlying his analysis concerns the circumstances in which you are justified in believing that A will continue to believe P: you are so justified, he claims, just in case in all future courses of events that you do not believe will not come about (which are "feasible", in Bovens's terms), A will in fact continue to believe that P.

Armed with this epistemic principle, Bovens attempts to block the backward induction. Before going through the paradoxical argument, he points out, the players do not believe that cooperation will not occur at some round; that is, cooperation is feasible. Suppose, then, that B does cooperate before the penultimate round. This provides player A with better reason to believe that B will cooperate in the last round than that she will not. So A will not continue to believe, by the penultimate round, that there will be no cooperation in the last round. Hence, the players are not justified in believing that A will continue to have this pre-game belief.

How exactly is this relevant to the argument of the iterated dilemma? To make the connection, we must keep in mind that the *players* need to be able to work through the argument. In particular, at each step k of the argument, we must be able to maintain that the players are justified in believing step $k - 1$. So the players must be able to replicate our reasoning, and hence must be justified in believing the premises required for that reasoning. If the players cannot be warranted in accepting retention, then, the argument is brought to a standstill after the first step.

But the epistemic claims on which Bovens bases his solution are not very credible. Particularly striking is the assertion that having witnessed cooperative play by her opponent before the penultimate round, a player has better reason to believe the opponent will cooperate on the last round than not. Would one isolated act of cooperation, preceded by several acts of defection, really lead us to expect cooperation in the last round? Why should we project in this way? Indeed, even repeated cooperation might not lead us to anticipate cooperation in the last round.

Also implausible is Bovens's principle that you are justified in believing that A will continue to believe P just in case, in all future courses of events that you do not believe will not occur, A will in fact continue to believe P. This comes uncomfortably close to claiming that justification requires the truth of what is believed. But leaving this aside, suppose a neurological event of type N will occur in your brain this week and will wipe out all memories of your family. You have no reason to suspect this event will occur; nor do you believe it won't, since you do not even have the concept of an event of type N. Surely this does not mean that you are not now justified in believing that you will continue to believe through the week that you have two daughters. Of course, under some description ("event that will cause me to lose all memory of my family"), you believe the event will not occur. But this just shows that Bovens's principle does not admit of clear interpretation as it stands; nor is it evident how it can be tightened up.

The most significant progress towards a solution of the iterated dilemma seems to be found in the work of Pettit and Sugden; let us return to their analysis.[21] Their position is that the BIA requires strong belief retention premises: specifically, it must be assumed that the common belief in (R) will persist, *no matter what either player does*. But, they argue, the fact is that any act of cooperation will cause this common belief to break down.

The "no matter what" clause, I suggested earlier, seems necessary because the BIA must demonstrate that at each round prior to n, player A believes that she cannot hope to affect B's future actions; thus A must believe, at each round, that B will defect at subsequent rounds no matter what she does now. But this requires that A believe that B will retain her initial beliefs no matter what A does.

If the soundness of the BIA does indeed require this strong interpretation of the belief retention premises, the argument is easily overturned. The players are supposed to be epistemically ideal believers. But to be epistemically ideal, one's beliefs must be open to the impact of new evidence. Surely B, an ideal believer, could not continue to believe that A is a rational agent, if A were repeatedly to act irrationally by B's lights. If B's beliefs were somehow invulnerable to A's actions, B could not be considered ideally rational. It needs no intricate argument to expose the fallacy in any version of the BIA that relies on belief retention premises modified by the "no matter what" rider.

Let us concede to Pettit and Sugden, then, that certain premises that are sufficient for the BIA cannot all be true.[22] We have a strong intuition that each player's beliefs about her opponent should be open to revision as a result of the opponent's actions. To express the belief retention premises of the argument in terms of a "no matter what the other player does" clause violates this intuition, although it does apparently give us premises that are sufficiently strong for the BIA. Still, the issue remains whether there is another set of premises that is both sufficient for the argument and more plausible. Might there be a better statement of the belief retention premises for the BIA?

The goal is, first, to have a coherent set of premises that is sufficiently strong to imply the conclusion. Of course, the stronger the premises, the less philosophical punch the paradox has; for it becomes increasingly difficult to imagine a situation in which the premises are true, and our intuitions weaken. For this and other reasons detailed in Chapter 1, we aim for a balance, for a set of premises which is as weak as possible, while still sufficient to yield the paradoxical conclusion.

I shall argue that (a) the premises formulated at the beginning of this section are coherent, and (b) there is reason to think they are sufficient to support *a version* of the BIA. Rather than strengthen the premises, it is possible that the *reasoning* of the argument should be revised and supplemented. Specifically, the possibility of an agent compelling her opponent to alter her beliefs must be taken into account. For simplicity, it will be assumed in what follows that if any belief revision results from a player's actions, it will be with respect to the belief in rationality.

To begin with (a), let us hold the assumption of the survival of a player's belief in her opponent's rationality in abeyance. If a rational player of whom *all the other* premises are true would, in the situation envisaged, give up her belief in her opponent's rationality, then the coherence of the full set of premises is in doubt. So let us explore the question. It is a given of the iterated dilemma that each player is epistemically ideal: her memory and logical abilities are perfect, and she believes only what she is justified in believing. Consequently, a player's initial beliefs will be retained unless she encounters new evidence. It is a further assumption of the problem, one that is normally left implicit, that the only new relevant evidence the players acquire throughout the game consists in the actions of the players at each round. Thus *B*'s initial belief in *A*'s rationality will survive *unless A* acts in a way that compels revision.

Will *A* act at a given round so as to get *B* to give up her initial belief in *A*'s rationality? The only way to do so is to provide counter-evidence; if *A* acts as she is expected to act, then nothing will change. But she is expected to act rationally. So if *A* acts rationally, nothing will change. In order for *A*'s action at a given round to force belief revision on *B*, then, *A* must act irrationally.

But it can never be rational to act irrationally. Therefore, *A* will not act irrationally and, as a consequence, *B*'s initial belief in *A*'s rationality will not be revised. *A* will not bring it about, at any round, that *B* gives up the belief in *A*'s rationality. The continued survival of the belief in rationality follows from, and is therefore coherent with, other assumptions of the problem.

It may be objected here that *A* does not need to act irrationally in order to get *B* to revise her beliefs; she need only act irrationally *by B's lights*. That is, she need only act irrationally relative to *what* B *takes her to believe*. But *A* will consider belief revision as an option only if it has not yet taken place. Assuming, then, that belief revision has not yet occurred, *A* and *B* share all the relevant beliefs, and *B* believes this. The situation is, in this sense, transparent. So it follows that *A* must act irrationally. A first revision of *B*'s initial beliefs will require *A* to act irrationally, and therefore will not occur.

Let us now turn to (b). It has been argued is that it is irrational for a player to attempt belief revision. This has bearing on the question of whether the premises as originally formulated are sufficient for the BIA. In providing a rationale for Pettit and Sugden's strengthened retention premise, it was pointed out that without it, there is a gap in reasoning. For the argument proceeds from (i) *B* will defect on future rounds, to (ii) the only consequences of *A*'s present action are those given by the payoff matrix, to (iii) *A* ought to defect. But the first inference is warranted, it was argued, only if premise (i) is given the sense of "*B* will defect on future rounds no matter what *A* does now". This still seems correct as an analysis of the reasoning. Rather than close the gap with an implausibly strong premise, however, it may be possible to replace or revise the line of reasoning.

The critical moves of the BIA, given the results of the preceding discussion, might instead go as follows: (i) *B* will defect on future rounds *unless* A *compels her to revise her belief in* A's *rationality*. But (ii) it is not rational for *A* to try to revise *B*'s belief; *A* ought not to try to do so. Thus, (iii) the only consequences of *A*'s action *that it is rational for* A *to consider* are those given by the payoff matrix. Therefore, (iv) *A* ought to defect.

This rather more subtle line of reasoning takes a different route to the conclusion that *A* ought to defect, a route that does not require the implausibly strong belief retention premise.

One way to contrast the two versions of the BIA is this. As originally formulated, the key steps of the argument seem designed to show that *A cannot* prevent *B*'s future defection, for it is argued that the only consequences of *A*'s action on the current round are given in the payoff matrix. In contrast, the new line of reasoning, if successful, would show at most that *A cannot rationally* prevent *B* from defecting. It is still possible to maintain that *A can* bring it about that *B* revises her beliefs, for *A* can act irrationally. What is impossible is that *A* act rationally *and* bring about belief revision.

The new line of reasoning offers a promising route for reinstating the BIA, and merits further study.

Some final brief remarks. Part of what makes the iterated prisoner's dilemma so baffling is that there seems to be a significant reward for acting irrationally. If *A* were to act irrationally, she would, let us suppose, force *B* to give up her belief that *A* is rational, and defeat *B*'s reasons for defecting at later stages of the game. Clearly, it is in *A*'s best interest that *B* not defect on future rounds. So in such a case it seems that one ought to act irrationally. But it is contradictory to suppose that it is rational to act irrationally.

The iterated prisoner's dilemma, viewed in this way, is reminiscent of Gideon's paradox. Imagine that you have a choice between $1,000 ($G_1$) and $100 ($G_2$). You prefer more money to less money. Before you choose, a bystander offers you a reward of $1,000,000 for acting irrationally. So it seems you ought to act irrationally. That is, the choice you make between G_1 and G_2 will be rational if and only if it is irrational.[23]

One point of similarity between the two situations is that it is tempting in both to come to the conclusion that it is rational to act irrationally. A second common feature is that, in each case, the consequences of an act depend, in part, on whether the act is irrational or not. Normally, however, it is assumed that the rationality of an act is a function of its possible consequences. It is hard to see how to assess rationality if the possible consequences of the alternative acts are not already given.

To sum up, it has been argued in this section that the survival of the belief in rationality fits nicely with other features of the dilemma, indeed follows from them, and that it is irrational for a player to attempt belief revision. Although the original formulation of the BIA requires a belief retention premise asserting the survival of the belief in rationality come what may, there appears to be an alternative line of reasoning available that does not depend on this implausibly strong assumption. The BIA has not been defeated; the paradox of the iterated prisoner's dilemma is with us still.

The sorites paradox

The paradox

Suppose that your height is 6'3". Clearly, you are tall. Your friend Tom, however, is only 5'4" and is concerned about his height. You offer him the following philosophical argument. If two people differ in height by only 0.1", you point out, then either both are tall or neither is. A difference in height of 0.1" cannot make the difference between being tall and not being tall. So a person who is 0.1" shorter than you are (6'3" − 0.1") is tall. But then a person who is 0.1" shorter than that (6'3" − 0.2") is also tall. You continue in this way until you reach 5'4", and can reassure Tom that he is indeed tall. Your friend is neither comforted nor amused.

This sort of paradoxical reasoning can be traced back to the logician Eubulides, a contemporary of Aristotle. It is sometimes referred to as "the paradox of the heap", since it is commonly illustrated in terms of a heap of sand. ("Sorites" derives from "soros", the Greek term for "heap".) Suppose you have a heap of sand consisting of 10,000 grains. Removing one grain surely cannot turn a heap into something that is not a heap. So 10,000 − 1 grains constitute a heap. But then so do 10,000 − 2 grains. Continuing with this reasoning will eventually lead to the absurd conclusion that one grain of sand suffices for a heap.

Another classic illustration of the sorites reasoning makes use of the concept of baldness. Suppose that as well as being tall, you are blessed with a luxuriant mop of hair; it is clear that you are not bald. There are, let us suppose, n hairs on your head. You reason that the difference between being bald and not being bald cannot consist in one hair. Thus $n - 1$ hairs suffice for not being bald. But by the same reasoning, $n - 2$ hairs is sufficient. Finally, you conclude that a man with one hair on his head is not bald.

In each of these examples, the argument hinges on the presumed "tolerance" or "insensitivity" of the key term. That is, a minute difference cannot make a difference, cannot affect the applicability of the predicate. It is not difficult to see that sorites arguments can be constructed for a variety of other predicates: child (consider a difference in age of one minute); red (consider a series of coloured cards ranging in colour from red to yellow, ordered in such a way that any two adjacent cards are indiscriminable in colour). Still other predicates that have been considered susceptible to sorites reasoning, although not always obviously so, include: rich, intelligent, small number, most, moustache, table, tadpole and dead. Sorites reasoning can also involve moral predicates. Grant that it would be morally wrong to have an abortion on (or after) the nth day of pregnancy (or the mth minute, where m is the number of minutes in n days). But if it is wrong at the mth minute, then surely it is also wrong at the $(m - 1)$th minute. Thus it is morally wrong, at any point in a pregnancy, to have an abortion; abortion is never morally acceptable.[1]

Sorites reasoning can be cast in two different forms. First:

(A) (1) A person who is worth $\$M$ is rich.
  (2) If a person worth $\$M$ is rich, then so is a person worth $\$(M - 1)$.
∴ (3) A person worth $\$(M - 1)$ is rich.
  (4) If a person worth $\$(M - 1)$ is rich, then so is a person worth $\$(M - 2)$.
∴ (5) A person worth $\$(M - 2)$ is rich.
     ⋮
  (n) A person worth $\$1$ is rich.

In this form, the argument consists in a sequence of sub-arguments, each of the form *modus ponens*, and each containing a different categorical and conditional premise. The first step of the argument is straightforward and rarely disputed. The sequence of conditionals, which is more likely to draw critical fire, reflects the view that the predicate in question is insensitive to small differences. An insensitive or tolerant predicate is not fine-grained, not responsive to fine discriminations; but of course, as the argument shows, enough minute differences can add up to a large difference that *is* sufficient to affect the applicability of the predicate.

Sorites arguments can also be expressed in the more compact schema of mathematical induction:

(B)   (1) A person who has m hairs on his head is not bald.
         (2) For any x, if a person with x hairs on his head is not bald, then neither is a person with $x - 1$ hairs on his head.
    ∴ (3) A person with one hair on his head is not bald.

Premise (1) is the base step and premise (2) the inductive step. Given suitable values for m, both premises seem clearly true, yet the conclusion is absurd.

As presented in either of these forms, the sorites paradox is a type I falsidical paradox, and is uncontroversial (although there are a few individuals who consider the argument to be sound, as we will see). For the most part, the paradox will be treated below in the form given by (A).

One intriguing feature of the sorites paradox is that, whether expressed as a series of *modus ponens* inferences or as a mathematical induction, it can be stood on its head. Argument (B), for instance, is absurd because a person with only one hair on his head is clearly bald. But if we start with this obvious truth, another sorites argument can be constructed:

(C)   (1) A person with one hair on his head is bald.
         (2) For any x, if a person with x hairs on his head is bald, so is a person with $x + 1$ hairs on his head.
    ∴ (3) A person with m hairs on his head is bald.

Supposing that m is the number of hairs on Bill Clinton's head, the conclusions of (C) and (B) are equally absurd. Every sorites argument seems to be reversible in this way: a paradoxical argument can be formulated as a positive sorites argument (in terms of being bald) or as a negative sorites argument (in terms of not being bald). The positive and negative versions are so closely analogous that it seems they must stand or fall together. On the face of it, then, it is an uphill road for those few commentators who want to accept *only* the negative sorites argument as sound.

The sorites paradox may also be understood as consisting in two opposing arguments such as (B) and (C). Taken this way, it is of course a type II paradox. It is still falsidical, however, for the conclusions cannot both be true, and it is also uncontroversial.

One final, rather unusual, example of a sorites argument may drive home the pervasiveness of the paradoxical reasoning, and the extent of the potential damage. A child of one year, let us suppose, does not have the ability to speak English, although five years later, she is a fluent speaker. Suppose we serially order the child's life by seconds. It seems obvious that there is no second of her life such that:

> She does not speak English at t and she does speak English at $t + 1$.

A difference of a second cannot make the difference between having and not having the ability to speak English. But then starting from the fact that she does not speak English at t, and proceeding by increments of one second, it seems we can conclude that she does not have command of the language five years later.[2]

Vulnerability to sorites reasoning is thus widespread, threatening the coherence of most of our everyday beliefs and language. If a minute difference makes no difference to the applicability of the predicate P, then, it appears, it cannot be consistently maintained that P applies to some items in an ordered series and not to others. The sorites paradox is arguably the most disturbing of the paradoxes considered in this book.

In all sorites arguments, the key concept is a vague predicate: tall, red, rich. Thus much of the attempt to come to terms with the paradox has focused on vagueness, and borderline cases are taken to be essential to vagueness. For instance, Shirley may not be clearly tall, but yet not clearly not tall; and there may be no additional information we can acquire that would help us decide how she should be characterized with respect to height. Even knowing her height to the nearest millimetre would not settle the matter.

Similarly, although we see an object in the best perceptual circumstances imaginable, we may be unable to determine whether it is red or orange. These are borderline cases of tallness and redness, respectively.

Although the notion of a borderline case is critical to understanding vagueness, no definition of "borderline case" will be attempted here. For it is not clear that one can give a crisp definition of the concept that does not prejudge the substantive philosophical theories concerning vagueness. The examples of predicates susceptible to sorites reasoning introduced above, however, should suffice to point the reader in the right direction.[3]

The dominant philosophical theory of vagueness is that in borderline cases, the vague predicate cannot be truly or falsely applied. Our ignorance of whether Shirley is tall, for instance, is simply a result of there being nothing to know; there is no fact of the matter in a borderline case. This is the semantic conception of vagueness: vagueness is a function of the way in which words relate to the world. In borderline cases, vague predicates relate to the world in such a way that perfectly meaningful statements are neither true nor false.

An alternative view is given by the epistemic theory. On this account, vague terms only appear to be insensitive; in fact a vague predicate has a precise boundary determining its correct application. The appearance of insensitivity is a consequence of our irremediable ignorance concerning the correct boundaries. Vagueness is rooted in epistemology.

This gives a preview of some of the philosophical terrain to be covered in this chapter. But it is time to face the paradox head on. Strategies for dealing with the sorites paradox, considered as a type I paradox, can be grouped in three categories. It can be argued that:

- the argument is sound and the paradox is veridical; or
- there is a flaw in the reasoning; or
- at least one of the premises is not true.

Each of these alternatives will be considered in turn.

A veridical paradox

The most radical response to the paradox is offered by Peter Unger.[4] On the basis of sorites reasoning, he maintains that the common-sense view of reality is in error: there are no such things as stones, twigs, tables or swizzle sticks. In short, there are no ordinary things.

Unger's argument is simple. To begin, consider the concept of a heap. Clearly, one grain of sand is insufficient for a heap. But if there isn't a heap before us, adding one grain will not create a heap. Hence, no (finite) number of grains is sufficient for a heap. There are thus no heaps, and our concept of a heap is incoherent.

Unger considers this a *direct argument* for his conclusion concerning heaps. But we may also begin by supposing that there are heaps, and that a million grains of sand, properly arranged, constitute a heap. Given that we have a heap of a million grains before us, removing one grain of sand will not leave us with no heap. Nor will removing one more. And so on, until finally we reach the conclusion that one grain of sand will suffice for a heap. This, says Unger, is preposterous; our original supposition that there exists a heap is thus reduced to absurdity. This reasoning is considered an *indirect argument* that there are no heaps, and that the concept of heap is incoherent.

To endorse Unger's direct argument is to treat a negative sorites argument as a sound argument, and a veridical paradox. The negative sorites argument is taken to provide an impeccable demonstration that there are no heaps, no tall people, and so on. The corresponding positive sorites argument, in contrast, is regarded as a *reductio ad absurdum* of the first premise. There is clearly an asymmetry here, a lack of congruity, and it is difficult to see how it can be justified, given the obvious parallels between the two arguments.

But even if we grant that Unger has disposed of heaps, how does he arrive at the more sweeping conclusion that there are no ordinary things? Sorites arguments are typically cast in terms of predicates such as being a heap, or being bald, where the unit of increment (or decrement) is obvious: a grain of sand, a hair. Unger, however, maintains that the argument can be extended to ordinary items such as stones, tables and swizzle sticks. Classic sorites reasoning is adapted to, for instance, a stone, by taking a single atom as the unit of increment. We begin with just a single atom; clearly, that is not a stone. Now the addition of one atom to something that is not a stone cannot create a stone; one atom cannot make the difference between there being a stone and there not being a stone. Thus, no collection of atoms can constitute a stone; there are no stones.

Unger's ultimate conclusion is stated dramatically: there are no stones, tables or swizzle sticks, there are no ordinary things. But this is to be understood as a striking way of expressing what is essentially a semantic thesis: terms such as "stone" and "table" are *incoherent* and therefore have no extension, cannot apply to anything real. Understood semantically, the thesis might be better supported by maintaining, first, that the negative and positive sorites arguments are valid, have entirely plausible premises and incompatible conclusions, and then inferring from this that the key concept is incoherent. This approach would obviate the need for an asymmetry in the treatment of the two arguments.

Unger attempts to soften the blow of his radical conclusion by pointing out that the common-sense view is not entirely devastated, for nothing has been said to rule out the existence of physical objects of various shapes and sizes. Nonetheless, his position flies in the face of common sense and should be considered only as a last resort, only if there is no way to block the paradoxical argument. It is worth noting here that, aside from the conflict with our everyday beliefs, there are also logical difficulties for the view that vague predicates are incoherent. The result of conjoining two incoherent or inconsistent predicates, it would seem, should itself be an incoherent predicate. If vague predicates are all incoherent, then "is an integer slightly more than 104" is incoherent, as is "is an integer slightly less than 106". Hence, the conjunctive predicate "is an integer slightly more than 104 and slightly less than 106" should also be incoherent. But clearly it has a non-empty extension: 105.[5]

A flaw in the reasoning

Close scrutiny of the reasoning in order to find a fallacy may not seem a promising route to resolution of the sorites paradox. It is true that mathematical induction has been the subject of some controversy, both in the context of sorites reasoning and elsewhere;

some have gone so far as to reject it as completely invalid.[6] But the sorites paradox, we have seen, can equally well be formulated in terms of a sequence of arguments of the form *modus ponens*. Surely denying the validity of *modus ponens* can only be seen as a desperate move.

However, invalidity is not the only possible flaw in reasoning. In the chain of *modus ponens* arguments, one might grant that each sub-argument is valid, the initial premise and the conditional premises true, and yet deny that the reasoning is adequate to establish the truth of the final conclusion. Consider a typical sorites argument:

(1) A person who is worth $1,000,000 is rich.
(2) If a person who is worth $1,000,000 is rich, then so is a person worth $1,000,000 − 1.
∴ (3) A person worth $1,000,000 − 1 is rich.
(4) If person worth $1,000,000 − 1 is rich, then so is a person worth $1,000,000 − 2.

.
.
.

∴ (*n*) A person worth $1 is rich.

The objection here is that, given the length of the argument, the degree of confirmation afforded the final conclusion must be low, and it thus cannot be regarded as having been established. For in the first sub-argument, (3) will receive a degree of confirmation equal to that of the conjunction of (1) and (2). Assuming that neither of the two premises has maximal probability of 1, this means that the probability of (3) is less than that of either (1) or (2). Similarly, it can be shown that the probability of (5) is less than that of either (3) or (4). And so on. The essential idea is that, despite valid reasoning, the degree of confirmation will diminish with the length of the argument, and thus it cannot be assumed that step (*n*) has been established.

We need not get entangled in disputes concerning the model of confirmation here.[7] Even if we are entitled to ascribe to (*n*) only a low degree of confirmation on the basis of the sorites argument, the paradox remains. It is no great consolation to be told that the paradoxical argument does not *prove* the truth of (*n*), for the verdict of common sense is that (n) is *false*. But how can this be? If *modus ponens* is valid, and premises (1), (2), (4), (6), (8), ... are true, then (n) must also be true. Granting the validity of *modus ponens*, then, (n) can be false only if at least one of the premises cited is not true. But each such premise seems to be a transparent truth. The paradox presents a conflict of reasons, which appeal to confirmation theory does nothing to dispel.

Degrees of truth

At this point, the only option left is to abandon one of the premises of the sorites paradox. Attempts to defuse the paradox by rejecting a premise have focused on the conditional premises, since the first premise of a sorites argument is generally regarded as beyond question.

It has been argued that within the framework of a many-valued logic, one can find independent reason to reject certain of the conditional premises. Vague predicates admit borderline cases, cases in which it is, in some sense, impossible to know whether the attribution of the predicate results in a true or a false statement. The best explanation of this unavoidable ignorance, it is maintained, is that the statement is *neither* true nor false. Of course, to accept this explanation it is necessary to reject a fundamental principle of classical logic:

> *Bivalence*: Every statement is either true or false.

The theories examined in this and the next section, both of which locate the flaw in the sorites argument in a conditional premise, agree in rejecting bivalence, and recognizing more than two truth-values.

The degrees of truth theory, the topic of this section, maintains that statements about borderline cases, although neither true nor false, have *degrees of truth or falsity*. Borderline cases can often be precisely compared: A may be clearly taller than B, although both are borderline cases of "tall". The statement that A is tall thus seems closer to the truth than the statement that B is tall, or, put differently, to have more truth in it. From this, it seems natural to infer that "A is tall" has a *greater degree of truth* than "B is tall".

So we arrive at the notion of degrees of truth. Since the sorites paradox presents us with a continuum of cases, it seems appropriate to have a continuum of truth-values to assign to statements about borderline cases. The convention standardly adopted is that degrees of truth are represented by the real numbers $0 \le x \le 1$. The value 1 is assigned to strictly true statements, 0 to strictly false statements. Intermediate truth-values are assigned to attributions of vague predicates in borderline cases according to their approximation to the truth. The initial attribution of a vague predicate in a sorites series will have value 1; but values will gradually decline as one proceeds down the series, ultimately reaching 0.

Although degrees of truth theory departs from classical logic in its rejection of bivalence, the system of logic that emerges from the theory is an attempt to minimize the discrepancy. The logical constants are usually treated as truth-functional: the degree of truth of a compound statement is a function of the degree of truth of its components. Where the degree of truth of P is $[P]$, the favoured proposal is:

$$[\sim P] = 1 - [P]$$

$$[P \ \& \ Q] = \min \{[P], [Q]\}$$

$$[P \lor Q] = \max \{[P], [Q]\}$$

$$[P \supset Q] = 1 \text{ when } [Q] \ge [P]$$
$$= 1 - \{[P] - [Q]\} \text{ when } [P] > [Q]$$

The rationale for this last assignment is that since a conditional is clearly false when its antecedent is true and its consequent false, if the antecedent has a higher degree of truth than the consequent, the conditional cannot be entirely true. Where $[P]$ is greater than $[Q]$, the degree of truth of the conditional decreases as the gap between $[P]$ and $[Q]$ grows, since there is greater decay of truth from antecedent to consequent.

How does the degrees of truth theory dispel the sorites paradox? Consider a typical conditional in a sorites argument where the individuals referred to are borderline cases:

$$\Phi x_n \supset \Phi x_{n+1}$$

If the antecedent is true and the consequent false, the conditional is of course false. But in borderline cases, the components of the conditional have a truth-value less than 1 and greater than 0. Further, Φx_n is closer to the truth, has a higher degree of truth, than Φx_{n+1}. The truth-value assigned to the conditional is thus less than 1; that is, the conditional is not true. Hence the sub-argument in which the conditional is a premise is not sound, and the sorites argument is overturned.

Still, the conditional premises in the chain of arguments are, at the least, very nearly true, while the final conclusion is strictly false. How is this possible? Consider the following argument, which deals only with borderline cases:

$$\Phi x_n$$
$$\Phi x_n \supset \Phi x_{n+1}$$
$$\therefore \quad \Phi x_{n+1}$$

Suppose $[\Phi x_n]$ is 0.9, and $[\Phi x_{n+1}]$ is 0.8. Then the value of the first premise is 0.9, as is the value of the second. But the conclusion is just the consequent of the conditional and thus its value is 0.8, which is lower than either of the premises. The conditional of the next sub-argument has an antecedent whose value is 0.8, and a consequent with value of, say, 0.7. So, in the next sub-argument, the conditional premise again has a value of 0.9, but the value of the conclusion is 0.7. In general, the value of the conclusion of each sub-argument will continue to decline as the argument progresses. However, since the antecedent and consequent will presumably continue to differ *by the same amount*, say 0.1, the value of each conditional will be high.

The degrees of truth theory may have the virtue that it can derail the sorites argument, but it is beset with internal difficulties. Of particular concern is the revised system of logic which arises as an offshoot of the theory. Attempting to mirror classical logic, degree theory typically defines a valid argument as one in which the conclusion must have a degree of truth not less than that of the least true premise. The difficulty is that on this account, *modus ponens* is not valid, as the previous paragraph illustrates. Perhaps it would be more perspicuous to say that the conclusion of a valid argument must have a degree of truth no less than the conjunction of its premises.[8] Such a definition, of course, would yield different results from the first only if coupled with an account of conjunction distinct from the one usually proposed by degree theory. But, in any case, the standard treatment of the logical constants in degree theory has its own counter-intuitive implications.

Classical logic takes $P \lor \sim P$ to be a logical truth, an instance of the law of excluded middle. However, in degree theory, if both disjuncts have a value of 0.5 (both concern borderline cases), $[P \lor \sim P] = 0.5$; the disjunction is not true. Similarly, $[P \mathbin{\&} \sim P] = 0.5$; contradictions need not be false. Nor are such counter-intuitive results limited to cases where there is a logical relation between the components. Suppose x, y and z are balls of different colours and sizes and that:

[x is red] = 1	[x is small] = 0.5
[y is red] = 0.5	[y is small] = 0.5
[z is red] = 0.5	[z is small] = 0

Intuitively, the value of "x is red & x is small" should be higher than "y is red & y is small", but on standard degree theory they are the same. Similarly, "y is red $\lor$ y is small" has the same value as "z is red $\lor$ z is small", although intuitively the former should be higher.[9] Possibly degree theory can develop a more credible account by abandoning the assumption that the logical connectives are truth-functional, that is, that the value of a compound is determined by the value of the components.[10] But clearly there is difficult terrain here for degree theory to navigate.

A final source of concern has to do with higher-order vagueness. Imagine a sorites series for the predicate "tall". At one end, the attribution of tallness to the individual has the value 1 (the individual is tall); at some point, moving along the series, such an attribution has a value of less than 1. Where, one might ask, is the last statement with value 1? If there is such a last statement, then there is a sharp boundary between clear cases of being tall and borderline cases. But this seems contrary to our understanding of vague predicates. Just as there is no precise transition point between being tall and not being tall, so, it seems, there is none between clear cases of being tall and borderline cases. Alternatively, it may be that "has truth-value of 1" is itself vague, and there is thus no last statement with value 1. If so, then the meta-language in which the theory is expressed must itself be vague, and yet must be so constructed that sorites reasoning at the meta-level is not sound.

Truth-value gaps: supervaluationism

Adopting the framework of degrees of truth makes it possible to reject some of the conditional premises of the sorites argument. But an alternative route to the same end is provided by the theory of supervaluationism, which posits only truth-value gaps: statements that are neither true nor false.[11]

Vague predicates may be thought of as having positive extension (things to which the term clearly applies), negative extension (things to which the term clearly does not apply), and penumbral extension (things to which the term neither clearly applies nor clearly fails to apply). For the supervaluationist, statements attributing a vague predicate to a penumbral object are neither true nor false. That is, vague predicates permit truth-value gaps; there simply is no fact of the matter as to whether or not a vague predicate applies to an object in its penumbra.

There is, however, a variety of ways to convert a vague predicate into a precise one, only some of which are acceptable. For instance, it might be useful, for certain purposes, to make the term "morning" more precise. One acceptable way to do this might be to take 6am as the cut-off between night and morning. Another might be to have 5am as the transition point. In any context, however, 11am is unacceptable, for it is ruled out by our understanding of the term "morning". A *sharpening* of a predicate, in order to be *acceptable*, must not be precluded by the meaning of the predicate; objects originally in the positive extension must remain so and those originally in the negative extension must remain there. In effect, any acceptable sharpening must draw a line either through the penumbra or on one extreme edge of it.

The key idea of supervaluationism is that a statement with a vague predicate is true just in case it is true in all sharpenings, and false just in case it is false in all sharpenings. ("Sharpening" now has the sense of "acceptable sharpening".) Otherwise the statement is neither true nor false. Attributing a vague predicate to a penumbral object will yield a true statement under some sharpenings, and a false statement under others; consequently such statements are neither true nor false.

What does this logical machinery accomplish? First, it successfully blocks sorites reasoning by disqualifying at least one of the conditional premises. Suppose that x and y are immediately adjacent individuals in a sorites series for "tall", that both are borderline cases, and that x is taller than y. Consider the conditional:

x is tall $\supset y$ is tall

There are sharpenings of "tall" in which both antecedent and consequent are true, as well as sharpenings in which both are false. But there is, in particular, a sharpening that draws the line precisely between x and y, in which case the antecedent is true, the consequent false, and the conditional therefore false. So it is not the case that the conditional is true in all sharpenings; therefore it is not (simply) true. Any sorites argument that uses it as a premise is thus derailed. (Note that we cannot say that the conditional is false either; for, assuming it is a material conditional, we can see from the above that there are sharpenings in which it is true.)

A second virtue of supervaluationism is that, although bivalence is rejected, the law of excluded middle still holds, as does the law of non-contradiction. Where x is in the penumbra for "tall", consider:

x is tall $\vee \sim x$ is tall

For any sharpening, exactly one of the two disjuncts will be true, for either x will be in the expanded positive extension (in which case the first disjunct is true), or x will be in the expanded negative extension (in which case the second disjunct is true). So the disjunction is true in all sharpenings, and is thus simply true. What is peculiar is that the disjunction is true without either disjunct being true: "x is tall" is not true in all sharpenings, and nor is "x is not tall".

Similarly, an instance of the law of non-contradiction

$\sim(x$ is tall $\& \sim x$ is tall$)$

is true in all sharpenings, and is thus true. Thus far, the principles of classical logic are preserved by supervaluationism.

These consequences of the theory are generally considered to be positive, and weigh in its favour. Other implications of supervaluationism, however, are problematic. Consider a statement that seems to assert a sharp boundary between the tall and the not tall:

(S) $(\exists x)$(A person x millimetres in height is tall and a person $x - 1$ millimetres in height is not tall)

For any sharpening, there is a precise division between the tall and the not tall. That boundary determines the value of x that makes the existential claim true in the sharpening. That is, in every sharpening, there is a value of x that makes (S) true. So (S) is true in every sharpening, and is thus simply true.

This is a highly counter-intuitive result. The theory of supervaluations maintains that there is no number that constitutes the cut-off for "tall". (S) is true, according to the theory, even though there is *no particular number* that satisfies the existential generalization. This means that the behaviour of quantifiers in vague contexts constitutes a radical departure from classical logic. Similarly, we saw earlier that, in the logic of supervaluationism, a disjunction may be true even though neither of its disjunctions is true. Given such disparities, it can hardly be maintained that the theory manages to preserve classical logic in its entirety.

Another area of concern is supervaluationism's account of truth. For many, a necessary condition of any such account being acceptable is that it satisfy Tarski's schema (T), according to which biconditionals of the form

"Snow is white" is true if and only if snow is white

are true. However, (T) ensures that any statement that is not true is false, and thus that there are no truth-value gaps. The reasoning that establishes this connection is:[12]

(1) Suppose "Snow is white" is not true.
(2) "Snow is white" is true if and only if snow is
    white.   (T)

(3) ~Snow is white.   from 1 and 2
(4) "~Snow is white" is true if and only if ~snow
     is white.   (T)
(5) "~Snow is white" is true.   from 3 and 4
(6) "Snow is white" is false.   from 5

The supervaluationist, it is argued, has no reason to reject any step in this reasoning. In order to make room for the truth-value gaps that are essential to his theory, he can only reject (T). For many, this means that the supervaluationist conception of truth is fundamentally misguided.

Finally, supervaluationism, like the degrees of truth theory, faces problems with higher-order vagueness. The concept of an admissible sharpening presupposes that there are precise boundaries between the positive extension, penumbra and negative extension of a vague predicate. But this does not seem to fit with our understanding of vague predicates. A statement such as "Tom is clearly tall" may itself be vague. There is unresolvable uncertainty, it seems, about where the penumbral area begins and where it ends. Some borderline cases are clearly borderline. But it may be uncertain whether an individual falls within the positive extension of "tall", or the penumbra. That person would be a borderline clear case, and a borderline borderline case of tallness. If there is indeed such higher-order vagueness, then the notion of an admissible sharpening will itself be vague. This raises the prospect of sorites reasoning breaking out again at the meta-level.

The epistemic theory

To provide a basis for rejecting one of the premises of the sorites argument, the theories of the previous two sections require complex systems of logic and semantics. In contrast, the epistemic theory is simplicity itself. It licenses the rejection of a premise without any need to tamper with classical logic or semantics. The essence of the theory is that vague terms, contrary to standard conception, do indeed have sharp boundaries; and statements containing vague terms are either true or false. The distinctive feature of a borderline case of a vague predicate, what makes it a borderline case, is that we are *unavoidably ignorant* of the truth-value of the ascription of the predicate to the individual. Vagueness is essentially a matter of ignorance.[13]

If vague terms have precise cut-offs, as the epistemic theory maintains, the sorites argument is easily defused. A typical conditional premise in a sorites series has the form:

$$\Phi x_n \supset \Phi x_{n+1}$$

Given that there is a sharp boundary dividing Φs from non-Φs, it is apparent that exactly one of these conditionals is false, and the argument is therefore unsound. For the same reason, if the argument is cast in the form of a mathematical induction, the inductive step will fail.

The chief virtue of the epistemic theory is conservativeness. The principle of bivalence is preserved, which in turn permits the retention of Tarski's schema for truth. Classical logic and semantics stand without need for revision. This is powerful inducement to regard the theory favourably; yet the standard reaction to the epistemic theory ranges from scepticism to hostility.

What prompts this negative response to the epistemic theory? Timothy Williamson distinguishes four considerations as follows.[14]

Meaning and use

The first objection to the theory contends that words have the meaning we give them; the meaning of a term is determined by how we use it. However, if b is a borderline case for a vague term, we typically refrain from either affirming or denying the statement that applies the term to b. How can a sharp cut-off possibly be determined by this pattern of use? How can our use determine the location of a boundary when we do not seem to draw a line? To suppose that there is a fact of the matter in borderline cases is to suppose that the meaning of a vague term draws a line where competent speakers of the language do not.

The first response to this objection on behalf of the epistemic theory equates the thesis that meaning is determined by use with the view that meaning *supervenes* on use. The latter is then understood to say that the same use implies the same meaning, that is, that there can be no difference in meaning without a difference in use. But, the defender of the epistemic theory points out, it is entirely consistent with the theory to suppose that there can be no difference in the meaning of vague terms without a difference in use.

Still, the critic might persist, there is no account offered of *how* the truth-conditions of a vague term may be derived from its use. To this, the counter is that even for precise terms, there is no recipe for calculating the meaning of a term from its use. In particular, neither universal assent nor majority assent guarantees correct application of a term, or truth. The inability to show how the meaning of a vague expression is derived from its use hardly impugns the epistemic theory if there is no known formula, outside the context of vagueness, for extracting meaning from use.

The question remains: does the epistemic theory make it *impossible in principle* to give an account of the connection between meaning and use for vague terms?

Vague properties supervene on precise properties

If two objects are identical with regard to precise properties, then they are identical with regard to vague properties. That is, vague properties supervene on precise properties. Suppose Bernard's height is h, and he is a borderline case of tallness. According to the epistemic theory, either he is tall or he is not tall. This means that being tall (or not tall, as the case may be) is a necessary consequence of having height h. So if I determine Bernard's exact height, I should be able to determine for certain whether or not he is tall. In reality, however, I can know all the precise facts on which the vague fact supervenes without being able to determine the vague fact. I can know Bernard's exact height without knowing whether he is tall. How can this be squared with the epistemic theory?

Williamson's response to this objection is straightforward. Suppose that

(H)   Anyone with height h is tall

is a necessary truth given the meaning of "tall". Still, the fact that (H) is necessary does not guarantee that it can be known a priori. Williamson maintains, as he must, that (H) is unknowable by us all; this is what explains how I can know that Bernard's height is h without being able to determine whether or not he is tall.

But this, of course, raises a crucial question: how can the epistemic theory possibly provide a convincing explanation of why simple necessary statements such as (H) should be unknowable by us all?

We cannot know what we mean

The objection here is that since the meaning of "tall" determines a sharp cut-off, and since I cannot locate that cut-off, I use the term without completely understanding it. Worse, no one in the community of competent speakers fully understands the term. What we mean goes beyond what we can know.

Here the answer to the previous objection bears repeating: there is no guarantee that (H) can be known, even if it is a necessary truth. Williamson also points out that to know what a word means is not to know a complete set of necessary truths. Rather, to understand the meaning of a term is to participate in a practice that does determine the meaning, that is, to acquire a set of dispositions that at least roughly matches those of other competent speakers.

Again, the question remains: why it is that (H) is unknowable by us all? This is clearly a critical issue for the epistemic theory.

Why are we ignorant of the cut-off?

What blocks the progress of the sorites argument is the existence of an unknowable but true statement giving the location of a sharp boundary. Where $x_1, \ldots, x_n$ is a sorites series for a predicate F, there is a true but unknowable statement of the form:

$$Fx_i \ \& \ \sim Fx_{i+1}$$

But what exactly is the obstacle to our knowing the relevant conjunctions given that they are true? In general, why it is impossible to have knowledge of borderline cases? Unless we can find an *epistemic account* of why such statements are unknowable, it may be more plausible to suppose simply that they have no truth-value.

Responding to the challenge, Williamson constructs an analysis within the framework of a margin for error. In order for a given true belief to qualify as knowledge, he maintains, it must be reliable; insofar as a belief's being true is just a matter of luck or accident, it cannot have the status of knowledge. In the particular context of vagueness, reliability requires a *margin for error*. Consider the sorites series $x_1, \ldots, x_n$ for the predicate F. You have a margin for error in believing Fx_i only if all individuals sufficiently close to x_i are also F. For suppose that you truly believe Fx_i, and that Fx_{i+1} is false. Then if things had been *very slightly different*, Fx_i might also have been false, and yet you might still have believed Fx_i. For instance, suppose you truly believe that Sam is not bald, Sam has m hairs on his head, and baldness begins with $m - 1$ hairs. Given that you cannot perceptually distinguish between m and $m - 1$ hairs, you might have believed that Sam was not bald even if he had one fewer hairs. So if things had been slightly different, your belief would have been false. Your belief is thus not reliable; your getting it right is a matter of luck.[15]

In the context of vagueness, knowledge requires a margin for error; and there is a margin for error in believing Fx_i only if both Fx_{i-1} and Fx_{i+1} are true. So we have:

(M)   If it is known that Fx_i, then Fx_{i+1}.

This principle provides the basis for explaining our ignorance of sharp cut-offs. To know the location of a boundary is to know a statement of the form:

$$Fx_i \ \& \ {\sim}Fx_{i+1}$$

Clearly, knowledge of a conjunction requires knowledge of each conjunct. By (M), knowledge of the first conjunct implies the truth of Fx_{i+1}. So if the first conjunct is known, then it is impossible to know ${\sim}Fx_{i+1}$, for the simple reason that it is false.[16]

Williamson's derivation of the margin for error principle for vagueness is an adroit and perceptive application of the traditional view that knowledge cannot be a matter of luck, and provides the basis for a credible explanation of our ignorance of sharp boundaries. But the victory is at best partial. For not only is it impossible to have knowledge of the location of a cut-off point, but it is also impossible to have *reasonable belief* on the matter. *Any* belief concerning exactly what height is necessary and sufficient to make a person tall is surely unreasonable. There is more here for the epistemic theory to explain than just lack of knowledge.

The impossibility of reasonable belief concerning the location of a cut-off point appears to present a more intractable problem for the epistemic theory. For one thing, reasonable belief that P, unlike knowledge, has no immediate implications for the truth of P. It should also be noted that justified belief can be right as a matter of luck or accident. Indeed, this is the basis of the Gettier counter-examples to the traditional definition of knowledge. Suppose Sam is justified in believing both:

(S)   Smith will be promoted to associate vice-president.
(T)   Smith has ten coins in his pocket.

From this Sam infers, and is therefore also justified in believing:

(J)   The man who will get the job of associate vice-president has ten coins in his pocket.

But (J) is true, let us suppose, because Brown, whom Sam does not know, will get the job and, as it happens, Brown has ten coins in his pocket. This is just the sort of story that persuades us that knowledge cannot be a matter of luck. The judgement that Sam is warranted in believing (J), on the other hand, is unaffected by our knowledge that it is Brown who will get the promotion. Once it is granted that justified belief may be false, it seems clear that it can also be true as a matter of accident or luck.

Williamson concedes that reasonable belief does not satisfy a margin for error principle. In general, there is a margin for error for a belief P in situation s if P is true in all cases sufficiently similar to s. If reasonable belief that P in situation s required a margin for error, then, since s is sufficiently similar to itself, P would have to be true in s. But it is clear that reasonable belief can be false. How, then, can the epistemic theory account for the impossibility of reasonable belief about the location of boundaries for vague predicates? In tackling this issue, Williamson provides the outline of an intricate analysis that rests on an *externalist* theory of evidence and justification. There are two central theses. First, one's evidence is restricted to what one knows, and thus to true statements.

Secondly, a belief P is justified just in case P is highly probable relative to the evidence. Suppose now that you are in situation s, and you know just those statements that leave a margin for error d. Then, says Williamson, what you know is that your situation is within d of s. So the belief P will be highly probable conditional on what you know if P is true in *most* situations within d of s.[17] From this, Williamson derives:

(R) A belief is reasonable in a situation s just in case it is true in most worlds within d of s.[18]

This principle forges the critical link between justification and truth, thus providing the key for Williamson's explanation of the impossibility of reasonable belief concerning sharp boundaries. Briefly, the analysis runs as follows. Consider the belief that having height h is sufficient for being tall, but a height of $h - 1$ is not. Suppose that you are in situation s, and that h and $h - 1$ are indistinguishable to the unaided eye. Since there is only a minute, imperceptible difference between h and $h - 1$, in some of the worlds closest to s, $h - 1$ is the minimum height which qualifies a person as tall; in some it is $h + 1$; and so on. Williamson goes on to argue that the statement that height h makes a person tall, while $h - 1$ does not, cannot be true in most worlds sufficiently close to s. Given (R), it follows that the belief in a cut-off point cannot be justified, even if true.

The argument is intricate, but at its core is the externalist conception of evidence and justification, which limits evidence to the known, and thus to the true. The implications of this externalism, however, run counter to our strong intuitions in many situations, including the Gettier scenario just outlined. There it seems clear that Sam is justified in believing (J), despite the fact that he infers (J) from (S) and (T), and (S) is false. It should also be noted that the denial that (J) is reasonable conflicts with the deductive closure principle for justified belief. Nevertheless, Williamson must deny that it is reasonable for Sam to believe (J), since (S) cannot count as evidence given that it is false. He has the company of those commentators who have taken this line as a way of evading the Gettier counter-examples, and protecting the traditional definition of knowledge.

Let us try to clarify the issues here by reflecting on what is to be understood by "justified belief". First, it is clearly epistemic justification that is at issue here. Secondly, justification, as thus understood, is closely linked to rationality. If you believe only what you are justified in believing, you cannot be charged with irrationality *qua* believer; you have done all that can be demanded of you. Put differently, to be justified in your beliefs means that you are epistemically faultless: not biased, not dogmatic or close-minded, not credulous, not gullible, not overly sceptical or incredulous. In short, to be justified in your beliefs is to be immune to criticism on purely intellectual grounds, on grounds of any type of irrationality.

Call this "subjective justification". It is possible that there are other concepts of justification that play a different role. Some (not Williamson) would maintain that there is a concept of justification that suffices to convert true belief to knowledge. For the sake of argument, let us make a concession to Williamson and grant that there is *a* concept of justification that is externalist, and that (J) is accordingly not justified in that sense. Still, it surely must be acknowledged that the belief in (J) has *some positive epistemic status*: surely (J) is subjectively justified. Sam is not irrational in believing (J), he is not at fault *qua* believer. Subjective justification for *P* evidently does not impose truth conditions either on *P*, or on the evidence for *P*.

To return to vagueness and the epistemic theory: There is a type of justification, subjective justification, which (J) has, but which any belief concerning a cut-off point for a vague predicate lacks. Any belief concerning the exact number of grains of sand necessary and sufficient for there to be a heap seems irrational, or subjectively unjustified. What Williamson's theory of vagueness has yet to come to grips with is how the impossibility of subjectively justified beliefs concerning borderline cases may be explained. This may well prove an intractable problem for the epistemic theory.

We have canvassed the most prominent theories of vagueness, none of which seems, at the moment, to provide a wholly satisfactory solution to the sorites paradox. Yet the sorites may well be the most troubling of the paradoxes studied in this work. Our everyday language and concepts are riddled with vagueness; if the argument stands, most of our ordinary concepts and beliefs are incoherent. But the prospect of yielding our most fundamental beliefs to the inexorable steps of the sorites is surely unthinkable.

Appendix

Here are some further paradoxes. Some are versions of paradoxes already considered; others are unrelated to what has gone before.

The racetrack paradox
Suppose Achilles is trying to break the record for the 100m dash. Not only will he not succeed, but he will not even finish the course. To complete the course, he first has to run half the track, or 50m; then he has to complete half the remaining distance, or 25m; then he has to complete half the remaining distance, or 12½m; and so on. First he is half-way there, then three-quarters of the way, then seven-eighths of the way. But however many of these segments of the track he completes, there will always be some distance left to the finish line. Thus, Achilles will never complete the course.

The racetrack, and the Achilles and the tortoise paradox from Chapter 1, are two of the paradoxes attributed to Zeno of Elea (*c.* 470BC). See W. Salmon, *Zeno's Paradoxes* (Indianapolis: Bobbs-Merrill, 1970).

Grelling's paradox
Some words, it seems, apply to themselves. For instance, the word "short" is short and the word "polysyllabic" is polysyllabic. Words that have this feature are called "autological". Many words, however, do not apply to themselves. The word "long" is not long and the word "monosyllabic" is not monosyllabic. Call such words "heterological".

Is "heterological" heterological? If it is, then it does not apply to itself, and is thus not heterological. If it is not, then it does not apply to itself, and is thus heterological. So "heterological" is heterological if and only if it is not.

See W. V. Quine, *The Ways of Paradox and Other Essays* (New York: Random House, 1966).

Russell's paradox

Most familiar classes are not members of themselves. The class of all pianos is not a member of itself, because a class is not a piano. Similarly, the class of all classes with exactly one member presumably has more than one member, and is thus not a member of itself. Some classes, on the other hand, are members of themselves; for instance, the class of all classes with more than three members surely has more than three members, and is thus a member of itself.

Now consider the class of all classes that are not members of themselves. Is this class a member of itself? If it is, then it is not; and if it is not, then it is. So the class of all classes is a member of itself if and only if it is not.

This paradox first appeared in B. Russell, *The Principles of Mathematics* (Cambridge: Cambridge University Press, 1903). For an accessible account of this and related paradoxes, see I. Copi, *The Theory of Logical Types* (London: Routledge & Kegan Paul, 1971).

The paradox of Pseudo-Scotus

Argument I.　　(i)　Argument I is valid.
　　　　　　　　(ii)　Therefore, squares have five sides.

Suppose premise (i) is true. Then the argument is valid, and since the premise is true, the conclusion must also be true. Suppose, on the other hand, that the premise is not true, and the argument is therefore invalid. If the argument is invalid, then it is possible for the premise to be true and the conclusion false. But this is not possible, as was shown above. So the argument is valid, and the premise is true; consequently, the conclusion must also be true.

This paradox seems closely related to the liar paradox (described in Chapter 2).

The toxin puzzle

Suppose a rational person, Indy, has been offered $1,000,000 to intend at midnight tonight to drink a vial of toxin tomorrow. Drinking the toxin will make him ill, but only for a day. The reward, in any case, is for having the intention at midnight to drink the toxin the next day. It seems it would be foolish to actually drink the toxin tomorrow, since the reward is determined by whatever already happened at midnight. So Indy knows he won't drink the toxin tomorrow. But it is impossible to intend to do something you know that you will not do. It seems, then, that Indy, a fully rational person, cannot take advantage of this wonderful offer and win the $1,000,000.

The paradox was first stated in G. Kavka, "The Toxin Puzzle", *Analysis* **43** (1983), 33–6, and may have some bearing on the paradox of deterrence described below.

The two-envelope paradox

There are two sealed envelopes, *A* and *B*. Each contains a sum of money, and one has exactly twice as much as the other. You have chosen *A*, but at the last minute you are offered a chance to switch envelopes. Should you switch? If x is the amount of money in *A*, then either there is $0.5x$ in *B*, or there is $2x$ in *B*. Both possibilities are equally likely. So the expected utility of switching is:

$$(0.5)(0.5x) + (0.5)(2x) = 1.25x$$

On the other hand, the expected utility of staying with *A* is just x. So it seems that rationality requires that you accept the offer to switch envelopes. But if you were to switch to *B*, you could use the same sort of argument to show that you should switch back to *A*. Surely it is no more rationally required to switch than it is to choose a particular envelope at the outset.

See J. Broome, "The Two Envelope Paradox", *Analysis* **55** (1995), 6–11.

The paradox of preference

It seems a highly plausible and intuitive principle that the preferences of a rational person are always transitive. That is, if a person prefers A to B, and also prefers B to C, and she is fully rational, then she prefers A to C. But suppose you are contemplating marriage. You prefer to marry Albert rather than Bob, for you find Albert much more interesting than Bob. You also prefer to marry Bob rather than Carl, for Bob is much more interesting than Carl. In fact, however, given a choice between marrying Albert and Carl, you would choose Carl, who is much less interesting, but also vastly richer. You may be mercenary, but are you also irrational?

The investment paradox

Aunt Maud passes a hat to her nephews, Albert, Bob and Carl. She invites them each to make a contribution; she will then double the sum in the hat and distribute the profits equally among the three. So, for instance, if each contributes $100, each will receive $200 – a wonderful opportunity. But Albert, a highly rational person, reasons as follows. In the end, I receive only 2/3 of my original investment, plus 2/3 of whatever else is in the hat. I would be better off, then, to put nothing in the hat and just take my share of whatever else is there. Of course, if the other nephews are equally rational, they will reason similarly. So if all the nephews are rational, nothing will be put in the hat, no one will make any money, and the fabulous opportunity will prove worthless.

See M. Hollis, "Penny Pinching and Backward Induction", *Journal of Philosophy* **88** (1981), 437–88, for an interesting discussion of this and related paradoxes.

The mañana paradox

You need to visit the dentist, and should do so soon. Of course, one day more or less won't make any difference. So seeing the dentist tomorrow would be just as good as seeing him today. But if it is acceptable to see the dentist tomorrow, then it is surely all right to see him the day after tomorrow, since a difference of one day is insignificant. And so on. Your visit to the dentist can be postponed indefinitely.

See D. Edgington, "Validity, Uncertainty and Vagueness", *Analysis* **52** (1992), 193–204.

Wang's paradox

(i)   1 is a small integer.
(ii) If n is a small integer, then so is $n + 1$.
(iii) Therefore every integer is a small integer.

See M. Dummett, "Wang's Paradox", *Synthese* **30** (1975), 301–24.

The unpredictable numbers paradox

Two game show contestants are each asked to think of a positive integer between 1 and 100, and to inform the host privately of the number they chose. The host then announces, "You have each chosen a different positive integer between 1 and 100, and neither of you can tell whose number is greater." One of the contestants, *A*, ponders the implications of this announcement. If *B* had chosen 1, *A* reasons, he would know that I had chosen the greater number. So *B* did not choose 1. Similarly, he can determine that I did not choose 1. But now if *B* had chosen 2, he would know that I had chosen the greater number. So *B* did not choose 2. Similarly, he can determine that I did not choose 2. And so on. *A* concludes that what the host said cannot be true.

This paradox was first presented in M. Hollis, "A Paradoxical Train of Thought", *Analysis* **44** (1984), 205–6.

The paradox of the ravens

Confirmation theory deals with the question of what constitutes evidence or support for a statement. A principle that has been widely accepted as fundamental to confirmation theory is Nicod's criterion: A generalization is confirmed by any positive instance. According to this principle, "All *A* are *B*" is confirmed, or supported, by "This *A* is *B*". So the generalization "All ravens are black" is supported by finding a particular raven that is black. Further, it seems an unquestionable principle of confirmation theory that whatever confirms a statement

S also confirms any logically equivalent statement *S'*. Now "All ravens are black" (*R*) is logically equivalent, by contraposition, to "All non-black things are non-ravens" (*R'*). So finding a positive instance of *R'* should provide confirmation for *R*. But this means that finding a white shoe (a non-black non-raven) confirms the hypothesis that all ravens are black. And not only is a white shoe evidence that all ravens are black, but it is also evidence that all ravens are blue, since a white shoe is a non-blue non-raven.

Also known as the paradoxes of confirmation, these highly counter-intuitive consequences were discovered by Carl Hempel and can be found in his "Studies in the Logic of Confirmation", *Mind* 54 (1945), 1–26, 97–121.

The paradox of omniscience and freedom

Suppose there is an omniscient God. Then God knows all truths, past, present and future. In particular, if I am going to do *x* at *t*, then God knows this. But if God knows that I am going to do *x* at *t*, then I must do it; I cannot do otherwise. So if there is an omniscient God, no one ever acts freely.

The paradox of the stone

To say that a being is omnipotent is to say that he is all-powerful, that he can do anything. Suppose there is an omnipotent God. Now consider the question "Can God make a stone heavier than He can lift?" If God cannot make a stone heavier than He can lift, then there is one thing He cannot do, and He is therefore not omnipotent. On the other hand, if God can create a stone heavier than He can lift, then there is one thing He cannot do, namely, lift that stone, and He is therefore not omnipotent. So God cannot be omnipotent. More generally, it is impossible that there should be an omnipotent being.

See C. W. Savage, "The Paradox of the Stone", *Philosophical Review* 76 (1967), 74–9.

Forrester's paradox

It is a given that Sam is going to murder his rival Archie. But if he is going to do so, then he ought at least to do so without incurring unnecessary suffering for Archie. That is, if he is going to murder Archie, then he ought to murder him gently. It follows by *modus ponens* that Sam ought to murder Archie gently. Further, it seems unquestionable that if you ought to do *X*, then you ought to do whatever is necessary in order to perform *X*. But Sam cannot murder gently without murdering. It follows that Sam ought to commit murder.

See J. W. Forrester, "Gentle Murder and the Adverbial Samaritan", *Journal of Philosophy* 81 (1984), 193–7, where the paradox first appeared.

A paradox of deterrence

You hope to dissuade your enemy from launching a nuclear strike against you by maintaining an arsenal of weapons, and threatening devastating retaliation in the event of a strike. But to carry out the threat, to respond in kind, would be morally inconceivable, in your view; for your country would be doomed in any case, and you would be killing or seriously harming millions of innocent people to no good end. The horror of the first strike would in no way warrant further devastation of those who are not responsible. For this reason, you are not in fact prepared to retaliate. Unfortunately, you believe that your enemy can discern whether you are bluffing; he will find your threat credible only if you sincerely intend to carry it out. Morally, it seems clear that you ought not to retaliate; and from this it apparently follows that you ought not to intend to retaliate. Thus, if you are perfectly moral, you will not do what is necessary and sufficient to prevent a great evil: a nuclear attack on your country. You will not intend to retaliate, despite the fact that having the intention would produce by far the most desirable outcome, and would harm no one.

This paradox is presented in G. Kavka, "Some Paradoxes of Deterrence", *Journal of Philosophy* 75 (1978), 285–302.

The moral luck paradox

The moral value of our character and our actions is not a matter of luck. In particular, we cannot be morally assessed, or held morally responsible, for that which is not fully under our control. These seem to be strong intuitions shared by all. But consider. Suppose in a fit of jealous rage, you fire your gun at the man who has stolen your love, intending perhaps only to frighten him, or to cause a superficial wound. But if he moves in just the right way at the critical moment, or if your aim is bad, the bullet may lodge in his heart and kill him. In such a case, you are morally responsible for his death, and judged severely. On the other hand, if you miss him entirely, the judgement is softened: you have been reckless, or indifferent to the welfare of others. But once you fire the gun, the consequences that follow are not within your control; they are entirely a matter of luck. Moral value, in such a case, seems to be a matter of luck in the way your actions turn out.

Moral evaluations also seem contingent on the circumstances and choices one faces. An officer in a concentration camp in Nazi Germany may commit vile acts, and deserve the harshest condemnation. However a teacher, living in Canada, may be relatively guilt free, even though, placed in the same circumstances as the soldier, he would behave just as badly. Again, the difference in moral status seems attributable to luck: luck in the choices and opportunities one encounters.

See T. Nagel, "Moral Luck", in *Mortal Questions*, T. Nagel, 24–38 (Cambridge: Cambridge University Press, 1976), for an excellent discussion of these issues.

Notes

Chapter 1: The nature of paradox

1. The issue here is what philosophers refer to as "quantitative identity". If *A* and *B* are quantitatively identical, then they are one and the same thing. The Morning Star, for example, is quantitatively identical to the Evening Star; it is the same heavenly body. There is another notion of identity that is called "qualitative identity": two suitcases (yours and mine) are qualitatively identical if they are exactly similar.

2. *The Globe and Mail*, 11 January 2000, A5.

3. W. V. Quine, "The Ways of Paradox", in *The Ways of Paradox and Other Essays*, W. V. Quine, 3–10 (New York: Random House, 1966), 3.

4. The example is found in S. Barker, *Induction and Hypothesis* (Ithaca, NY: Cornell University Press, 1957), 76.

5. Nicholas Rescher disagrees with this assessment. He takes examples like that of the Texan/philosopher to be paradoxes. Similarly, situations in which different witnesses give conflicting evidence constitute paradoxes in his eyes, as do cases of sensory illusion (a stick immersed in water looks bent, but feels straight). Whenever our sources of evidence conflict, according to Rescher, there is a paradox. In my view, taking every conflict of evidence to be a paradox represents a considerable departure from the standard philosophical conception of paradox. The notion I am trying to elucidate is clearly much narrower than Rescher's conception of paradox. See his *Paradoxes: Their Roots, Range and Resolution* (Chicago, IL: Open Court, 2001).

6. This point is made in D. Lewis, "Truth in Fiction", *American Philosophical Quarterly* 15 (1978), 37–46; the article provides an excellent discussion of fictional truth.

7. It has to be said that it is not entirely clear how significant this discrepancy is, for it is by no means apparent that counting such a statement as true in the taxi-cab paradox will have any impact on its resolution.

8. See, for example, the discussion of I. Levi, "Newcomb's Many Problems", *Theory and Decision* 6 (1975), 161–75, in Chapter 6, 117–18.

9. If, however, the appropriate general principles are not to be taken as necessary truths in the sense of being true in all possible worlds, then further specification of allowable background information is needed. One might wish, for instance, to allow as background information all a priori truths.

10. I borrow this terminology from Quine, "The Ways of Paradox", although my definition is not exactly the same as his. For one thing, Quine does not draw the distinction between narrative-paradoxes and paradoxes that are not based on a story, and thus does not recognize the need for a special sense of "true".

Chapter 2: Paradox and contradiction

1. In this chapter, "contradiction" refers only to explicit contradictions: statements of the form "*A* & ~*A*".

2. These diagrams can be found in G. Priest, "What Is So Bad About Contradictions?", *Journal of Philosophy* 95 (1998), 410–26.

3. An interesting critique of Priest's solution to the paradox is found in A. Everett, "A Dilemma for Priest's Dialetheism", *Australasian Journal of Philosophy* 74 (1996), 657–68.

4. G. Priest, *In Contradiction* (Dordrecht: Nijhoff, 1987), 122.

5. Interesting discussions pertaining to rejection are found in: T. Smiley, "Can Contradictions Be True?", *Supplementary Proceedings of the Aristotelian Society* 67 (1993), 17–33; and E. D. Mares, "Even Dialetheists Should Hate Contradictions", *Australasian Journal of Philosophy* 78 (2000), 503–16.

6. The reader may wish to think about how it can be that the tautologies of classical logic are all preserved in Priest's system, while some of the valid arguments of classical truth-functional logic are not.

7. G. Priest, "The Logic of Paradox", *Journal of Philosophical Logic* 8 (1979), 231.

8. Priest, "What Is So Bad About Contradictions?", 415.

9. *Ibid.*, 419.

10. G. Priest, "Perceiving Contradictions", *Australasian Journal of Philosophy* 77 (1999), 439–46. For an insightful critique, see J. C. Beall, "Is the Observable World Consistent?", *Australasian Journal of Philosophy* 78 (2000), 113–18.

11. Priest, *In Contradiction*, 144, and "What Is So Bad About Contradictions?", 424.

12. There is a peculiar pattern of argument here. Priest argues here from the (*past*) success of disjunctive syllogism to the low frequency of true contradictions, but then also uses the latter as the basis for his claim that disjunctive syllogism is *generally* successful. Would it not be equally plausible to argue directly from the past success of disjunctive syllogism to its general success?

13. Priest takes this line in *In Contradiction*, 118.

14. Given the above, possible (non-exclusive) truth-values of a statement include *tb*, *tf* and *fb*, as well as *t*, *b* and *f*. (The value *tbf* is equivalent to *tf*.) Although the truth-tables offered earlier should perhaps be expanded, this seems a

fairly straightforward matter. The truth-value of a conjunction with first conjunct *tb* and second conjunct *fb*, for instance, is presumably *fb*.

Chapter 3: Believing in surprises: the prediction paradox

1. M. Scriven, "Paradoxical Announcements", *Mind* 60 (1951), 403.
2. Parts of this chapter are taken from my "The Prediction Paradox Resolved", *Philosophical Studies* 44 (1983), 225–33, with kind permission of Kluwer Academic Publishers; and from "The Prediction Paradox: Resolving Recalcitrant Variations", *Australasian Journal of Philosophy* 64 (1986), 181–9, with permission of Oxford University Press.
3. See R. Sorensen, *Blindspots* (Oxford: Clarendon Press, 1988), 253.
4. Two "solutions" that first require us to grant that the argument is acceptable are: J. M. Chapman & R. J. Butler, "On Quine's 'So-Called Paradox'", *Mind* 74 (1965), 424–5; and R. L. Kirkham, "Paradoxes and a Surprise Exam", *Philosophia* 21 (1991), 31–52.
5. This variation is due to R. Sorensen, "Recalcitrant Variations of the Prediction Paradox", *Australasian Journal of Philosophy* 60 (1982), 355–62.
6. For instance, the analysis of C. Wright & A. Sudbury, "The Paradox of the Unexpected Examination", *Australasian Journal of Philosophy* 55 (1977), 41–58, which focuses on the retention of beliefs over time, is thus shown to be incomplete.
7. See A. Lyon, "The Prediction Paradox", *Mind* 68 (1959), 510–17.
8. See A. J. Ayer, "On a Supposed Antinomy", *Mind* 82 (1973), 125–6.
9. W. V. Quine, "On A So-Called Paradox", *Mind* 62 (1953), 65–8.
10. R. Shaw, "The Paradox of the Unexpected Examination", *Mind* 67 (1958), 382–4.
11. The (KK) thesis is usually discussed in the context of a formalized version of the argument. I shall try to present the issues informally, both to minimize the logical demands on the reader and to ensure that we remain close to the original intuitive argument.
12. Notice that we are here using a time-specific version of (KK): If *S* knows at *t* that *P*, then *S* knows at *t* that *S* knows at *t* that *P*.
13. J. McLelland & C. Chihara, "The Surprise Examination Paradox", *Journal of Philosophical Logic* 4 (1975), 71–89.
14. G. Harman, *Thought* (Princeton, NJ: Princeton University Press, 1973), 148.
15. See T. Williamson, "Inexact Knowledge", *Mind* 101 (1992), 217–42. The change in cognitive standpoint may involve a change in subject, or a change in time.
16. This variation can be found in Sorensen, "Recalcitrant Variations of the Prediction Paradox".
17. Others whose work falls in this general category include: R. Binkley, "The Surprise Examination in Modal Logic", *Journal of Philosophy* 65 (1968), 127–35; Wright & Sudbury, "The Paradox of the Unexpected Examination"; and R. A. Sorensen, "Conditional Blindspots and the Knowledge Squeeze:

A Solution to the Prediction Paradox", *Australasian Journal of Philosophy* **62** (1984), 126–35. The philosophical underpinnings, in each case, however, are quite different, as are the epistemological consequences.

18. Note that if one of the premises *Ai* proves to be false, then the claim that *S* is justified in believing *Ai* should also be regarded as false.

19. Some have misinterpreted my analysis in this way. See, for example, R. Weintraub, "Practical Solutions to the Surprise-Examination Paradox", *Ratio* **8** (1995), 161–9.

20. The analysis has been criticized on this point. C. Janaway, "Knowing about Surprises: A Supposed Antinomy Revisited", *Mind* **98** (1989), 391–409, takes this assumption to be crucial to my analysis, and rejects it on that basis. However, he overlooks the fact that the solution can also apply to cases of unequal evidence. Nothing hinges on whether there is equal evidence for (A) and (B) in the original version of the paradox.

21. Sorensen has one other variation, the paradox of the undiscoverable position, which also falls to this solution in essentially the same way. See my "The Prediction Paradox".

22. This argument has been advanced by C. Chihara, "Olin, Quine, and the Surprise Examination", *Philosophical Studies* **45** (1985), 191–9.

23. Most notably, by J. Cargile, "The Surprise Test Paradox", *Journal of Philosophy* **64** (1967), 550–63 and by E. Sober, "To Give a Surprise Exam, Use Game Theory", *Synthese* **115** (1998), 355–73.

Chapter 4: The preface paradox, fallibility and probability

1. Portions of this chapter are drawn from my "The Fallibility Argument for Inconsistency", *Philosophical Studies* **56** (1989), 95–102, with kind permission of Kluwer Academic Publishers; and from "Consistency, Fallibility and Probability", *The Logica 99 Yearbook* (Prague: Filosofia, 2000), 140–8. Classical logic (as opposed to dialetheism) is presupposed throughout the discussion.

2. Philosophers who subscribe to the traditional view include: R. Chisholm, *Theory of Knowledge*, 3rd edn (Englewood Cliffs, NJ: Prentice Hall, 1989); K. Lehrer, *Knowledge* (Oxford: Oxford University Press, 1974); and J. L. Pollock, "Epistemology and Probability", *Synthese* **55** (1983), 231–52.

3. Some of those who take the radical position are: R. Foley, *The Theory of Epistemic Rationality* (Cambridge, MA: Harvard University Press, 1987); P. Klein, "The Virtues of Inconsistency", *The Monist* **68** (1985), 105–35; and P. Moser, *Epistemic Justification* (Dordrecht: D. Reidel, 1985).

4. The paradox was first formulated by D. C. Makinson, "The Paradox of the Preface", *Analysis* **25** (1965), 205–7.

5. See A. R. Lacey, "The Paradox of the Preface", *Mind* **79** (1970), 614–15.

6. S. Ryan, "The Preface Paradox", *Philosophical Studies* **64** (1991), 293–307. This suggestion is also advanced by S. Evnine, "Believing Conjunctions", *Synthese* **118** (1999), 201–27.

7. Klein, "The Virtues of Inconsistency".
8. This apparent implication of our fallibility has been noted and taken up by several philosophers, including: R. Foley, "Justified Inconsistent Beliefs", *American Philosophical Quarterly* 16 (1979), 247–57; C. Ginet, *Knowledge, Perception and Memory* (Dordrecht: D. Reidel, 1975); and Klein, "The Virtues of Inconsistency".
9. There are possible problems arising from self-reference here. If the body of beliefs referred to in (2) included (2) itself, then (2) could not be false (if it were false, it would be true). Further, if all my beliefs other than (2) were true, then (2) would be true if and only if it were false. But there is paradox enough here without having to worry about self-reference. My way of avoiding these problems is to use the phrase "the body of *other* reasonable beliefs", where this phrase is understood to exclude each statement in the argument. In the preface paradox, these issues were circumvented by speaking of the statements in the *body* of the book.
10. I have stated the argument in the simplest possible form for ease of exposition. A more explicit account would have each of the four steps prefaced with "*T* is justified in believing . . .", and would also specify *T*'s epistemic attributes and the relevant epistemic principles.
11. See, for example, the authors cited in note 8. In the preface paradox, the corresponding assumption is that the author can cite every statement in her book – which is also unrealistic.
12. This argument could of course be developed between $R_1, \ldots, R_n$ and any other set that contains, for each i, exactly one of R_i or its negation. Note that the issue is not whether there is good reason to believe there is error in the set, but whether the *tea-leaf reading* provides good reason for this belief.
13. I ignore here possible qualifications that are irrelevant to the argument, for instance, the sort of qualification suggested by the treatment of the prediction paradox in Chapter 3.
14. A statement p is probabilistically independent of q if q is neither positively nor negatively relevant to p; that is, if q neither confirms nor disconfirms p. "Probability" is to be understood as "epistemic probability" throughout.
15. That is, each statement is independent of every other statement, and each is also independent of a conjunction of any of others.
16. Examples of this kind of argument can be found in: R. Campbell, "Can Inconsistency be Reasonable?", *Canadian Journal of Philosophy* 11 (1981), 245–70; K. Lehrer, "Reason and Inconsistency", in *Analysis and Metaphysics*, K. Lehrer (ed.), 57–74 (Dordrecht: D. Reidel, 1975); and J. N. Williams, "Inconsistency and Contradiction", *Mind* 90 (1981), 600–602.
17. Unfortunately, the prospects for finding a set of necessary and sufficient conditions for the product of an indefinitely large sequence of x_is ($0 < x < 1$) approaching 0, conditions that are also easily applicable to the probability of a conjunction, are not promising. There is, however, a sufficient condition that can be straightforwardly applied:

> If there is a number h ($h < 1$) such that each $x_i \leq h$, then the product of an indefinitely large sequence of x_is approaches 0.

One way to satisfy this condition is to have all the x_is equal. (I thank George O'Brien and Philip Olin for clarifying the mathematics of the situation.)

18. Let me briefly recap Goodman's argument. Goodman introduces the predicate "grue", which is defined as follows. An item is grue if it is examined before t and is green, or is not examined before t and is blue. Suppose it is now t and many emeralds have been examined, found to be green, and thus to be grue. Does this fact provide any confirmation, any positive evidence, that all emeralds are grue? Hardly. For if it did, then we would have evidence that the *emeralds examined after* t *are also grue*, and thus are blue. But in fact, our available data confirm that emeralds examined after t are green. So "grue" is not a projectible predicate: finding an emerald to be grue does not provide any confirmation that the next emerald is grue, nor that all are grue. See N. Goodman, *Fact, Fiction and Forecast* (New York: Bobbs-Merrill, 1965), Chapter 3.

19. A conversation with Haim Gaifman, concerning an earlier version of the analogous argument, was helpful with regard to the issue of independence.

20. See, for example, J. L. Pollock, "Epistemology and Probability" and R. Chisholm, *Perceiving: A Philosophical Study* (Ithaca, NY: Cornell University Press, 1957).

21. This is in accord with L. Jonathan Cohen's treatment of what he calls "inductive probability"; Cohen denies that the probability of a statement and its negation are complementary. See his *The Probable and the Provable* (Oxford: Clarendon Press, 1977).

22. Note that the assumption of a connection between degree of confirmation and warranted belief has not been questioned in this section. Without it, no conclusions concerning warranted belief will follow, either in the EPA or in argument (I). But (I) will still show that, in the case described, there is *strong confirmation* that there is either a cure for AIDS or a cure for cancer. And this is a clearly intolerable result. It can be avoided, it appears, only by rejecting the fit between degree of confirmation and the calculus.

Chapter 5: The lottery paradox

1. The paradox was first stated in H. Kyburg, *Probability and the Logic of Rational Belief* (Middleton, CT: Wesleyan University Press, 1961), 167.

2. Dana K. Nelkin presents a "knowledge version" of the lottery paradox as well as a version in terms of rational belief. But the knowledge version is easily dispatched: we cannot *know* each T_i for the simple reason that only true statements can be known, and one of the T_is is false. See Nelkin, "The Lottery Paradox, Knowledge, and Rationality", *The Philosophical Review* 109 (2002), 373–409.

3. A similar example is given in J. Cornman, G. S. Pappas & K. Lehrer, *Philosophical Problems and Arguments,* 3rd edn (New York: Macmillan, 1982), 30–1.

4. Lehrer, *Knowledge*, is a prime example of the conservative position on the lottery paradox, while Kyburg, *Probability and the Logic of Rational Belief*, takes the radical approach.

5. See G. Harman, *Change in View* (Cambridge, MA: MIT Press, 1986), 71, for this sort of response.
6. This principle is just (A5), encountered earlier in the discussion of the prediction paradox.
7. Note that the prohibition against believing contradictory statements, accepted by all parties, means that no two inconsistent statements can be rationally believed. Suppose, for instance, that P and Q cannot both be true; then Q logically implies $\sim P$. If P and Q are both justified for S, and S sees that Q implies $\sim P$, then it follows by (WDCP) that $\sim P$ is also justified for S. But then S is justified in believing a contradiction: P, $\sim P$. So the radical cannot grant that two inconsistent statements can be warranted. What this means is that the definition of a type II paradox offered in Chapter 1 can stand *even if* the radical position is correct.
8. Campbell, "Can Inconsistency be Reasonable?", 256. This sort of argument against (CP) can also be found in: A. A. Derksen, "The Alleged Lottery Paradox Resolved", *American Philosophical Quarterly* 15 (1978), 72; and Foley, *The Theory of Epistemic Rationality*, 243.
9. See Cohen, *The Probable and the Provable* and Pollock, "Epistemology and Probability".
10. R. Foley, "The Epistemology of Belief and the Epistemology of Degrees of Belief", *American Philosophical Quarterly* 29 (1992), 111–24.
11. Very briefly, a Gettier case is one in which a true justified belief fails to be knowledge because the justification is defective in certain ways. For instance: I am justified in believing that Jones owns a Ford based on having seen him driving a Ford, hearing him say that he owns a Ford and so on. From this, I justifiably infer: either Jones owns a Ford or Brown is in Barcelona. Suppose that the disjunction is true, but *only because* Brown is in Barcelona; Jones does not own a Ford, having sold it last week. It seems clear that I do not know the disjunction, despite my true justified belief. In Gettier cases, it is a matter of luck or coincidence that the belief is true.
12. A version of this sort of argument can be found in S. Ryan, "The Epistemic Virtues of Consistency", *Synthese* 109 (1996), 136.
13. It is sometimes argued that the fourth condition of the analysis will rule out the lottery as well as the Gettier cases. But the case has not been successfully made, since the proposals for the fourth condition appealed to are open to objection. See, for example, Chisholm, *Theory of Knowledge*.
14. D. Lewis, "Elusive Knowledge", *Australasian Journal of Philosophy* 74 (1996), 549–67, offers this sort of explanation of why we lack knowledge in lottery situations.
15. See K. DeRose, "Knowledge, Assertion and Lotteries", *Australasian Journal of Philosophy* 74 (1996), 568–80, for a discussion of how the subjunctive conditionals account applies to the lottery.
16. This difference in attitude is noted in R. Stalnaker, *Inquiry* (Cambridge, MA: MIT Press, 1984), 91. (E) has probability less than 1 because it is not absolutely certain.
17. Note that the fact that the T_is are regarded as highly probable helps to explain how they can be relevant to the rationality of certain actions even

though they are not justifiably believed.

18. Lehrer, *Knowledge*, Ch. 8. Lehrer appears to understand (C) as providing necessary and sufficient conditions for justification. According to this view, then, strong support by the evidence is not sufficient for justification. Another advocate of the comparative approach is I. Levi, *Gambling with Truth* (New York, Knopf, 1967).

19. More precisely, the implication also requires the premise that one of the thousand tickets will win.

20. J. L. Pollock, "The Paradox of the Preface", *Philosophy of Science* 53 (1986), 250. A minimal inconsistent set is one in which if any statement were removed, the set would no longer be inconsistent. Others who take this general approach are Evnine, "Believing Conjunctions", and Ryan, "The Epistemic Virtues of Consistency".

21. This case is based on a similar example in K. B. Korb, "The Collapse of Collective Defeat: Lessons from the Lottery Paradox", *Proceedings of the Biennial Meetings of the Philosophy of Science Association* 1 (1992), 230–6.

22. Foley, "Justified Inconsistent Beliefs", 251–2, and *The Theory of Epistemic Rationality*, 245–6. Others who consider the connection between scepticism and (HP) include: L. Bonjour, "Externalist Theories of Empirical Knowledge", *Midwest Studies in Philosophy* 5 (1980), 53–73; and Ryan, "The Epistemic Virtues of Consistency".

23. It is now apparent that Foley's earlier argument in this section makes use of the unquestioned assumption that high statistical probability is a source of good evidence. This assumption can seem unavoidable when statistical and epistemic probabilities are run together in (HP). It can now also be seen that the chief difference between (HP) and principle (E) of Chapter 4 is that the latter was explicitly restricted to epistemic probability when introduced.

24. See Nelkin, "The Lottery Paradox", for a recent discussion that locates the problem in statistical inference. Nelkin starts with an externalist position on knowledge: For S's belief that P to be knowledge, there must be a causal or explanatory connection between the truth of P and S's belief. This connection is missing when one's belief is based on purely statistical considerations, as in the lottery situation; thus we do not know any of the T_is. But Nelkin recognizes the implausibility of such an externalist condition for rational belief. Instead, she requires, for rational belief that P, only that S believe (rationally) that there is a causal connection between the truth of P and his belief that P. The implications for the lottery case are that we are not justified in believing any T_i. But the proposed condition has the unfortunate consequence that in order for a belief that P to be warranted, one must have a warranted meta-belief about the belief that P. The prospect of an infinite regress looms.

25. J. Vogel, "Are There Counter-Examples to the Closure Principle?", in *Doubting*, M. D. Roth & G. Ross (eds) (Dordrecht: Kluwer, 1990), 16.

26. See *ibid.*, 22, for the core of the argument. Vogel is concerned with knowledge, rather than justified belief; for this and other reasons the argument presented here is best construed as an adaptation of Vogel's argument.

27. A similar example is found in DeRose, "Knowledge, Assertion and Lotter-

ies", although it is used for a different purpose. DeRose takes it that George *knows* that he will be unable to pay off the mortgage.

28. Recently, there has been a good deal of interest in closure as a principle applied to knowledge. See F. Dretske, "Epistemic Operators", *Journal of Philosophy* 69 (1970), 1007–22; Vogel, "Are There Counterexamples to the Closure Principle?"; DeRose, "Knowledge, Assertion and Lotteries"; and Lewis, "Elusive Knowledge". There has not, however, been particular attention paid to closure as a principle concerning justified belief.

29. But perhaps justification is context sensitive in a different way. We might try to extend the strategy of recent contextualist accounts of knowledge, according to which what is known *in a given situation* is a function of the context or perspective from which that situation is viewed. (See Lewis, "Elusive Knowledge".) So *different* judgements about one and the same situation are possible, depending on the context, and the closure principle for knowledge is understood to apply only within a specific context.

How might this work for justified belief? Clearly, there are contexts in which (1) is justified. Suppose this is so when, and only when, the context has feature F; and suppose also that (3) is justified in the same contexts. Thus far, closure is preserved. But turn now to the Max scenario. It seems that (1*) should also be warranted in contexts that have feature F (or the analogue of F), given that (3) is. The difficulty, however, is that (3*) does not appear to be warranted. For the situation has not been changed, statistical evidence remains the only evidence available, and (3*) apparently cannot be justified on the basis of lottery-style evidence. To make this version of contextualism work, it seems, it would have to be shown that feature F somehow cannot even occur in the Max story.

Chapter 6: Newcomb's problem

1. Parts of this chapter are drawn from my "Newcomb's Problem: Further Investigations", *American Philosophical Quarterly* 13 (1976), 129–33, with permission of the executive editor of the journal.

2. R. Nozick, "Newcomb's Problem and Two Principles of Choice", in *Essays in Honor of Carl G. Hempel*, N. Rescher (ed.) (Dordrecht: D. Reidel, 1969), 114–46. The discussion of Nozick's views is limited to this article.

3. This and the following horse-race example can be found in Nozick, "Newcomb's Problem".

4. To say that a number of outcomes are exclusive is to say that no two can both occur; if they are exhaustive, at least one must occur.

5. Note that $Pr(S_1/A) = Pr(S_1)$; that is, the conditional and unconditional probabilities are the same in this case.

6. These definitions, it should be clear, presuppose only that you can rank order the value of the different outcomes. Note also that strong dominance implies weak dominance.

7. A state S is probabilistically independent of acts A and B if $Pr(S/A) = Pr(S/B)$.

8. R. Jeffrey, *The Logic of Decision* (New York: McGraw-Hill, 1965).
9. This example can be found in A. Gibbard & W. L. Harper, "Counterfactuals and Two Kinds of Expected Utility", in *Paradoxes of Rationality and Cooperation*, R. Campbell & L. Sowden (eds) (Vancouver, BC: University of British Columbia Press, 1985).
10. G. Schlesinger, "The Unpredictability of Free Choice", *British Journal for the Philosophy of Science* 25 (1974), 209–21. A similar argument is found in M. Gardner, "Free Will Revisited with a Mind-Bending Prediction Paradox by William Newcomb", *Scientific American* 229 (1973), 104–8. Note that if the Newcomb scenario involves a contradiction, the paradox will count as veridical.
11. Levi, "Newcomb's Many Problems". A similar point is made by J. Cargile, "Newcomb's Paradox", *British Journal for the Philosophy of Science* 26 (1975), 234–9.
12. See Nozick, "Newcomb's Problem", footnote 8.
13. J. L. Mackie, "Newcomb's Problem and the Direction of Causation", *Canadian Journal of Philosophy* 7 (1977), 213–25; see also Cargile, "Newcomb's Paradox".
14. See, for example, I. Levi, "A Note on Newcomb Mania", *Journal of Philosophy* 79 (1982), 337–42.
15. The role of conditionals in Newcomb's problem will be addressed more fully in the next section. For the moment, these brief comments may be regarded as a promissory note to be cashed later in the chapter.
16. This objection can be found in R. Richter, "Rationality Revisited", *Australasian Journal of Philosophy* 62 (1984), 392–403.
17. *Ibid.*, 392.
18. Note that (MEU) does not yield this result. The expected utility of each act is the same; thus neither act is rationally preferable, and there is no instability.
19. E. Eells, "Causality, Decision, and Newcomb's Paradox", in *Paradoxes of Rationality and Cooperation*, Campbell & Sowden (eds), 183–213.
20. Gibbard & Harper, "Counterfactuals and Two Kinds of Expected Utility".
21. See Eells, "Causality, Decision, and Newcomb's Paradox", 193. In what follows, I use the term "counterfactual conditional" (as opposed to "subjunctive conditional") when it is the favoured term of the author under discussion. The points made, however, could equally well be expressed using "subjunctive conditional".
22. I, for one, do not find my intuitions in the Solomon–charismatic kings example any stronger than in the Newcomb situation; similarly for the medical versions.
23. Here I take the traditional line about belief in inconsistent statements.
24. I take it as an essential feature of the Newcomb case that the predictor bases his prediction on the results of some sort of examination of the player.
25. This excursion into the logic of conditionals will also prove useful for Chapter 7.
26. N. Goodman, "The Problem of Counterfactual Conditionals", in *Fact, Fiction and Forecast*, N. Goodman (New York: Bobbs-Merrill, 1955), 3–27.

Others who subscribe to similar views include: R. Chisholm, "The Contrary to Fact Conditional", *Mind* 55 (1946), 289–307; and N. Rescher, *Hypothetical Reasoning* (Amsterdam: North Holland, 1964).

27. Recall the discussion of "The predictor will predict correctly" (115–16), and the Death in Aleppo case (120–23). The flaw, in each case, could be described as assuming that *any* truth can be held constant or fixed in reasoning with conditionals.

28. D. Lewis, *Counterfactuals* (Cambridge, MA: Harvard University Press, 1973).

29. K. Fine, Review of David Lewis's *Counterfactuals*, *Mind* 84 (1975), 451–8.

30. D. Lewis, "Counterfactual Dependence and Time's Arrow", *Noûs* 13 (1979), 455–76.

31. T. Horgan, "Counterfactuals and Newcomb's Problem", *Journal of Philosophy* 78 (1981), 331–56.

Chapter 7: The prisoner's dilemma

1. The example is drawn from J. Heath, *The Efficient Society* (Toronto: Viking Press, 2001).

2. See J. Tilley, "Altruism and the Prisoner's Dilemma", *Australasian Journal of Philosophy* **69** (1991), 264–87.

3. I leave it to the reader to classify this and subsequent paradoxes. If the prisoner's dilemma requires exactly two players, then this is not an instance of that paradox. But clearly it is a closely related dilemma.

4. This paradox is presented in R. Selten, "The Chain Store Paradox", *Theory and Decision* 9 (1978), 128–59.

5. This paradox is found in R. Sharvey, "The Bottle Imp", *Philosophia* **12** (1983), 401.

6. This paradox is the topic of M. Hollis, "Penny Pinching and Backward Induction", *Journal of Philosophy* 88 (1981), 473–88.

7. The most comprehensive defense of the symmetry argument is found in L. Davis, "Prisoners, Paradox, and Rationality", *American Philosophical Quarterly* 14 (1977), 319–27; it is also presented in A. Rapoport, *Two Person Game Theory* (Ann Arbor, MI: University of Michigan Press, 1970).

8. See Davis, "Prisoners, Paradox, and Rationality" and "Is the Symmetry Argument Valid?" in *Paradoxes of Rationality and Cooperation*, Campbell & Sowden (eds), 255–63. Note that if cooperation is prescribed in the one-play case, there is no basis for the backward induction argument in the iterated case.

9. See Davis, "Prisoners, Paradox, and Rationality" and "Is the Symmetry Argument Valid?", and J. Leslie, "Ensuring Two Bird Deaths With One Throw", *Mind* **100** (1991), 73–80. Neither thinks in terms of the dominance argument, and neither attempts to spell out *why* dominance should be inapplicable in certain situations.

10. See Davis, "Is the Symmetry Argument Valid?".

11. Note also that it is unclear how to refashion (3s) as a material conditional. One might try: $(\exists x)(\exists y)[(\text{I cooperate} \supset \text{I get } x) \ \& \ (\text{I defect} \supset \text{I get } y) \ \&$

(x is preferable to y)]. But this won't do as the basis for an assessment of rationality, for it is compatible with: $(\exists u)(\exists v)$[I cooperate $\supset$ I get u) & (I defect $\supset$ I get v) & (v is preferable to u)].

12. Of course, this revised version still does not constitute an analysis of conditionals, since a conditional is used in its formulation. But it does serve to clarify the logic of conditionals.

13. This first sub-argument is of the form $P \rightarrow Q$, $(P \& Q) \rightarrow R$, $\therefore P \rightarrow R$. This form is necessary to get a valid inference, since it has been shown that hypothetical syllogism $(P \rightarrow Q, Q \rightarrow R, \therefore P \rightarrow R)$ is invalid. See Lewis, *Counterfactuals*.

14. See, for instance, J. L. Bermudez, "Rationality and the Backwards Induction Argument", *Analysis* 59 (1999), 243–8.

15. Note that neither (CBR) nor (CBE) is required for the reasoning of (1). There is often confusion on this point in presentations of the dilemma.

16. See R. Hardin, *Collective Action* (Baltimore, MD: Johns Hopkins University Press, 1982), 148.

17. See Sorensen, *Blindspots*, and "The Iterated Versions of Newcomb's Problem and the Prisoner's Dilemma", *Synthese* 63 (1985), 157–66.

18. P. Pettit & R. Sugden, "The Backward Induction Paradox", *Journal of Philosophy* 96 (1989), 169–82.

19. Howard Sobel seems to agree on the need for a "no matter what" rider, although his version of the premise asserting common belief in rationality is different. See his "Backward-Induction Arguments: A Paradox Regained", *Philosophy of Science* 60 (1993), 114–33.

20. L. Bovens, "The Backward Induction Argument for the Finite Iterated Prisoner's Dilemma and the Surprise Exam Paradox", *Analysis* 57 (1997), 179–86.

21. Others who find a strong analogy between the prediction paradox and the iterated prisoner's dilemma, but cannot be considered here, include: Williamson, "Inexact Knowledge"; and F. Schick, "Surprise, Self-Knowledge, and Commonality", *Journal of Philosophy* 97 (2000), 440–53.

22. Sobel, who follows Pettit and Sugden in requiring a "no matter what" qualification or, as he puts it, a subjunctive interpretation of the belief retention premises, introduces more complex versions of the premises. But I would claim that his premises also cannot all be true of an epistemically ideal believer. See Sobel, "Backward-Induction Arguments".

23. See M. Bar-Hillel & A. Margalit, "Gideon's Paradox – A Paradox of Rationality", *Synthese* 63 (1985), 139–55; and R. Sorensen, "A Cure for Incontinence!", *Mind* 106 (1997), 743.

Chapter 8: The sorites paradox

1. It is, of course, controversial whether this argument constitutes a paradox.

2. This example is found in J. Cargile, "The Sorites Paradox", *British Journal for the Philosophy of Science* 20 (1965), 195. Cargile suggests that the reasoning can be applied to any case of change over time.

3. I agree here with Timothy Williamson that it is best to begin by introducing

examples, and then proceed on that basis to assess theories concerning the underlying nature of vagueness and borderline cases. See his *Vagueness* (London: Routledge, 1994), 202.

4. P. Unger, "There Are No Ordinary Things", *Synthese* **41** (1979), 117–54.
5. This objection can be found in Sorensen, *Blindspots*, 229.
6. J. W. Smith, "The Surprise Exam on the Paradox of the Heap", *Philosophical Papers* **13** (1984), 43–56.
7. For objections to this model, and an alternative view, see Pollock, "Epistemology and Probability". See also the discussion in Chapter 4.
8. See D. H. Sanford, "Many Values Versus Super-Truth", *Synthese* **33** (1976), 195–210; and D. Edgington, "Validity, Uncertainty and Vagueness", *Analysis* **52** (1992), 193–204.
9. See Edgington, "Validity, Uncertainty and Vagueness".
10. See Sanford, "Many Values Versus Super-Truth", and Edgington, "Validity, Uncertainty and Vagueness".
11. See K. Fine, "Vagueness, Truth and Logic", *Synthese* **30** (1975), 265–300 for a good discussion of this approach.
12. See R. M. Sainsbury & T. Williamson, "Sorites", in *A Companion to Philosophy of Language*, B. Hale & C. Wright (eds) (Oxford: Blackwell, 1997), 458–84.
13. The epistemic theory has been endorsed by: Cargile, "The Sorites Paradox"; Sorensen, *Blindspots*; and, most notably, Williamson, *Vagueness*.
14. The following objections and responses are based on Williamson's *Vagueness*, and on his "Vagueness and Ignorance", *Supplementary Proceedings of the Aristotelian Society* **66** (1992), 145–62.
15. Williamson's margin for error principle is discussed in the works previously cited in this chapter, as well as in "Inexact Knowledge", and in *Identity and Discrimination* (Oxford: Blackwell, 1990). In his later work, *Vagueness*, Ch. 8, the account of the rationale for the margin for error principle in the context of vagueness is more intricate, and appeals to slight differences in the use of the vague term. For simplicity, I describe the earlier account here.
16. Recall that Williamson also needs to maintain the unknowability of necessary truths such as (H). How can this be explained by the margin for error principle?
17. Note that there is no implication that *P* is true in the actual situation.
18. See Williamson, *Vagueness*, 244–7, for a fuller account of the argument. There is no standard way of explicating the distinction between internalist and externalist conceptions of justification. For present purposes a rough characterization will suffice. Theories of justified belief that place some sort of truth-condition on the statement believed, or on the evidence for it (for instance, that the belief be formed by a reliable process, or be true in most worlds sufficiently close to the actual world), are externalist. An internalist conception focuses on the perspective or viewpoint of the subject.

Bibliography

Armour-Garb, B. & J. C. Beall 2002. "Further Remarks on Truth and Contra-diction", *Philosophical Quarterly* **52**: 217–25.

Ayer, A. J. 1973. "On a Supposed Antinomy", *Mind* **82**: 125–6.

Bar-Hillel, M. & A. Margalit 1985. "Gideon's Paradox – A Paradox of Ration-ality", *Synthese* **63**: 139–55.

Barker, S. 1975. *Induction and Hypothesis*. Ithaca, NY: Cornell University Press.

Beall, J. C. 2000. "Is the Observable World Consistent?", *Australasian Journal of Philosophy* **78**: 113–18.

Beall, J. C. 2001. "Dialetheism and the Probability of Contradictions", *Australasian Journal of Philosophy* **79**: 114–18.

Bermudez, J. L. 1999. "Rationality and the Backwards Induction Argument", *Analysis* **59**: 243–8.

Binkley, R. 1968. "The Surprise Examination in Modal Logic", *Journal of Philosophy* **65**: 127–35.

Bonjour, L. 1980. "Externalist Theories of Empirical Knowledge", *Midwest Studies in Philosophy* **5**: 53–73.

Bovens, L. 1997. "The Backward Induction Argument for the Finite Iterated Prisoner's Dilemma and the Surprise Exam Paradox", *Analysis* **57**: 179–86.

Bromand, J. 2002. "Why Paraconsistent Logic Can Only Tell Half The Truth", *Mind* **111**: 741–9.

Broome, J. 1995. "The Two Envelope Paradox", *Analysis* **55**: 6–11.

Campbell, R. 1981. "Can Inconsistency be Reasonable?", *Canadian Journal of Philosophy* **11**: 245–70.

Campbell, R. & L. Sowden (eds) 1985. *Paradoxes of Rationality and Coopera-tion*. Vancouver, BC: University of British Columbia Press.

Cargile, J. 1965. "The Sorites Paradox", *British Journal for the Philosophy of Science* **20**: 193–202.

Cargile, J. 1967. "The Surprise Test Paradox", *Journal of Philosophy* **64**: 550–63.

Cargile, J. 1975. "Newcomb's Paradox", *British Journal for the Philosophy of Science* **26**: 234–9.

Chapman, J. M. & R. J. Butler 1965. "On Quine's 'So-Called Paradox'", *Mind* **74**: 424–5.

Chihara, C. 1985. "Olin, Quine, and the Surprise Examination", *Philosophical Studies* **45**: 191–9.

Chisholm, R. 1946. "The Contrary to Fact Conditional", *Mind* **55**: 289–307.

Chisholm, R. 1957. *Perceiving: A Philosophical Study*. Ithaca, NY: Cornell University Press.

Chisholm, R. 1989. *Theory of Knowledge*, 3rd edn. Englewood Cliffs, NJ: Prentice Hall.

Clark, M. 2002. *Paradoxes from A to Z*. London: Routledge.

Cohen, L. J. 1977. *The Probable and the Provable*. Oxford: Clarendon Press.

Copi, I. 1971. *The Theory of Logical Types*. London: Routledge & Kegan Paul.

Cornman, J., G. S. Pappas, K. Lehrer 1982. *Philosophical Problems and Arguments*, 3rd edn. New York: Macmillan.

Davis, L. 1977. "Prisoners, Paradox, and Rationality", *American Philosophical Quarterly* **14**: 319–27.

Davis, L. 1985. "Is the Symmetry Argument Valid?" See Campbell & Sowden (eds) (1985), 255–63.

Derksen, A. A. 1978. "The Alleged Lottery Paradox Resolved", *American Philosophical Quarterly* **15**: 67–74.

DeRose, K. 1996. "Knowledge, Assertion and Lotteries", *Australasian Journal of Philosophy* **74**: 568–80.

Dretske, F. 1970. "Epistemic Operators", *Journal of Philosophy* **69**: 1007–22.

Dummett, M. 1975. "Wang's Paradox", *Synthese* **30**: 301–24.

Edgington, D. 1992. "Validity, Uncertainty and Vagueness", *Analysis* **52**: 193–204.

Eells, E. 1985. "Causality, Decision, and Newcomb's Paradox". See Campbell & Sowden (eds) (1985), 183–213.

Everett, A. 1996. "A Dilemma for Priest's Dialetheism", *Australasian Journal of Philosophy* **74**: 657–68.

Evnine, S. 1999. "Believing Conjunctions", *Synthese* **118**: 201–27.

Fine, K. 1975. Review of David Lewis's *Counterfactuals*, *Mind* **84**: 451–8.

Fine, K. 1975. "Vagueness, Truth and Logic", *Synthese* **30**: 265–300.

Foley, R. 1979. "Justified Inconsistent Beliefs", *American Philosophical Quarterly* **16**: 247–57.

Foley, R. 1987. *The Theory of Epistemic Rationality*. Cambridge, MA: Harvard University Press.

Foley, R. 1992. "The Epistemology of Belief and the Epistemology of Degrees of Belief", *American Philosophical Quarterly* **29**: 111–24.

Forrester, J. W. 1984. "Gentle Murder and the Adverbial Samaritan", *Journal of Philosophy* **81**: 193–7.

Gardner, M. 1973. "Free Will Revisited with a Mind-Bending Prediction Paradox by William Newcomb", *Scientific American* **229**: 104–8.

Gibbard, A. & W. L. Harper 1985. "Counterfactuals and Two Kinds of Expected Utility". See Campbell & Sowden (eds) (1985), 133–58.

Ginet, C. 1975. *Knowledge, Perception and Memory*. Dordrecht: D. Reidel.

Goodman, N. 1965. *Fact, Fiction and Forecast*. New York: Bobbs-Merrill.

Goodman, N. 1955. "The Problem of Counterfactual Conditionals". In *Fact, Fiction and Forecast*, N. Goodman, 3–27. New York: Bobbs-Merrill.

Hall, N. 1999. "How to Set a Surprise Exam", *Mind* 108: 645–703.

Hardin, R. 1982. *Collective Action*. Baltimore, MD: Johns Hopkins University Press.

Harman, G. 1973. *Thought*. Princeton, NJ: Princeton University Press.

Harman, G. 1986. *Change in View*. Cambridge, MA: MIT Press.

Hawthorne, J. 2002. "Lewis, the Lottery and the Preface", *Analysis* 62: 242–51.

Hawthorne, J. & L. Bovens 1999. "The Preface, the Lottery and the Logic of Belief", *Mind* 108: 241–64.

Heath, J. 2001. *The Efficient Society*. Toronto: Viking Press.

Hempel, C. 1945. "Studies in the Logic of Confirmation", *Mind* 54: 1–26, 97–121.

Hollis, M. 1981. "Penny Pinching and Backward Induction", *Journal of Philosophy* 88: 473–88.

Hollis, M. 1984. "A Paradoxical Train of Thought", *Analysis* 44: 205–6.

Hollis, M. & R. Sugden 1993. "Rationality in Action", *Mind* 102: 1–35.

Horgan, T. 1981. "Counterfactuals and Newcomb's Problem", *Journal of Philosophy* 78: 331–56.

Jacquette, D. 1994. "On the Designated Student and Related Induction Paradoxes", *Canadian Journal of Philosophy* 24: 583–92.

Janaway, C. 1989. "Knowing about Surprises: A Supposed Antinomy Revisited", *Mind* 98: 391–409.

Jeffrey, R. 1965. *The Logic of Decision*. New York: McGraw-Hill.

Kavka, G. 1978. "Some Paradoxes of Deterrence", *Journal of Philosophy* 75: 285–302.

Kavka, G. 1983. "The Toxin Puzzle", *Analysis* 43: 33–6.

Kirkham, R. L. 1991. "Paradoxes and a Surprise Exam", *Philosophia* 21: 31–52.

Klein, P. 1985. "The Virtues of Inconsistency", *The Monist* 68: 105–35.

Korb, K. B. 1992. "The Collapse of Collective Defeat: Lessons from the Lottery Paradox", *Proceedings of the Biennial Meetings of the Philosophy of Science Association* 1: 230–6.

Kyburg, H. 1961. *Probability and the Logic of Rational Belief*. Middleton, CT: Wesleyan University Press.

Lacey, A. R. 1970. "The Paradox of the Preface", *Mind* 79: 614–15.

Lehrer, K. 1974. *Knowledge*. Oxford: Oxford University Press.

Lehrer, K. 1975. "Reason and Inconsistency". In *Analysis and Metaphysics*, K. Lehrer (ed.), 57–74. Dordrecht: D. Reidel.

Leslie, J. 1991. "Ensuring Two Bird Deaths With One Throw", *Mind* 100: 73–80.

Levi, I. 1967. *Gambling with Truth*. New York: Knopf.

Levi, I. 1975. "Newcomb's Many Problems", *Theory and Decision* 6: 161–75.

Levi, I. 1982. "A Note on Newcomb Mania", *Journal of Philosophy* 79: 337–42.

Lewis, D. 1973. *Counterfactuals*. Cambridge, MA: Harvard University Press.

Lewis, D. 1978. "Truth in Fiction", *American Philosophical Quarterly* **15**: 37–46.

Lewis, D. 1979. "Counterfactual Dependence and Time's Arrow", *Noûs* **13**: 455–76.

Lewis, D. 1996. "Elusive Knowledge", *Australasian Journal of Philosophy* **74**: 549–67.

Lyon, A. 1959. "The Prediction Paradox", *Mind* **68**: 510–17.

Mackie, J. L. 1977. "Newcomb's Problem and the Direction of Causation", *Canadian Journal of Philosophy* **7**: 213–25.

Makinson, D. C. 1965. "The Paradox of the Preface", *Analysis* **25**: 205–7.

Mares, E. D. 2000. "Even Dialetheists Should Hate Contradictions", *Australasian Journal of Philosophy* **78**: 503–16.

Margalit, A. & M. Bar-Hillel 1983. "Expecting the Unexpected", *Philosophia* **13**: 263–88.

Martin, R. M. 1992. *There are Two Errors in the Title of this Book*. Peterborough, ON: Broadview Press.

McLelland, J. & C. Chihara 1975. "The Surprise Examination Paradox", *Journal of Philosophical Logic* **4**: 71–89.

Moser, P. 1985. *Epistemic Justification*. Dordrecht: D. Reidel.

Nagel, T. 1976. "Moral Luck". In *Mortal Questions*, T. Nagel, 24–38. Cambridge: Cambridge University Press.

Nelkin, D. K. 2002. "The Lottery Paradox, Knowledge, and Rationality", *The Philosophical Review* **109**: 373–409.

Nozick, R. 1969. "Newcomb's Problem and Two Principles of Choice". In *Essays in Honor of Carl G. Hempel*, N. Rescher (ed.), 114–46. Dordrecht: D. Reidel.

Olin, D. 1976. "Newcomb's Problem: Further Investigations", *American Philosophical Quarterly* **13**: 129–33.

Olin, D. 1983. "The Prediction Paradox Resolved", *Philosophical Studies* **44**: 225–33.

Olin, D. 1986. "The Prediction Paradox: Resolving Recalcitrant Variations", *Australasian Journal of Philosophy* **64**: 181–9.

Olin, D. 1986. "On a Paradoxical Train of Thought", *Analysis* **46**: 18–20.

Olin, D. 1988. "Predictions, Intentions and the Prisoner's Dilemma", *The Philosophical Quarterly* **38**: 111–16.

Olin, D. 1989. "The Fallibility Argument for Inconsistency", *Philosophical Studies* **56**: 95–102.

Olin, D. 2000. "Consistency, Fallibility and Probability", *The Logica 99 Yearbook*, 140–8. Prague: Filosofia.

Peacocke, C. 1981. "Are Vague Predicates Incoherent?", *Synthese* **46**: 121–41.

Pettit, P. & R. Sugden 1989. "The Backward Induction Paradox", *Journal of Philosophy* **96**: 169–82.

Pollock, J. L. 1983. "Epistemology and Probability", *Synthese* **55**: 231–52.

Pollock, J. L. 1986. "The Paradox of the Preface", *Philosophy of Science* **53**: 246–58.

Poundstone, W. 1988. *Labyrinths of Reason*. New York: Doubleday.

Priest, G. 1979. "The Logic of Paradox", *Journal of Philosophical Logic* **8**: 219–41.

Priest, G. 1984. "The Logic of Paradox Revisited", *Journal of Philosophical Logic* **13**: 153–79.

Priest, G. 1987. *In Contradiction*. Dordrecht: Nijhoff.

Priest, G. 1989. *"Reductio ad Absurdum et Modus Tollendo Ponens"*. In *Paraconsistent Logics*, G. Priest & R. Routley (eds), 613–26. Munich: Philosophia-Verlag.

Priest, G. 1993. "Can Contradictions Be True?", *Supplementary Proceedings of the Aristotelian Society* **67**: 35–54.

Priest, G. 1998. "What Is So Bad About Contradictions?", *Journal of Philosophy* **95**: 410–26.

Priest, G. 1999. "Perceiving Contradictions", *Australasian Journal of Philosophy* **77**: 439–46.

Priest, G. 2000. "Truth and Contradiction", *Philosophical Quarterly* **50**: 305–19.

Quine, W. V. 1953. "On A So-Called Paradox", *Mind* **62**: 65–8.

Quine, W. V. 1966. "The Ways of Paradox". In *The Ways of Paradox and Other Essays*, W. V. Quine, 3–10. New York: Random House.

Rapoport, A. 1970. *Two Person Game Theory*. Ann Arbor, MI: University of Michigan Press.

Rescher, N. 1964. *Hypothetical Reasoning*. Amsterdam: North Holland.

Rescher, N. 2001. *Paradoxes: Their Roots, Range and Resolution*. Chicago, IL: Open Court.

Richter, R. 1984. "Rationality Revisited", *Australasian Journal of Philosophy* **62**: 392–403.

Russell, B. 1903. *The Principles of Mathematics*. Cambridge: Cambridge University Press.

Ryan, S. 1991. "The Preface Paradox", *Philosophical Studies* **64**: 293–307.

Ryan, S. 1996. "The Epistemic Virtues of Consistency", *Synthese* **109**: 121–41.

Sainsbury, R. M. 1995. *Paradoxes*, 2nd edn. Cambridge: Cambridge University Press.

Sainsbury, R. M. & T. Williamson 1997. "Sorites". In *A Companion to Philosophy of Language*, B. Hale & C. Wright (eds), 458–84. Oxford: Blackwell.

Salmon, W. 1970. *Zeno's Paradoxes*. Indianapolis: Bobbs-Merrill.

Sanford, D. H. 1976. "Many Values Versus Super-Truth", *Synthese* **33**: 195–210.

Savage, C. W. 1967. "The Paradox of the Stone", *The Philosophical Review* **76**: 74–9.

Schick, F. 2000. "Surprise, Self-Knowledge, and Commonality", *Journal of Philosophy* **97**: 440–53.

Schlesinger, G. 1974. "The Unpredictability of Free Choice", *British Journal for the Philosophy of Science* **25**: 209–21.

Scriven, M. 1951. "Paradoxical Announcements", *Mind* **60**: 403–7.

Selten, R. 1978. "The Chain Store Paradox", *Theory and Decision* **9**: 128–59.

Shapiro, S. C. 1998. "A Procedural Solution to the Unexpected Hanging and Sorites Paradoxes", *Mind* **107**: 751–61.

Sharvey, R. 1983. "The Bottle Imp", *Philosophia* **12**: 401.

Shaw, R. 1958. "The Paradox of the Unexpected Examination", *Mind* **67**: 382–4.

Slater, B. H. 1995. "Paraconsistent Logics?", *Journal of Philosophical Logic* **24**: 451–4.

Smiley, T. 1993. "Can Contradictions Be True?", *Supplementary Proceedings of the Aristotelian Society* **67**: 17–33.

Smith, J. W. 1984. "The Surprise Exam on the Paradox of the Heap", *Philosophical Papers* **13**: 43–56.

Smullyan, R. 1978. *What is the Name of this Book?* Englewood Cliffs, NJ: Prentice Hall.

Sobel, H. 1993. "Backward-Induction Arguments: A Paradox Regained", *Philosophy of Science* **60**: 114–33.

Sober, E. 1998. "To Give a Surprise Exam, Use Game Theory", *Synthese* **115**: 355–73.

Sorensen, R. 1982. "Recalcitrant Variations of the Prediction Paradox", *Australasian Journal of Philosophy* **60**: 355–62.

Sorensen, R. 1984. "Conditional Blindspots and the Knowledge Squeeze: A Solution to the Prediction Paradox", *Australasian Journal of Philosophy* **62**: 126–35.

Sorensen, R. 1985. "The Iterated Versions of Newcomb's Problem and the Prisoner's Dilemma", *Synthese* **63**: 157–66.

Sorensen, R. 1987. "Anti-Expertise, Instability, and Rational Choice", *Australasian Journal of Philosophy* **65**: 301–15.

Sorensen, R. 1988. *Blindspots*. Oxford: Clarendon Press.

Sorensen, R. 1997. "A Cure for Incontinence!", *Mind* **106**: 743.

Stalnaker, R. 1984. *Inquiry*. Cambridge, MA: MIT Press.

Tilley, J. 1991. "Altruism and the Prisoner's Dilemma", *Australasian Journal of Philosophy* **69**: 246–87.

Unger, P. 1979. "There Are No Ordinary Things", *Synthese* **41**: 117–54.

Vogel, J. 1990. "Are There Counter-Examples to the Closure Principle?". In *Doubting*, M. D. Roth & G. Ross (eds), 13–27. Dordrecht: Kluwer.

Weintraub, R. 1995. "Practical Solutions to the Surprise-Examination Paradox", *Ratio* **8**: 161–9.

Williams, J. N. 1981. "Inconsistency and Contradiction", *Mind* **90**: 600–602.

Williamson, T. 1992. "Inexact Knowledge", *Mind* **101**: 217–42.

Williamson, T. 1990. *Identity and Discrimination*. Oxford: Blackwell.

Williamson, T. 1992. "Vagueness and Ignorance", *Supplementary Proceedings of the Aristotelian Society* **66**: 145–62.

Williamson, T. 1994. *Vagueness*. London: Routledge.

Wright, C. & A. Sudbury 1977. "The Paradox of the Unexpected Examination", *Australasian Journal of Philosophy* **55**: 41–58.

Index